Frommer's®

Portable
Big Island of Hawaii

7th Edition

by Jeanette Foster

Here's what critics say about Frommer's:

"Amazingly easy to use. Very portable, very complete."
—*Booklist*

"Detailed, accurate, and easy-to-read information for all price ranges."
—*Glamour Magazine*

WILEY

John Wiley & Sons, Inc.

Published by:

JOHN WILEY & SONS, INC.

111 River St.
Hoboken, NJ 07030-5774

ISBN 978-1-118-02882-7 (pbk); 978-1-118-17548-4 (ebk); 978-1-118-17549-1 (ebk); 978-1-118-17550-7 (ebk)
Production Editor: Lindsay Beineke
Cartographer: Andy Dolan
Photo Editor: Richard Fox
Production by Wiley Indianapolis Composition Services

Front cover photo: Lymans surf location, Kailua Kona, The Big Island of Hawaii. ©Bryan Lowry / Alamy Images

For information on our other products and services or to obtain technical support, please contact our Customer Care Department within the U.S. at 877/762-2974, outside the U.S. at 317/572-3993 or fax 317/572-4002.

Wiley also publishes its books in a variety of electronic formats. Some content that appears in print may not be available in electronic formats.

Manufactured in the United States of America

5 4 3 2 1

CONTENTS

LIST OF MAPS

ABOUT THE AUTHOR

A resident of the Big Island, **Jeanette Foster** has skied the slopes of Mauna Kea—during a Fourth of July ski meet, no less—and gone scuba diving with manta rays off the Kona Coast. A prolific writer widely published in travel, sports, and adventure magazines, she's also the editor of *Zagat's Survey to Hawaii's Top Restaurants.* In addition to writing this guide, Jeanette is the author of *Frommer's Hawaii; Frommer's Maui; Frommer's Kauai; Frommer's Hawaii with Kids; Frommer's Honolulu, Waikiki & Oahu; Frommer's Maui Day by Day;* and *Frommer's Honolulu & Oahu Day by Day.*

HOW TO CONTACT US

In researching this book, we discovered many wonderful places—hotels, restaurants, shops, and more. We're sure you'll find others. Please tell us about them, so we can share the information with your fellow travelers in upcoming editions. If you were disappointed with a recommendation, we'd love to know that, too. Please write to:

Frommer's Portable Big Island of Hawaii, 7th Edition
John Wiley & Sons, Inc. • 111 River St. • Hoboken, NJ 07030-5774

AN ADDITIONAL NOTE

Travel information can change quickly and unexpectedly, and we strongly advise you to confirm important details locally before traveling, including information on visas, health and safety, traffic and transport, accommodations, shopping, and eating out. We also encourage you to stay alert while traveling and to remain aware of your surroundings. Avoid civil disturbances, and keep a close eye on cameras, purses, wallets, and other valuables.

While we have endeavored to ensure that the information contained within this guide is accurate and up-to-date at the time of publication, we make no representations or warranties with respect to the accuracy or completeness of the contents of this work and specifically disclaim all warranties, including without limitation warranties of fitness for a particular purpose. We accept no responsibility or liability for any inaccuracy or errors or omissions, or for any inconvenience, loss, damage, costs, or expenses of any nature whatsoever incurred or suffered by anyone as a result of any advice or information contained in this guide.

The inclusion of a company, organization, or website in this guide as a service provider and/or potential source of further information does not mean that we endorse them or the information they provide. Be aware that information provided through some websites may be unreliable and can change without notice. Neither the publisher nor author shall be liable for any damages arising herefrom.

FROMMER'S STAR RATINGS, ICONS & ABBREVIATIONS

Every hotel, restaurant, and attraction listing in this guide has been ranked for quality, value, service, amenities, and special features using a star-rating system. In country, state, and regional guides, we also rate towns and regions to help you narrow down your choices and budget your time accordingly. Hotels and restaurants are rated on a scale of zero (recommended) to three stars (exceptional). Attractions, shopping, nightlife, towns, and regions are rated according to the following scale: zero stars (recommended), one star (highly recommended), two stars (very highly recommended), and three stars (must-see).

In addition to the star-rating system, we also use seven feature icons that point you to the great deals, in-the-know advice, and unique experiences that separate travelers from tourists. Throughout the book, look for:

special finds—those places only insiders know about

fun facts—details that make travelers more informed and their trips more fun

kids—best bets for kids and advice for the whole family

special moments—those experiences that memories are made of

overrated—places or experiences not worth your time or money

insider tips—great ways to save time and money

great values—where to get the best deals

The following abbreviations are used for credit cards:

AE	American Express	DISC	Discover	V	Visa
DC	Diners Club	MC	MasterCard		

TRAVEL RESOURCES AT FROMMERS.COM

Frommer's travel resources don't end with this guide. Frommer's website, **www.frommers.com**, has travel information on more than 4,000 destinations. We update features regularly, giving you access to the most current trip-planning information and the best airfare, lodging, and car-rental bargains. You can also listen to podcasts, connect with other Frommers.com members through our active-reader forums, share your travel photos, read blogs from guidebook editors and fellow travelers, and much more.

HAWAII, THE BIG ISLAND

The Big Island, the largest in the Hawaiian archipelago, has it all: fiery volcanoes, sparkling waterfalls, black-lava deserts, snowcapped mountains, tropical rainforests, alpine meadows, a glacial lake, and miles of golden, black, and even green-sand beaches. It attracts visitors to its unmatched diversity of terrain and climate, not to mention its mystery. Inland is snow-capped Mauna Kea, the world's tallest sea mountain, and the vast Volcanoes National Park. Its world-class golf courses are some of the best in the country.

BEACHES   For the island's best swimming, snorkeling, and bodysurfing head to **Hapuna Beach,** a ½-mile crescent of gold sand. Families flock to **Kahaluu Beach,** on the Kona Coast, where brilliantly colored tropical fish convene in the reef. **Green Sands Beach** is a spectacle to behold—tiny olivine pieces in the sand give the beach its shimmering green shade.

THINGS TO DO   Be sure to visit **Puuhonua O Honaunau National Historical Park,** a sacred site that was once a refuge for ancient Hawaiian warriors. Or discover the **Puako Petroglyph Archaeological District,** home to more than 3,000 petryoglyphs. A jacket, beach mat, and binoculars are all you need to see every star and planet from **Mauna Kea.**

EATING & DRINKING   Good soil, creative chefs, and rich cultural tradition combine to make the Big Island a culinary destination. High-end restaurants are concentrated in the **Kohala Coast,** while those for all budgets can be found in **Kailua-Kona.** Most of the island's delicacies—including **laulau, kalua pork, lomi salmon, squid luau,** and **kulolo**—can be

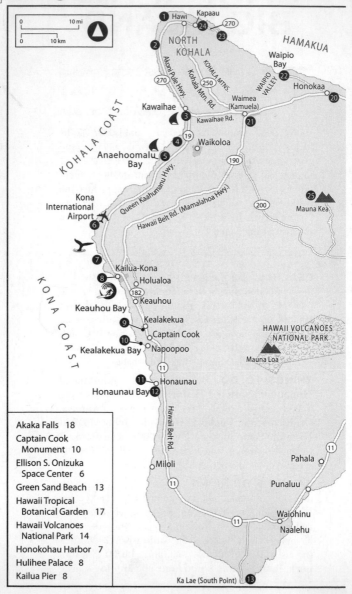

Akaka Falls 18

Captain Cook
  Monument 10

Ellison S. Onizuka
  Space Center 6

Green Sand Beach 13

Hawaii Tropical
  Botanical Garden 17

Hawaii Volcanoes
  National Park 14

Honokohau Harbor 7

Hulihee Palace 8

Kailua Pier 8

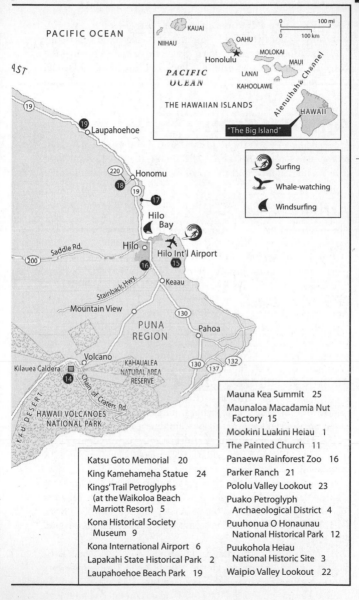

PACIFIC OCEAN

KAUAI

NIIHAU

OAHU

MOLOKAI

Honolulu

PACIFIC OCEAN

LANAI

MAUI

KAHOOLAWE

THE HAWAIIAN ISLANDS

HAWAII

"The Big Island"

0   100 mi
0   100 km

Alenuihaha Channel

AST

Surfing

Whale-watching

Windsurfing

19

19 Laupahoehoe

220

Honomu

18

19

17

Hilo Bay

Saddle Rd.

200

Hilo

Hilo Int'l Airport

16

15

Keaau

Stainback Hwy.

Mountain View

130

PUNA REGION

Pahoa

Volcano

130   132

Kilauea Caldera

KAHAUALEA NATURAL AREA RESERVE

137

14

Chain of Craters Rd.

KAU DESERT

HAWAII VOLCANOES NATIONAL PARK

Katsu Goto Memorial   20

King Kamehameha Statue   24

Kings' Trail Petroglyphs
(at the Waikoloa Beach
Marriott Resort)   5

Kona Historical Society
Museum   9

Kona International Airport   6

Lapakahi State Historical Park   2

Laupahoehoe Beach Park   19

Mauna Kea Summit   25

Maunaloa Macadamia Nut
Factory   15

Mookini Luakini Heiau   1

The Painted Church   11

Panaewa Rainforest Zoo   16

Parker Ranch   21

Pololu Valley Lookout   23

Puako Petroglyph
Archaeological District   4

Puuhonua O Honaunau
National Historical Park   12

Puukohola Heiau
National Historic Site   3

Waipio Valley Lookout   22

found at a luau, the best of which is at the **Kona Village Resort.** In **Hilo** you'll find **Japanese** and other **ethnic restaurants** that provide delicious, simple offerings in low-key surroundings.

NATURE   Take a **catamaran tour** or treat yourself to a **whale-watching adventure.** Carve through the jungle and experience **Waipio Valley.** After dark, don't miss the volcanic eruption at the **Hawaii Volcanoes National Park's Kamoamoa Fissure,** where red rivers of molten lava flow, inching down the mountain and pouring into the Pacific.

ORIENTATION

Most people arrive on the Big Island at Kona International Airport, on the island's west coast. From the airport, the ritzy Kohala Coast is to the left (north) and the town of Kailua-Kona is to the right (south).

Arriving

The Big Island has two major airports for jet traffic between the islands, in Kona and Hilo.

The **Kona International Airport** receives direct overseas flights from Japan on **Japan Airlines** (✆ 800/525-3663; www.jal.co.jp/en) and from Vancouver on **Air Canada** (✆ 888/247-2262; www.aircanada.com). Carriers from the mainland include **American Airlines** (✆ 800/433-7300; www.aa.com), with flights from Los Angeles; **Delta Air Lines** (✆ 800/221-1212; www.delta.com), with nonstop flights from Salt Lake City (originating in Atlanta); **Northwest Airlines** (✆ 800/225-2525; www.nwa.com), with flights from Seattle; **U.S. Airways/American West** (✆ 800/428-4322; www.usairways.com), with flights from Phoenix; and **United Airlines** (✆ 800/241-6522; www.united.com), with nonstop flights from Denver, Los Angeles, and San Francisco, and a direct flight from Chicago.

The **Hilo International Airport** used to have a direct flight from Oakland via ATA, but with the demise of that airline, it is now served only by interisland carriers.

If you cannot get a direct flight to the Big Island, you'll have to pick up an interisland flight in Honolulu. **Hawaiian Airlines** (✆ 800/367-5320; www.hawaiianair.com) and **go!** (✆ 888/I-FLY-GO-2; www.iflygo.com) offer jet service to both Big Island airports.

All major American rental-car companies, such as Alamo, Avis, Budget, Dollar, Enterprise, Hertz, National, and Thrifty, have cars available at both airports. Also see "Getting There" and "Getting Around Hawaii" (p. 15 and p. 16) for details on interisland travel, insurance, and driving in Hawaii. For shuttle services from the Kona Airport, see "Getting Around," below.

Visitor Information

The **Big Island Visitors Bureau** (© 800/648-2441; www.big island.org) has two offices on the Big Island: one at 250 Keawe St., Hilo, HI 96720 (© **808/961-5797;** fax 808/961-2126), and the other at 65–1158 Mamalahoa Hwy., Suite 37-B, Kamuela, HI 96743 (© **808/885-1655**).

On the west side of the island, there are two additional sources to contact for information: the **Kohala Coast Resort Association,** 68–1310 Mauna Lani Dr., Suite 101, Kohala Coast, HI 96743 (© **800/318-3637** or 808/885-6414; fax 808/885-6145; www.kohalacoastresorts.com), and **Destination Kona Coast,** P.O. Box 2850, Kailua-Kona, HI 96745 (© **808/329-6748;** fax 808/328-0614). The Big Island's best free tourist publications are *This Week,* the *Beach and Activity Guide,* and *101 Things to Do on Hawaii the Big Island.* All three offer lots of useful information, as well as discount coupons on a variety of island adventures. Copies are easy to find all around the island.

THE ISLAND IN BRIEF

THE KONA COAST ★★ Kona is synonymous with great coffee and big fish—both of which are found in abundance along this 70-mile-long stretch of black-lava-covered coast.

A collection of tiny communities devoted to farming and fishing along the sun-baked leeward side of the island, the Kona Coast has an amazingly diverse geography and climate for such a compact area. The oceanfront town of **Kailua-Kona,** a quaint fishing village that now caters more to tourists than boat captains, is its commercial center. The lands of Kona range from stark, black, dry coastal desert to cool, cloudy upcountry where glossy green coffee, macadamia nuts, tropical fruit, and a riotous profusion of flowers cover the steep, jagged slopes. Among the coffee fields, you'll find the funky, artsy village of **Holualoa.** Higher yet in elevation are native forests of giant trees filled with tiny, colorful birds, some perilously close to extinction. About 7 miles south of Kailua-Kona, bordering the ocean, is the resort area of **Keauhou,** a suburban-like series of upscale condominiums, a shopping center, and million-dollar homes.

Kona means "leeward side" in Hawaiian—and that means full-on sun every day of the year. This is an affordable vacation spot: An ample selection of midpriced condo units, peppered with a few older hotels and B&Bs, line the shore, which is mostly rocky lava reef, interrupted by an occasional pocket beach. Here, too, stand two world-class resorts: Kona Village, the site of one of the best luaus in the islands, and the Four Seasons at Hualalai, one of Hawaii's luxury retreats.

Away from the bright lights of the town of Kailua lies the rural **South Kona Coast,** home to coffee farmers, macadamia-nut growers, and people escaping to the country. The serrated South Kona Coast is indented with numerous bays, from **Kealakekua,** a marine-life preserve that's the island's best diving spot, down to **Honaunau,** where a national historical park recalls the days of old Hawaii. Accommodations in this area are mainly B&Bs. This coast is a great place to stay if you want to get away from the crowds and experience peaceful country living. You'll be within driving distance of beaches and the sights of Kailua.

THE KOHALA COAST ★★　Fringes of palms and flowers, brilliant blankets of emerald green, and an occasional flash of white buildings are your only clues from the road that this black-lava coast north of Kona is more than bleak and barren. But, oh, is it! Down by the sea, pleasure domes rise like palaces no Hawaiian king ever imagined. This is where the Lear-jet set escapes to play in world-class beachfront hotels set like jewels in the golden sand. But you don't have to be a billionaire to visit the Waikoloa, Mauna Lani, and Mauna Kea resorts: The fabulous beaches and abundant historic sites are open to the public, with parking and other facilities, including restaurants, golf courses, and shopping, provided by the resorts.

NORTH KOHALA ★★　Seven sugar mills once shipped enough sugar from three harbors on this knob of land to sweeten all the coffee in San Francisco. **Hawi,** the region's hub and home to the Kohala Sugar Co., was a flourishing town. Today Hawi's quaint, 3-block-long strip of sun-faded, false-fronted buildings and 1920s vintage shops lives on as a minor tourist stop in one of Hawaii's most scenic rural regions, located at the northernmost reaches of the island. North Kohala is most famous as the birthplace of King Kamehameha the Great; a statue commemorates the royal site. It's also home to the islands' most sacred site, the 1,500-year-old **Mookini Heiau.**

WAIMEA (KAMUELA) ★★　This old upcountry cow town on the northern road between the coasts is set in lovely country: rolling green pastures, wide-open spaces dotted by *puu* (hills), and real cowpokes who ride mammoth **Parker Ranch,** Hawaii's largest working ranch. The town is also headquarters for the **Keck Telescope,** the largest and most powerful in the world. Waimea is home to several affordable B&Bs, and Merriman's restaurant is a popular foodie outpost at Opelo Plaza.

THE HAMAKUA COAST ★★   This emerald coast, a 52-mile stretch from Honokaa to Hilo on the island's windward northeast side, was once planted with sugar cane; it now blooms with flowers, macadamia nuts, papayas, and marijuana, also known as *pakalolo* (still Hawaii's number-one cash crop). Resort-free and virtually without beaches, the Hamakua Coast still has a few major destinations. Picture-perfect **Waipio Valley** has impossibly steep sides, taro patches, a green riot of wild plants, and a winding stream leading to a broad, black-sand beach; and the historic plantation town of **Honokaa** is making a comeback as the B&B capital on the coastal trail. **Akaka Falls** and **Laupahoehoe Beach Park** are also worth seeking out.

HILO ★★   When the sun shines in Hilo, it's one of the most beautiful tropical cities in the Pacific. Being here is an entirely different kind of island experience: Hawaii's largest metropolis after Honolulu is a quaint, misty, flower-filled city of Victorian houses overlooking a half-moon bay, with a restored historic downtown and a clear view of Mauna Loa's often snowcapped peak. Hilo catches everyone's eye until it rains—it rains a lot in Hilo, and when it rains, it pours.

Hilo is one of America's wettest towns, with 128 inches of rain annually. It's ideal for growing ferns, orchids, and anthuriums, but not for catching a few rays. But there's a lot to see and do in Hilo, so grab your umbrella. The rain is warm (the temperature seldom dips below 70°F/21°C), and there's usually a rainbow afterward.

Hilo's oversize airport and hotels are remnants of a dream: The city wanted to be Hawaii's major port of entry. That didn't happen, but the facilities here are excellent. Hilo is also Hawaii's best bargain for budget travelers. It has plenty of hotel rooms—most of the year, that is. Hilo's magic moment comes in spring, the week after Easter, when hula *halau* (schools) arrive for the annual **Merrie Monarch Hula Festival** hula competition (see "Big Island Calendar of Events" on p. 10). This is a full-on Hawaiian spectacle and a wonderful cultural event. Plan ahead if you want to go: Tickets are sold out by the first week in January, and the hotels within 30 miles are usually booked solid.

Hilo is also the gateway to Hawaii Volcanoes National Park; it's just an hour's drive up-slope.

HAWAII VOLCANOES NATIONAL PARK ★★★   This is America's most exciting national park, where a live volcano called Kilauea erupts daily. If you're lucky, it will be a spectacular sight. At other times, you may not be able to see the molten lava at all, but there's always a lot to see and learn. Ideally, you should plan to spend 3 days at the park exploring the trails, watching the volcano, visiting the rainforest, and just enjoying this spectacular place. But even if you have only a day, get here—it's worth the trip. Bring your sweats or jacket (honest!); it's cool up here, especially at night.

If you plan to dally in the park, then you'll want to stay in the sleepy hamlet of **Volcano Village,** just outside the national park entrance. Several extremely cozy B&Bs, some with fireplaces, hide under tree ferns in this cool mountain hideaway. The tiny highland community (elevation 4,000 ft.), first settled by Japanese immigrants, is now inhabited by artists, soul-searchers, and others who like the crisp air of Hawaii's high country. It has just enough civilization to sustain a good life: a few stores, a handful of eateries, a gas station, and a golf course.

KA LAE: SOUTH POINT ★★ This is the Plymouth Rock of Hawaii, where the first Polynesians arrived in seagoing canoes, probably from the Marquesas Islands or Tahiti, around A.D. 500. You'll feel like you're at the end of the world on this lonely, wind-swept place, the southernmost point of the United States (a geographic claim that belonged to Key West, Florida, before Hawaii became a state). Hawaii ends in a sharp, black-lava point. Bold 500-foot cliffs stand against the blue sea to the west and shelter the old fishing village of Waiahukini, which was populated from A.D. 750 until the 1860s. Ancient canoe moorings, shelter caves, and *heiau* (temples) poke through windblown pili grass. The east coast curves inland to reveal a green-sand beach, a world-famous anomaly that's accessible only by foot or four-wheel-drive. For most, the only reason to venture down to the southern tip is to experience the empty vista of land's end.

Everything in **Naalehu** and **Waiohinu,** the two wide spots in the road that pass for towns at South Point, claims to be the southernmost this or that. Except for a monkeypod tree planted by Mark Twain in 1866, there's not much else to crow about. There is, thankfully, a gas station, along with a couple of places to eat, a fruit stand, and a few B&Bs. These end-of-the-world towns are just about as far removed from the real world as you can get.

WHEN TO GO

Most visitors don't come to Hawaii when the weather's best in the islands; rather, they come when it's at its worst everywhere else. Thus, the **high season**—when prices are up and resorts are often booked to capacity—is generally from mid-December to March or mid-April. The last 2 weeks of December, in particular, are the prime time for travel to Hawaii. If you're planning a holiday trip, make your reservations as early as possible, expect crowds, and prepare to pay top dollar for accommodations, car rentals, and airfare.

The **off season,** when the best rates are available and the islands are less crowded, is spring (mid-Apr to mid-June) and fall (Sept to mid-Dec)—a paradox because these are the best seasons to be in Hawaii, in terms of reliably great weather. If you're looking to save money, or if you just want to avoid the crowds, this is the time to visit. Hotel rates and airfares tend to be significantly lower, and good packages are often available.

Note: If you plan to come to Hawaii between the last week in April and early May, be sure you book your accommodations, inter-island air reservations, and car rentals in advance. In Japan, the last week of April is called **Golden Week** because three Japanese holidays take place one after the other. Waikiki is especially busy with Japanese tourists during this time, but the neighboring islands also see dramatic increases.

Due to the large number of families traveling in **summer** (June–Aug), you won't get the fantastic bargains of spring and fall. However, you'll still do much better on packages, airfare, and accommodations than you will in the winter months.

Climate

Because Hawaii lies at the edge of the tropical zone, it technically has only two seasons, both of them warm. There's a dry season that corresponds to **summer** (Apr–Oct) and a rainy season in **winter** (Nov–Mar). It rains every day somewhere in the islands any time of the year, but the rainy season sometimes brings enough gray weather to spoil your tanning opportunities. Fortunately, it seldom rains in one spot for more than 3 days straight.

The **year-round temperature** doesn't vary much. At the beach, the average daytime high in summer is 85°F (29°C), while the average daytime high in winter is 78°F (26°C); nighttime lows are usually about 10° cooler. But how warm it is on any given day really depends on *where* you are on the island.

Each island has a leeward side (the side sheltered from the wind) and a windward side (the side that gets the wind's full force). The **leeward** sides (the west and south) are usually hot and dry, while the **windward** sides (east and north) are generally cooler and moist. When you want arid, sunbaked, desertlike weather, go leeward. When you want lush, wet, junglelike weather, go windward.

 Travel Tip

Your best bet for total year-round sun is the Kona-Kohala Coast.

Daylight Saving Time

Since 1966, most of the United States has observed daylight saving time from the first Sunday in April to the last Sunday in October. In 2007, these dates changed, and now daylight saving time lasts from 2am on the second Sunday in March to 2am on the first Sunday in November. **Note that Hawaii does *not* observe daylight saving time.** So when daylight saving time is in effect in most of the U.S., Hawaii is 3 hours behind the West Coast and 6 hours behind the East Coast. When the U.S. reverts to standard time in November, Hawaii is 2 hours behind the West Coast and 5 hours behind the East Coast.

Hawaii is also full of **microclimates,** thanks to its interior valleys, coastal plains, and mountain peaks. Kauai's Mount Waialeale is the wettest spot on earth, yet Waimea Canyon, just a few miles away, is almost a desert. On the Big Island, Hilo is one of the wettest cities in the nation, with 180 inches of rainfall a year, but at Puako, only 60 miles away, it rains less than 6 inches a year. If you travel into the mountains, the climate can change from summer to winter in a matter of hours because it's cooler the higher you go. So if the weather doesn't suit you, just go to the other side of the island—or head into the hills.

On rare occasions, the weather can be disastrous, as when Hurricane Iniki crushed Kauai in September 1992 with 225-mph winds. Tsunamis have swept Hilo and the south shore of Oahu. But those are extreme exceptions. Mostly, one day follows another here in glorious, sunny procession, each quite like the other.

Big Island Calendar of Events

Please note that as with any schedule of upcoming events, the following information is subject to change; always confirm the details before you plan your trip around an event.

For an exhaustive list of events beyond those listed here, check http://events.frommers.com, where you'll find a searchable, up-to-the-minute roster of what's happening in cities all over the world.

MARCH

Kona Brewers Festival, King Kamehameha's Kona Beach Hotel Luau Grounds, Kailua-Kona. This annual event features microbreweries from around the world, with beer tastings, food, and entertainment. Call *𝒞* **808/334-1133** (www.konabrewersfestival.com). Mid-March.

Kona Chocolate Festival, Kona. A 3-day celebration of the chocolate (cacao) that is grown and produced in Hawaii. Days 1 and 2 are filled with symposiums and seminars on chocolate and its uses. Day 3 features a gala party with samples of chocolate creations by Big Island chefs, caterers, and ice-cream and candy makers. A chocoholic's dream! For information and tickets, call ✆ **808/324-4606** (www.konachocolate festival.com). Mid-March to early April.

Prince Kuhio Day Celebrations, all islands. On this state holiday, various festivals throughout Hawaii celebrate the birth of Jonah Kuhio Kalanianaole, who was born on March 26, 1871, and elected to Congress in 1902.

APRIL

Merrie Monarch Hula Festival, Hilo. Hawaii's biggest hula festival features 3 nights of modern (auana) and ancient (kahiko) dance competition in honor of King David Kalakaua, the "Merrie Monarch" who revived the dance. It takes place the week after Easter, but tickets sell out by January 30—reserve early. Call ✆ **808/935-9168** (www.merriemonarch festival.org). April 8–14, 2012.

MAY

Outrigger Canoe Season, all islands. From May to September, canoe paddlers across the state participate in outrigger canoe races nearly every weekend. Call ✆ **808/383-7798** (www.y2kanu.com) for this year's schedule of events.

Lei Day Celebrations, various locations on all islands. May Day is Lei Day in Hawaii, celebrated with lei-making contests, pageantry, and arts and crafts. Call ✆ **808/886-1655** for events. May 1.

JUNE

King Kamehameha Celebration, all islands. This state holiday (officially June 11, but celebrated on different dates on each island) features a massive floral parade, *hoolaulea* (party), and much more. Call ✆ **808/886-1655** for Big Island events. Most events in 2012 will be held on either June 9–10 or June 16–17.

Great Waikoloa Food, Wine & Music Festival, Hilton Waikoloa Village. One of the Big Island's best food and wine festivals features Hawaii's top chefs (and a few mainland chefs) showing off their culinary talents, wines from around the world, and an excellent jazz concert with fireworks. Not to be missed. Call ✆ **808/886-1234** (www.hiltonwaikoloa village.com or www.dolphindays.com). Mid-June.

AUGUST

Puukohola Heiau National Historic Site Anniversary Celebration, Kawaihae. This is a weekend of Hawaiian crafts, workshops, and games. Call ✆ **808/882-7218.** Mid-August.

Admissions Day, all islands. Hawaii became the 50th state on August 21, 1959. On the third Friday in August, the state takes a holiday (all state-related facilities are closed).

SEPTEMBER

Queen Liliuokalani Canoe Race, Kailua-Kona to Honaunau. It's the world's largest long-distance canoe race, with hundreds participating. Call ✆ **808/331-8849** (www.kaiopua.org). Labor Day weekend.

Parker Ranch Rodeo, Waimea. This is a hot rodeo competition in the heart of cowboy country. Call ✆ **808/885-7311** (www.parkerranch. com). Labor Day weekend.

Hawaiian Slack-Key Guitar Festival, Sheraton Keauhou Bay Resort & Spa, Kona. The best of Hawaii's folk music (slack-key guitar) performed by the best musicians in Hawaii. It's 5 hours long and free. Call ✆ **808/239-4336** (kahokuproductions@yahoo.com). Early September.

Aloha Festivals, various locations on all islands. Parades and other events celebrate Hawaiian culture and friendliness throughout the state. Call ✆ **808/589-1771** (www.alohafestivals.com).

Aloha Festivals' Poke Contest, Hapuna Beach Prince Hotel. Top chefs from across Hawaii and the U.S. mainland, as well as local amateurs, compete in making the Hawaiian delicacy, poke (pronounced *po*-kay): chopped raw fish mixed with seaweed and spices. Here's your chance to sample poke at its best. Call ✆ **808/880-3424.**

OCTOBER

Ironman Triathlon World Championship, Kailua-Kona. Some 1,500-plus world-class athletes run a full marathon, swim 2½ miles, and bike 112 miles on the Kona-Kohala Coast of the Big Island. Spectators can watch the action along the route for free. The best place to see the 7am start is along the seawall on Alii Drive, facing Kailua Bay; arrive before 5:30am to get a seat. The best place to see the bike-and-run portion is along Alii Drive (which will be closed to traffic; park on a side street and walk down). To watch the finishers come in, line up along Alii Drive from Holualoa Street to the finish at Palani Road/Alii Drive; the first finisher can arrive as early as 2:30pm, and the course closes at midnight. Call ✆ **808/329-0063** (www.ironman.com/worldchampionship). Saturday or Sunday closest to the full moon in October: October 7, 2012.

NOVEMBER

Kona Coffee Cultural Festival, Kailua-Kona. Celebrate the coffee harvest with bean-picking and lei contests, song and dance, and the Miss Kona Coffee Pageant. Call ✆ **808/326-7820** (www.konacoffeefest.com). Events throughout November.

Hawaii International Film Festival, various locations throughout the state. This cinema festival with a cross-cultural spin features filmmakers from Asia, the Pacific Islands, and the United States. Call ✆ **808/550-8457** (www.hiff.org). First 2 weeks in November.

Invitational Wreath Exhibit, Volcano Art Center, Hawaii Volcanoes National Park. Thirty-two artists, including painters, sculptors, glass artists, fiber artists, and potters, produce both whimsical and traditional "wreaths" for this exhibit. Park entrance fees apply. Call ✆ **866/967-7565** or 808/967-7565 (www.volcanoartcenter.org). Mid-November to early January.

ENTRY REQUIREMENTS

Passports

Virtually every air traveler entering the U.S. is required to show a passport. All persons, including U.S. citizens, traveling by air between the United States and Canada, Mexico, Central and South America, the Caribbean, and Bermuda are required to present a valid passport. Note: U.S. and Canadian citizens entering the U. S. at land and sea ports of entry from within the western hemisphere must now also present a passport or other documents compliant with the Western Hemisphere Travel Initiative (WHTI; see www.getyouhome.gov for details). Children 15 and under may continue entering with only a U.S. birth certificate, or other proof of U.S. citizenship.

Australia: Australian Passport Information Service (© **131-232;** www.passports.gov.au).

Canada: Passport Office, Department of Foreign Affairs and International Trade, Ottawa, ON K1A 0G3 (© **800/567-6868;** www.ppt.gc.ca).

Ireland: Passport Office, Setanta Centre, Molesworth Street, Dublin 2 (© **01/671-1633;** www.foreignaffairs.gov.ie).

New Zealand: Passports Office, Department of Internal Affairs, 47 Boulcott St., Wellington, 6011 (© **0800/225-050** in New Zealand or 04/474-8100; www.passports.govt.nz).

United Kingdom: Visit your nearest passport office, major post office, or travel agency or contact the Identity and Passport Service (IPS), 89 Eccleston Sq., London, SW1V 1PN (© **0300/222-0000;** www.ips.gov.uk).

United States: To find your regional passport office, check the U.S. State Department website (travel.state.gov/passport) or call the National Passport Information Center (© **877/487-2778**) for automated information.

Visas

For information on obtaining a visa, please see "Fast Facts" at the end of this chapter.

The U.S. State Department has a **Visa Waiver Program (VWP)** allowing citizens of the following countries to enter the United States without a visa for stays of up to 90 days: Andorra, Australia, Austria, Belgium, Brunei, Czech Republic, Denmark, Estonia, Finland, France, Germany, Greece, Hungary, Iceland, Ireland, Italy, Japan, Latvia, Liechtenstein, Lithuania, Luxembourg, Malta, Monaco, the Netherlands, New Zealand, Norway, Portugal, San Marino, Singapore, Slovakia, Slovenia, South Korea,

Spain, Sweden, Switzerland, and the United Kingdom. (*Note:* This list was accurate at press time; for the most up-to-date list of countries in the VWP, consult http://travel.state.gov/visa.) Even though a visa isn't necessary, in an effort to help U.S. officials check travelers against terror watch lists before they arrive at U.S. borders, visitors from VWP countries must register online through the Electronic System for Travel Authorization (ESTA) before boarding a plane or a boat to the U.S. Travelers must complete an electronic application providing basic personal and travel eligibility information. The Department of Homeland Security recommends filling out the form at least 3 days before traveling. Authorizations will be valid for up to 2 years or until the traveler's passport expires, whichever comes first. Currently, there is a US$14 fee for the online application. Existing ESTA registrations remain valid through their expiration dates. *Note:* Any passport issued on or after October 26, 2006, by a VWP country must be an **e-Passport** for VWP travelers to be eligible to enter the U.S. without a visa. Citizens of these nations also need to present a round-trip air or cruise ticket upon arrival. E-Passports contain computer chips capable of storing biometric information, such as the required digital photograph of the holder. If your passport doesn't have this feature, you can still travel without a visa if the valid passport was issued before October 26, 2005, and includes a machine-readable zone; or if the valid passport was issued between October 26, 2005, and October 25, 2006, and includes a digital photograph. For more information, go to **http://travel.state.gov/visa**. Canadian citizens may enter the United States without visas, but will need to show passports and proof of residence.

Citizens of all other countries must have (1) a valid passport that expires at least 6 months later than the scheduled end of their visit to the U.S and (2) a tourist visa.

Customs
WHAT YOU CAN BRING INTO THE U.S.

Every visitor more than 21 years of age may bring in, free of duty, the following: (1) liter of wine or hard liquor; (2) 200 cigarettes, 100 cigars (but not from Cuba), or 3 pounds of smoking tobacco; and (3) $100 worth of gifts. These exemptions are offered to travelers who spend at least 72 hours in the United States and who have not claimed them within the preceding 6 months. It is forbidden to bring into the country almost any meat products (including canned, fresh, and dried meat products such as bouillon, soup mixes, and so on). Generally, condiments including vinegars, oils, spices, coffee, tea, and some cheeses and baked goods are permitted. Avoid rice products, as rice can often harbor insects. Bringing fruits and vegetables is not advised, though not prohibited. Customs will allow produce depending where you got it and where you're going after you arrive in the U.S. International visitors may carry in or out up to $10,000 in U.S. or foreign currency with no formalities; larger sums must be declared to U.S. customs on entering or leaving, which includes filing form CM 4790. For details regarding U.S. Customs and Border Protection, consult your nearest U.S. embassy or consulate, or U.S. Customs (www.customs.gov).

WHAT YOU CAN TAKE HOME FROM HAWAII
You cannot take home fresh fruit, plants, or seeds (including some leis) unless they are sealed. You cannot seal and pack them yourself.

For information on what you're allowed to bring home, contact one of the following agencies:

U.S. Citizens: U.S. Customs & Border Protection (CBP), 1300 Pennsylvania Ave., NW, Washington, DC 20229 (© **877/ 287-8667;** www.cbp.gov).

Canadian Citizens: Canada Border Services Agency (© **800/ 461-9999** in Canada, or 204/983-3500; www.cbsa-asfc.gc.ca).

U.K. Citizens: HM Customs & Excise at © **0845/010-9000** (from outside the U.K., 020/8929-0152), or consult their website at www.hmce.gov.uk.

Australian Citizens: Australian Customs Service at © **1300/ 363-263,** or log on to www.customs.gov.au.

New Zealand Citizens: New Zealand Customs, The Customhouse, 17–21 Whitmore St., Box 2218, Wellington (© **04/473- 6099** or 0800/428-786; www.customs.govt.nz).

Medical Requirements
Unless you're arriving from an area known to be suffering from an epidemic (particularly cholera or yellow fever), inoculations or vaccinations are not required for entry into the United States.

GETTING THERE & GETTING AROUND
Getting to Hawaii
BY PLANE
Most major U.S. and many international carriers fly to **Honolulu International Airport** (HNL), on Oahu. Some also offer direct flights to **Kona International Airport** (KOA), near Kailua-Kona on the Big Island. If you can fly directly to the Big Island, you'll be spared a 2-hour layover in Honolulu and another plane ride.

United Airlines offers the most frequent service from the U.S. mainland, with nonstop service from Los Angeles and San Francisco to the Big Island. **American Airlines** offers flights from Dallas, Chicago, San Francisco, San Jose, Los Angeles, and St. Louis to Honolulu.

Continental Airlines offers the only daily nonstop from the New York area (Newark) to Honolulu. **Delta Air Lines** flies nonstop from the West Coast and from Houston and Cincinnati. **Hawaiian Airlines** offers nonstop flights to Honolulu from several West Coast cities (including new service from San Diego). **Northwest Airlines** has a daily nonstop from Detroit to Honolulu.

Airlines serving Hawaii from places other than the U.S. mainland include **Air Canada; Air New Zealand; Qantas Airways; Japan Air Lines; All Nippon Airways** (ANA); the Taiwan-based **China Airlines; Air Pacific,** which serves Fiji, Australia, New Zealand, and the South Pacific; **Korean Air;** and **Philippine Airlines. Hawaiian Airlines** also flies nonstop to Sydney, Tahiti, and American Samoa.

ARRIVING AT THE AIRPORT

IMMIGRATION & CUSTOMS CLEARANCE International visitors arriving by air should cultivate patience and resignation before setting foot on U.S. soil. U.S. airports have considerably beefed up security clearances in the years since the terrorist attacks of September 11, 2001, and clearing Customs and Immigration can take as long as 2 hours.

AGRICULTURAL SCREENING AT THE AIRPORTS At Honolulu International and the neighbor-island airports, baggage and passengers bound for the mainland must be screened by agricultural officials. Officials will confiscate local produce such as fresh avocados, bananas, and mangoes in the name of fruit-fly control. Pineapples, coconuts, and papayas inspected and certified for export; boxed flowers; leis without seeds; and processed foods (macadamia nuts, coffee, jams, dried fruit, and the like) will pass.

Getting around Hawaii
INTERISLAND FLIGHTS

The major interisland carriers have cut way back on the number of flights. The airlines warn you to show up at least 90 minutes before your flight, and believe me, with all the security inspections, you will need all 90 minutes to catch your flight.

Hawaii has three major interisland carriers: **Hawaiian Airlines** (✆ **800/367-5320;** www.hawaiianair.com), **go!** (✆ **888/I-FLY-GO-2** [435-9462]; www.iflygo.com), and **Mokulele Airlines** (✆ **808/426-7070;** www.mokuleleairlines.com).

Some large airlines offer transatlantic or transpacific passengers special discount tickets under the name **Visit USA,** which allows

Cruising Through the Islands

1

If you're looking for a taste of several islands in a single week, consider **Norwegian Cruise Line** (*C* **800/327-7030;** www.ncl. com), the only cruise line that operates year-round in Hawaii. NCL's 2,240-passenger ship *Pride of Aloha* circles the Hawaiian Islands, stopping on the Big Island, Maui, Kauai, and Oahu; some itineraries even go to Fanning Island in the Republic of Kiribati before returning to Honolulu. The disadvantage of a cruise is that you won't be able to see any of the islands in depth or at leisure; the advantage is that you can spend your days exploring the island where the ship is docked and your nights aboard ship sailing to the next port of call.

mostly one-way travel from one U.S. destination to another at very low prices. Unavailable in the U.S., these discount tickets must be purchased abroad in conjunction with your international fare. This system is the easiest, fastest, cheapest way to see the country.

BY CAR   You'll need a rental car on the Big Island; not having one will really limit you. All major car-rental firms, such as Alamo, Avis, Budget, Dollar, Enterprise, Hertz, National, and Thrifty, have agencies at the airports and at the Kohala Coast resorts. For tips on insurance and driving rules, see "Getting Around Hawaii" (p. 16).

There are more than 480 miles of paved road on the Big Island. The highway that circles the island is called the **Hawaii Belt Road.** On the Kona side of the island, you have two choices: the scenic "upper" road, **Mamalahoa Highway** (Hwy. 190), or the speedier "lower" road, **Queen Kaahumanu Highway** (Hwy. 19). The road that links east to west is called **Saddle Road** (Hwy. 200). Saddle Road looks like a shortcut from Kona to Hilo, but it usually doesn't make for a shorter trip. It's rough, narrow, and plagued by bad weather; as a result, most rental-car agencies forbid you from taking their cars on it.

GASOLINE   Gas prices in Hawaii, always much higher than the U.S. mainland, vary from island to island. As we went to press, gas on the Big Island was $3.99 per gallon.

INSURANCE   Hawaii is a no-fault state, which means that if you don't have collision-damage insurance, you are required to pay for all damages before you leave the state, whether or not the accident was your fault. Your personal car insurance may provide rental-car coverage; check before you leave home. Bring your insurance identification card if you decline the optional insurance, which usually costs from $12 to $20 a day. Obtain the name of your company's local claim representative before you go. Some credit card companies also provide collision-damage insurance for their customers; check with yours before you rent.

DRIVING RULES Hawaii state law mandates that all car passengers must wear a **seat belt** and all infants must be strapped into a car seat. You'll pay a $50 fine if you don't buckle up. **Pedestrians** always have the right of way, even if they're not in the crosswalk. You can turn **right on red** after a full and complete stop, unless otherwise posted.

ROAD MAPS The best and most detailed maps for activities are published by **Franko Maps** (www.frankosmaps.com); they feature a host of island maps, plus a terrific *Hawaiian Reef Creatures Guide* for snorkelers curious about those fish they spot underwater. Free road maps are published by *This Week Magazine,* a visitor publication available on the Big Island.

Another good source is the University of Hawaii Press maps, which include a detailed network of island roads, large-scale insets of towns, historical and contemporary points of interest, parks, beaches, and hiking trails. If you can't find them in a bookstore near you, contact **University of Hawaii Press,** 2840 Kolowalu St., Honolulu, HI 96822 (© **888/847-7737;** www.uhpress. hawaii.edu). For topographic and other maps of the islands, contact the **Hawaii Geographic Society,** P.O. Box 1698, Honolulu, HI 96806 (© **800/538-3950** or 808/538-3952).

If you're visiting from abroad and plan to rent a car in the United States, keep in mind that foreign driver's licenses are usually recognized in the U.S., but you may want to consider obtaining an international driver's license.

BY TAXI Taxis are readily available at both Kona and Hilo airports. In Kailua-Kona, call **Kona Airport Taxi** (© **808/329-7779**). In Hilo, call **Ace-1** (© **808/935-8303**). Taxis will take you wherever you want to go on the Big Island, but it's prohibitively expensive to use them for long distances.

BY BUS & SHUTTLE Door-to-door service from the airport to your hotel is provided by **SpeediShuttle** (© 808/329-5433; www.speedishuttle.com). Some sample per-person rates from the airport: $26 to Kailua-Kona, $24 to the Four Seasons, and $51 to the Mauna Lani Resort.

The islandwide bus system, the **Hele-On Bus** (© 808/961-8744; www.heleonbus.org), offers the best deal on the island— it's free—but, unfortunately, does not serve either airport. The recently created Kokua Zone allows riders in West Hawaii to travel from as far south as Ocean View to as far north as Kawai-hae for free; in East Hawaii, riders can ride free from Pahoa to

Hilo. Visitors can pick up the free, air-conditioned bus from the Kohala hotels and ride south to shopping destinations such as Costco, Lanihau Center, Kmart, Walmart, and Keauhou Shopping Center. The Hele-On Bus also stops at the Kona Community Hospital and provides wheelchair access.

In the Keauhou Resort area, there's a free, open-air, 44-seat **Keauhou Resort Trolley,** with stops at Keauhou Bay, Sheraton Keauhou Bay Resort & Spa, Kona Country Club, Keauhou Shopping Center, Outrigger Keauhou Beach Resort, and Kahaluu Beach Park. In addition, three times a day the trolley travels round-trip, via Alii Drive to Kailua Village, stopping at White Sands Beach on the way. For information, contact the concierge at either the Sheraton Keauhou Bay Resort & Spa (✆ **808/930-4900**) or the Outrigger Keauhou Beach Resort (✆ **808/322-3411**).

MONEY & COSTS

THE VALUE OF US$ VS. OTHER POPULAR CURRENCIES

US$	Can$	UK£	Euro (€)	Aus$	NZ$
1	C$1.17	£.65	€.74	A$1.32	NZ$1.69

Frommer's lists exact prices in the local currency. The currency conversions quoted below were correct at press time. However, rates fluctuate, so before departing consult a currency exchange website such as **www.oanda.com/convert/classic** to check up to-the-minute rates.

ATMs

ATMs (Cashpoints) are everywhere in Hawaii—at banks, supermarkets, Longs Drugs, Honolulu International Airport, and in some resorts and shopping centers. The **Cirrus** (✆ **800/424-7787;** www.mastercard.com) and **PLUS** (✆ **800/843-7587;** www.visa.com) networks span the country; you can find them even in remote regions. Go to your bank card's website to find ATM locations at your destination. Be sure you know your daily withdrawal limit before you depart.

Note: Many banks impose a fee every time you use a card at another bank's ATM, and that fee is often higher for international transactions (up to $5 or more) than for domestic ones (where they're rarely more than $2). In addition, the bank from which you withdraw cash may charge its own fee. To compare banks' ATM fees within the U.S., use **www.bankrate.com**. Visitors from outside the U.S. should also find out whether their bank assesses a 1% to 3% fee on charges incurred abroad.

Credit Cards & Debit Cards

The most widely used form of payment in the United States is credit cards: **Visa** (Barclaycard in Britain), **MasterCard** (Euro-Card in Europe, Access in Britain, Chargex in Canada), **American Express, Diners Club,** and **Discover.** Nearly every store, hotel, and restaurant in the city will accept all major credit cards and bank debit cards.

It's highly recommended that you travel with at least one major credit card. You must have one to rent a car, and hotels and airlines usually require a credit card imprint as a deposit against expenses. Credit cards also provide a convenient record of all your expenses, and they generally offer relatively good exchange rates. You can withdraw cash advances from your credit cards at banks or ATMs, provided you know your PIN. Visitors from outside the U.S. should inquire whether their bank assesses a 1% to 3% fee on charges incurred abroad.

ATM cards with major credit card backing, known as **debit cards,** are now a commonly accepted form of payment in most stores and restaurants. Debit cards draw money directly from your checking account. Some stores enable you to receive "cash back" on your debit card purchases as well. The same is true at most U.S. post offices. Credit cards are accepted everywhere except taxicabs (all islands) and some small restaurants and bed-and-breakfast accommodations.

HEALTH
Staying healthy
INSECTS & SCORPIONS

Like any tropical climate, Hawaii is home to lots of bugs. Most of them won't harm you. However, watch out for mosquitoes, centipedes, and scorpions, which do sting and may cause anything from mild annoyance to severe swelling and pain.

MOSQUITOES These pesky insects are not native to Hawaii but arrived as larvae stowed away in water barrels on the ship *Wellington* in 1826, when it anchored in Lahaina. There's not a whole lot you can do about them, except to apply commercial repellent, which you can pick up at any drugstore.

CENTIPEDES These segmented bugs with a jillion legs come in two varieties: 6- to 8-inch-long brown ones and 2- to 3-inch-long blue guys. Both can really pack a wallop with their sting. Centipedes are generally found in damp, wet places, such as under woodpiles or compost heaps; wearing closed-toe shoes can help prevent stings. If you're stung, apply ice at once to prevent swelling. See a doctor if you experience extreme pain, swelling, nausea, or any other severe reaction.

SCORPIONS   Rarely seen, scorpions are found in arid, warm regions; their stings can be serious. Campers in dry areas should always check their boots before putting them on and shake out sleeping bags and bed rolls. Symptoms of a scorpion sting include shortness of breath, hives, swelling, and nausea. In the unlikely event that you're stung, apply diluted household ammonia and cold compresses to the area of the sting and seek medical help immediately.

HIKING SAFETY

In addition to taking the appropriate precautions regarding Hawaii's bug population, hikers should always let someone know where they're heading, when they're going, and when they plan to return; too many hikers get lost in Hawaii because they don't let others know their basic plans. And make sure you know how strenuous the route and trail you will follow are—don't overestimate your ability.

Before you head out, always check weather conditions with the **National Weather Service** (☎ 808/973-4381 on Oahu). Do not hike if rain or a storm is predicted; flash floods are common in Hawaii. Hike with a pal, never alone. Plan to finish your hike at least an hour before sunset; because Hawaii is so close to the equator, it does not have a twilight period, and thus it gets dark quickly after the sun sets. Wear hiking boots, a sun hat, clothes to protect you from the sun and from getting scratches, and high-SPF sunscreen on all exposed areas of skin. Take plenty of water, basic first aid, a snack, and a bag to pack out what you pack in. Stay on the trail. Watch your step. It's easy to slip off precipitous trails and into steep canyons. Many experienced hikers and boaters today pack a cellphone in case of emergency; just dial ☎ **911.**

VOG

The volcanic haze dubbed "vog" is caused by gases released when molten lava—from the continuous eruption of Kilauea volcano on the Big Island—pours into the ocean. Some people claim that long-term exposure to the hazy, smoglike air has caused bronchial ailments, but it's highly unlikely to cause you any harm in the course of your visit.

There actually is a vog season in Hawaii: the fall and winter months, when the trade winds that blow the fumes out to sea die down. The vog is felt not only on the Big Island, but also as far away as Maui and Oahu.

One more word of caution: If you're pregnant or have heart or breathing problems, you should avoid exposure to the sulfuric fumes that are ever present in and around the Big Island's Hawaii Volcanoes National Park.

OCEAN SAFETY

Because most people coming to Hawaii are unfamiliar with the ocean environment, they're often unaware of the natural hazards it holds. With just a few precautions, your ocean experience can be a safe and happy one. An excellent book is *All Stings Considered: First Aid and Medical Treatment of Hawaii's Marine Injuries,* by Craig Thomas and Susan Scott (University of Hawaii Press, 1997).

SHARKS　Note that sharks are not a big problem in Hawaii; in fact, they appear so infrequently that locals look forward to seeing them. Since records have been kept, starting in 1779, there have been only about 100 shark attacks in Hawaii, of which 40% have been fatal. Most attacks occurred after someone fell into the ocean from the shore or from a boat; in these cases, the sharks probably attacked after the person was dead. But here are the general rules for avoiding sharks: Don't swim at sunrise, at sunset, or where the water is murky due to stream runoff—sharks may mistake you for one of their usual meals. And don't swim where there are bloody fish in the water, as sharks become aggressive around blood.

SEASICKNESS　The waters in Hawaii can range from as calm as glass (off the Kona Coast on the Big Island) to downright frightening (in storm conditions); they usually fall somewhere in between. In general, expect rougher conditions in winter than in summer. Some 90% of the population tends toward seasickness. If you've never been out on a boat, or if you've been seasick in the past, you might want to heed the following suggestions:

● The day before you go out on the boat, avoid alcohol, caffeine, citrus and other acidic juices, and greasy, spicy, or hard-to-digest foods.

● Get a good night's sleep the night before.

● Take or use whatever seasickness prevention works best for you—medication, an acupressure wristband, ginger-root tea or

---

Everything You've Always Wanted to Know About Sharks

The Hawaii State Department of Land and Natural Resources has launched a website, **www.hawaiisharks.com**, that covers the biology, history, and culture of these carnivores. It also provides safety information and data on shark bites in Hawaii.

The Pacific Whale Foundation has a free brochure called *Enjoying Maui's Unique Ocean Environment* that introduces visitors to Hawaii's ocean, beaches, tide pools, and reefs. Although written for Maui (with maps showing Maui's beaches), it's a great general resource on how to stay safe around the ocean, with hints on how to assess weather before you jump into the water and the best ways to view marine wildlife. To get the brochure, call ℂ **808/244-8390** or visit www.pacificwhale.org.

capsules, or any combination. But do it *before* **you board;** once you set sail, it's generally too late.

● While you're on the boat, stay as low and as near the center of the boat as possible. Avoid the fumes (especially if it's a diesel boat); stay out in the fresh air and watch the horizon. Do not read.

● If you start to feel queasy, drink clear fluids such as water, and eat something bland, such as a soda cracker.

What To Do If You Get Sick Away From Home

If you suffer from a chronic illness, consult your doctor before your departure. Pack prescription medications in your carry-on luggage, and carry them in their original containers, with pharmacy labels—otherwise, they won't make it through airport security. Visitors from outside the U.S. should carry generic names of prescription drugs. For U.S. travelers, most reliable health-care plans provide coverage if you get sick away from home. Foreign visitors may have to pay all medical costs up front and be reimbursed later. See "Insurance," in the "Fast Facts" section at the end of this chapter.

We list additional **emergency numbers** in the "Fast Facts" section, as well as listings of local **doctors, dentists, hospitals.**

SAFETY
General Safety

Although tourist areas are generally safe, visitors should always stay alert, even in laid-back Hawaii. It's wise to ask the island tourist office if you're in doubt about which neighborhoods are safe. Avoid deserted areas, especially at night. Don't go into any city park at night unless there's an event that attracts crowds. Generally speaking, you can feel safe in areas where there are many people and open establishments.

Avoid carrying valuables with you on the street, and don't display expensive cameras or electronic equipment. Hold on to your pocketbook, and place your billfold in an inside pocket. In theaters, restaurants, and other public places, keep your possessions in sight.

Oahu has seen a series of purse-snatching incidents, in which thieves in slow-moving cars or on foot have snatched handbags from female pedestrians. The Honolulu police department advises women to carry purses on the shoulder away from the street or, better yet, to wear the strap across the chest instead of on one shoulder. Women with clutch bags should hold them close to their chest.

Remember also that hotels are open to the public and that in a large property, security may not be able to screen everyone entering. Always lock your room door—don't assume that once inside your hotel, you're automatically safe.

Driving Safety

Recently, burglaries of tourists' rental cars in hotel parking structures and at beach parking lots have become more common. Park in well-lighted and well-traveled areas, if possible. Never leave any packages or valuables visible in the car. If someone attempts to rob you or steal your car, do not try to resist the thief or carjacker— report the incident to the police department immediately. Ask your rental agency about personal safety, and get written directions or a map with the route to your destination clearly marked.

What is Illegal

Generally, Hawaii has the same laws as the mainland United States. Nudity is illegal in Hawaii. There are *no* legal nude beaches (I don't care what you have read). If you are nude on a beach (or anywhere) in Hawaii you can be arrested.

Smoking marijuana also is illegal. Yes, there are lots of "stories" claiming that marijuana is grown in Hawaii, but the drug is illegal; if you attempt to buy it or light up, you can be arrested.

SPECIALIZED TRAVEL RESOURCES

In addition to the destination-specific resources listed below, please visit frommers.com for additional specialized travel resources.

Gay & Lesbian Travelers

Hawaii is known for its acceptance of all groups. The number of gay- or lesbian-specific accommodations on the islands is limited, but most properties welcome gays and lesbians like any other travelers.

Out in Honolulu (www.outinhonolulu.com) is a website with gay and lesbian news, blogs, features, shopping, classified, and other info.

For the Big Island, check out the website for **Out in Hawaii** (www.outinhawaii.com), which calls itself the "Queer Resources and Information for The State of Hawaii," with vacation ideas, a calendar of events, information on Hawaii, and even a chat room.

For more gay and lesbian travel resources, visit frommers.com.

Travelers with Disabilities

Most disabilities shouldn't stop anyone from traveling in the U.S. Thanks to provisions in the Americans with Disabilities Act, most public places are required to comply with disability-friendly regulations. There are more options and resources out there than ever before.

Travelers with disabilities are made to feel very welcome in Hawaii. There are more than 2,000 ramped curbs in Oahu alone, hotels are usually equipped with wheelchair-accessible rooms, and tour companies provide many special services. The **Hawaii Center for Independent Living,** 414 Kauwili St., Suite 102, Honolulu, HI 96817 (© **808/522-5400;** fax 808/586-8129), can provide information.

The only travel agency in Hawaii specializing in needs for travelers with disabilities is **Access Aloha Travel** (© **800/480-1143;** www.accessalohatravel.com), which can book accommodations, tours, cruises, airfare, and anything else you can think of.

The **America the Beautiful—National Park and Federal Recreational Lands Pass—Access Pass** (formerly the **Golden Access Passport**) gives visually impaired people or those with permanent disabilities (regardless of age) free lifetime entrance to federal recreation sites administered by the National Park Service, including the Fish and Wildlife Service, the Forest Service, the Bureau of Land Management, and the Bureau of Reclamation. This may include national parks, monuments, historic sites, recreation areas, and national wildlife refuges.

The America the Beautiful Access Pass can be obtained only in person at any NPS facility that charges an entrance fee. You need to show proof of medically determined disability. Besides free entry, the pass offers a 50% discount on some federal-use fees charged for such facilities as camping, swimming, parking, boat launching, and tours. For more information, go to www.nps.gov/fees_passes.htm, or call the United States Geological Survey (USGS), which issues the passes, at © **888/275-8747.**

For more on organizations that offer resources to travelers with disabilities, go to frommers.com.

Family Travel

Hawaii is paradise for children: beaches to run on, water to splash in, and unusual sights to see. To locate accommodations, restaurants, and attractions that are particularly child-friendly, refer to the "Kids" icon throughout this guide. And look for *Frommer's Hawaii with Kids* (John Wiley & Sons, Inc.).

The larger hotels and resorts offer supervised programs for children and can refer you to qualified babysitters. By state law, hotels can accept only children ages 5 to 12 in supervised activities programs, but they often accommodate younger kids by simply hiring babysitters to watch over them. You can also contact **People Attentive to Children (PATCH),** which can refer you to babysitters who have taken a training course on child care. On the Big Island, call © **808/329-7101,** or visit www.patchhawaii.org.

Baby's Away (www.babysaway.com) rents cribs, strollers, highchairs, playpens, infant seats, and the like; on the Big Island, call © **800/996-9030** or 808/987-9236. The staff will deliver whatever you need to wherever you're staying and pick it up when you're done.

Recommended family-travel websites include **Family Travel Forum** (www.familytravelforum.com), a comprehensive site that offers customized trip planning; **Family Travel Network** (www.familytravelnetwork.com), an online magazine providing travel tips; and **TravelWithYourKids.com** (www.travelwithyourkids.com), a comprehensive site written by parents for parents offering sound advice for long-distance and international travel with children. For a list of more family-friendly travel resources, turn to the experts at frommers.com.

Senior Travel

Discounts for seniors are available at almost all of Hawaii's major attractions and occasionally at hotels and restaurants. The Outrigger hotel chain, for instance, offers travelers ages 50 and older a 20% discount off regular published rates—and an additional 5% off for members of AARP. Always ask when making hotel reservations or buying tickets. And always carry identification with proof of your age—it can really pay off.

The U.S. National Park Service offers an **America the Beautiful—National Park and Federal Recreational Lands Pass—Senior Pass** (formerly the **Golden Age Passport**), which gives seniors 62 years or older lifetime entrance to all properties administered by the National Park Service—national parks, monuments, historic sites, recreation areas, and national wildlife refuges—for a one-time processing fee of $10. The pass must be purchased in person at any NPS facility that charges an entrance fee. Besides free entry, the America the Beautiful Senior Pass offers a 50% discount on some federal-use fees charged for such facilities as camping, swimming, parking, boat launching, and tours. For more information, go to www.nps.gov/fees_passes.htm or call the United States Geological Survey (USGS), which issues the passes, at *C* **888/275-8747.**

Frommers.com offers more information and resources on travel for seniors.

STAYING CONNECTED
Telephones

Generally, hotel surcharges on long-distance and local calls are astronomical, so you're better off using your **cellphone** or a **public pay telephone.** Many convenience groceries and packaging services sell **prepaid calling cards** in denominations up to $50; for international visitors, these can be the least expensive way to call home. Many public pay phones at airports now accept American Express, MasterCard, and Visa credit cards. **Local calls** made from pay phones in most locales cost 50¢ (no pennies, please).

All calls on-island are local calls; calls from one island to another via a landline are long distance and you must dial "1," then the Hawaii area code, 808, then the phone number.

Most long-distance and international calls can be dialed directly from any phone. **For calls within the United States and to Canada,** dial 1 followed by the area code and the seven-digit number. **For other international calls,** dial 011 followed by the country code, city code, and number you are calling.

Calls to area codes **800, 888, 877,** and **866** are toll-free. However, calls to area codes **700** and **900** (chat lines, bulletin boards, "dating" services, and so on) can be very expensive—usually a charge of 95¢ to $3 or more per minute, and they sometimes have minimum charges that can run as high as $15 or more.

For **reversed-charge or collect calls,** and for person-to-person calls, dial the number "0" and then the area code and number; an operator will come on the line, and you can specify whether you are calling collect, person-to-person, or both. If your operator-assisted call is international, ask for the overseas operator.

For **local directory assistance** ("information"), dial 411; for long-distance information, dial 1, then the appropriate area code, and 555-1212.

Cellphones

Just because your cellphone works at home doesn't mean it'll work everywhere in the U.S. (thanks to our nation's fragmented cellphone system). It's a good bet that your phone will work in major cities, but take a look at your wireless company's coverage map on its website before heading out; T-Mobile, Sprint, and Nextel are particularly weak in rural areas. If you need to stay in touch at a destination where you know your phone won't work, **rent** a phone that does from **InTouch USA** (© 800/872-7626; www.intouch global.com) or a rental-car location, but be aware that you'll pay $1 a minute or more for airtime.

If you're not from the U.S., you'll be appalled at the poor reach of our **GSM (Global System for Mobile Communications) wireless network,** which is used by much of the rest of the world. Your phone will probably work in most major U.S. cities; it definitely won't work in many rural areas. To see where GSM phones work in the U.S., check out www.t-mobile.com/coverage/national_popup.asp. And you may or may not be able to send SMS (text messaging) home.

Internet/E-Mail
WITHOUT YOUR OWN COMPUTER

To find cybercafes in your destination, check **www.cybercaptive. com** and **www.cybercafe.com**.

Most major airports have **Internet kiosks** that provide basic Web access for a per-minute fee that's usually higher than cybercafe prices. Check out copy shops like **Kinko's** (FedEx Kinkos), which offer computer stations with fully loaded software (as well as Wi-Fi).

WITH YOUR OWN COMPUTER

More and more hotels, resorts, airports, cafes, and retailers are going Wi-Fi (wireless fidelity), becoming "hotspots" that offer free high-speed Wi-Fi access or charge a small fee for usage. Wi-Fi is even found in campgrounds, RV parks, and entire towns. Most laptops sold today have built-in wireless capability. To find public Wi-Fi hotspots at your destination, go to **www.jiwire.com**; its Hotspot Finder holds the world's largest directory of public wireless hotspots.

For dial-up access, most business-class hotels in the U.S. offer dataports for laptop modems, and a few thousand hotels in the U.S. and Europe now offer free high-speed Internet access.

Wherever you go, bring a **connection kit** of the right power and phone adapters, a spare phone cord, and a spare Ethernet network cable—or find out whether your hotel supplies them to guests.

For information on electrical currency conversions, see "Electricity," in the "Fast Facts" section below.

[FastFACTS] THE BIG ISLAND

American Express Unfortunately, there currently is no office on the Big Island; however, to report lost or stolen traveler's checks, call ✆ **800/221-7282.**

Area Codes All the Hawaiian Islands are in the **808** area code. Note that if you're calling one island from another via a landline, you have to dial "1-808" before the local number.

ATM Networks/Cashpoints See "Money & Costs" on p. 19.

Automobile Organizations Motor clubs will supply maps, suggested routes, guidebooks, accident and bail-bond insurance, and emergency road service. The **American Automobile Association (AAA)** is the major auto club in the United States. If you belong to a motor club in your home country, inquire about AAA reciprocity before you leave. You may be able to join AAA even if you're not a member of a reciprocal club; to inquire, call AAA (✆ **800/222-4357;** www.aaa.com). AAA has a nationwide emergency road service telephone number (✆ **800/AAA-HELP**).

Business Hours Most offices are open Monday through Friday from 8am to 5pm. Bank hours are Monday through Thursday from 8:30am to 3pm and Friday from 8:30am to 6pm; some banks are open on Saturday as well. Shopping centers are open Monday through Friday from 10am to 9pm, Saturday from 10am to 5:30pm, and Sunday from noon to 5 or 6pm.

Dentists In an emergency, contact **Dr. Craig C. Kimura** at Kamuela Office Center (✆ **808/885-5947**). In Kona, call **Dr. Frank Sayre** at Frame 10 Center, behind Lanihau Shopping Center on Palani Road (✆ **808/329-8067**).

Doctors In Hilo, the **Hilo Medical Center** is at 1190 Waianuenue Ave. (✆ **808/974-4700**); on the Kona side, call **Hualalai Urgent Care,** 75–1028 Henry St., across the street from Safeway (✆ **808/327-HELP**).

Drinking Laws The legal age for purchase and consumption of alcoholic beverages is 21; proof of age is required and often requested at bars, nightclubs, and restaurants, so it's always a good idea to bring ID when you go out.

Bars are allowed to stay open daily until 2am; places with cabaret licenses are able to keep the booze flowing until 4am. Grocery and convenience stores are allowed to sell beer, wine, and liquor 7 days a week.

Do not carry open containers of alcohol in your car or any public area that isn't zoned for alcohol consumption. The police can fine you on the spot. Don't even think about driving while intoxicated.

Driving Rules   See "Getting There & Getting Around," p. 15.

Electricity   Like Canada, the United States uses 110 to 120 volts AC (60 cycles), compared to 220 to 240 volts AC (50 cycles) in most of Europe, Australia, and New Zealand. Downward converters that change 220–240 volts to 110–120 volts are difficult to find in the United States, so bring one with you.

Embassies & Consulates   All embassies are located in the nation's capital, Washington, D.C. Some consulates are located in major U.S. cities, and most nations have a mission to the United Nations in New York City. If your country isn't listed below, call for directory information in Washington, D.C. (☎ **202/555-1212**) or check **www.embassy.org/embassies**.

The embassy of **Australia** is at 1601 Massachusetts Ave. NW, Washington, DC 20036 (☎ **202/797-3000;** usa.embassy.gov/au).

The embassy of **Canada** is at 501 Pennsylvania Ave. NW, Washington, DC 20001 (☎ **202/682-1740;** www.canadianembassy.org). Other Canadian consulates are in Buffalo (New York), Detroit, Los Angeles, New York, and Seattle.

The embassy of **Ireland** is at 2234 Massachusetts Ave. NW, Washington, DC 20008 (☎ **202/462-3939;** www.irelandemb.org). Irish consulates are in Boston, Chicago, New York, San Francisco, and other cities. See website for complete listing.

The embassy of **New Zealand** is at 37 Observatory Circle NW, Washington, DC 20008 (☎ **202/328-4800;** www.nzembassy.com). New Zealand consulates are in Los Angeles, Salt Lake City, San Francisco, and Seattle.

The embassy of the **United Kingdom** is at 3100 Massachusetts Ave. NW, Washington, DC 20008 (☎ **202/588-7800;** www.britainusa.com). Other British consulates are in Atlanta, Boston, Chicago, Cleveland, Houston, Los Angeles, New York, San Francisco, and Seattle.

Emergencies   For ambulance, fire, and rescue services, dial ☎ **911** (if you dial 911 from a cellphone, it will route you to the nearest 911 center) or call ☎ **808/935-3311**. The **Poison Control Center** hot line is ☎ **800/222-1222** (if you call from a landline, you will be routed to a center based on the area code of the phone you are calling from; if you call from a cellphone with an area code that is different from 808, tell them, and they will direct you appropriately).

Gasoline (Petrol)   See "Gasoline" on p. 17.

Holidays   When Hawaii observes holidays (especially those over a long weekend), travel between the islands increases, interisland airline seats are fully booked, rental cars are at a premium, and hotels and restaurants are busier.

Federal, state, and county government offices are closed on all federal holidays. Federal holidays in 2012 include New Year's Day, Monday,

January 2; Martin Luther King, Jr., Day, Monday, January 16; Washington's birthday, Monday, February 20; Memorial Day, Monday, May 28; Independence Day, Wednesday, July 4; Labor Day, Monday, September 3; Columbus Day, Monday, October 8; Veterans Day, Monday, November 12; Thanksgiving Day, Thursday, November 22; and Christmas Day, Tuesday, December 25.

State and county offices are also closed on local holidays, including Prince Kuhio Day (Mar 26), honoring the birthday of Hawaii's first delegate to the U.S. Congress; King Kamehameha Day (June 11), a statewide holiday commemorating Kamehameha the Great, who united the islands and ruled them from 1795 to 1819; and Admissions Day (third Fri in Aug), which honors the admittance of Hawaii as the 50th state, on August 21, 1959. Also see "Big Island Calendar of Events" on p. 10.

Other special days that are celebrated in Hawaii by many people, but involve no closing of federal, state, and county offices are the Chinese New Year (which can fall in Jan or Feb), Girls' Day (Mar 3), Buddha's Birthday (Apr 8), Father Damien's Day (Apr 15), Boys' Day (May 5), Samoan Flag Day (in Aug), Aloha Festivals (Sept–Oct), and Pearl Harbor Day (Dec 7).

Hospitals　Hospitals offering 24-hour urgent-care facilities include the **Hilo Medical Center,** 1190 Waianuenue Ave., Hilo (© **808/974-4700**); **North Hawaii Community Hospital,** Waimea (© **808/885-4444**); and **Kona Community Hospital,** on the Kona Coast in Kealakekua (© **808/322-9311**).

Insurance　Travel insurance is a good idea if you think for some reason you may be cancelling your trip. It's cheaper than the cost of a no-penalty ticket and it gives you the safety net if something comes up, enabling you to cancel or postpone your trip and still recover the costs.

For information on traveler's insurance, trip-cancellation insurance, and medical insurance while traveling please visit www.frommers.com/planning.

Internet Access　Every major hotel and even many small B&Bs have Internet access. Many of them offer high-speed wireless; check ahead of time and check the charges, which can be exorbitant. The best Internet deal in Hawaii is the service at the **public libraries** (to find the location nearest you, check www.publiclibraries.com/hawaii.htm) which offer free access if you get a library card, available for purchase for $10 for 3 months. For free Internet access elsewhere try **Starbucks Coffee**—to find a Starbucks near you contact www.starbucks.com. My favorite Starbucks with Internet access are: Queens Marketplace, 201 Waikoloa Dr., Kohala (© **808/861-1888**), and on the other side of the island at 438 Kilauea Ave, Hilo (© **808/933-3094**).

Legal Aid　If you are "pulled over" for a minor infraction (such as speeding), never attempt to pay the fine directly to a police officer; this could be construed as attempted bribery, a much more serious crime. Pay fines by mail, or directly into the hands of the clerk of the court. If accused of a more serious offense, say and do nothing before consulting a lawyer. Here the burden is on the state to prove a person's guilt beyond a reasonable doubt, and everyone has the right to remain silent, whether he or she is suspected of a crime or actually arrested. Once arrested, a person can make one telephone call to a party of his or her choice. International visitors should call their embassy or consulate.

Mail   At press time, domestic postage rates were 28¢ for a postcard and 44¢ for a letter. For international mail, a first-class letter of up to 1 ounce costs 98¢ (75¢ to Canada and 79¢ to Mexico); a first-class postcard costs the same as a letter. For more information go to **www.usps.com**.

If you aren't sure what your address will be in the United States, mail can be sent to you, in your name, c/o General Delivery at the main post office of the city or region where you expect to be. (Call ✆ **800/275-8777** for information on the nearest post office.) The addressee must pick up mail in person and must produce proof of identity (driver's license, passport, and so on). Most post offices will hold your mail for up to 1 month, and are open Monday to Friday from 8am to 6pm, and Saturday from 9am to 3pm.

Always include zip codes when mailing items in the U.S. If you don't know your zip code, visit www.usps.com/zip4.

Newspapers & Magazines   Daily newspapers in Hawaii are as follows: on Oahu, the *Honolulu Advertiser* (www.honoluluadvertiser.com) and the *Honolulu Star-Bulletin* (www.honolulustarbulletin.com); on the Big Island, *West Hawaii Today* (www.westhawaiitoday.com) for the Kailua/Kona side, and the *Hawaii Tribune-Herald* (www.hilohawaiitribune.com) for the Hilo/Puna side; on Maui, the *Maui News* (www.mauinews.com); and on Kauai, the *Garden Island* (www.kauaiworld.com).

Publications for visitors include *This Week Oahu, This Week Big Island, This Week Maui,* and *This Week Kauai* (www.thisweek.com); *Oahu Visitor Magazine, Big Island Visitor Magazine, Maui Visitor Magazine,* and *Kauai Visitor Magazine* (www.visitormagazines.com); and *101 Things to Do* (with separate versions for Oahu, Big Island, Maui, and Kauai).

Lifestyle magazines include *Honolulu Magazine* (www.honolulu magazine.com); business publications include *Pacific Business News* (www.bizjournals.com/pacific) and *Hawaii Business* (www.hawaiibusiness.com).

Passports   See www.frommers.com/planning for information on how to obtain a passport. See "Embassies & Consulates," above, for whom to contact if you lose yours while traveling in the U.S. For other information, please contact the following agencies:

For Residents of Australia   Contact the **Australian Passport Information Service** at ✆ **131-232,** or visit the government website at www.passports.gov.au.

For Residents of Canada   Contact the central **Passport Office,** Department of Foreign Affairs and International Trade, Ottawa, ON K1A 0G3 (✆ **800/567-6868;** www.ppt.gc.ca).

For Residents of Ireland Contact the **Passport Office,** Setanta Centre, Molesworth Street, Dublin 2 (© **01/671-1633;** www.irlgov.ie/iveagh).

For Residents of New Zealand Contact the **Passports Office** at © **0800/225-050** in New Zealand or 04/474-8100, or log on to www.passports.govt.nz.

For Residents of the United Kingdom Visit your nearest passport office, major post office, or travel agency or contact the **United Kingdom Passport Service** at © **0870/521-0410** or search its website at www.ukpa.gov.uk.

For Residents of the United States To find your regional passport office, either check the U.S. State Department website or call the **National Passport Information Center** toll-free number (© **877/487-2778**) for automated information.

Police Dial © **911** in case of emergency; otherwise, call the **Hawaii Police Department** at © **808/935-3311** islandwide.

Post Office All calls to the U.S. Postal Service can be directed to © **800/275-8777.** There are local branches in Hilo at 1299 Kekuanaoa Ave., in Kailua-Kona at 74–5577 Palani Rd., and in Waimea on Lindsey Road.

Smoking It's against the law to smoke in public buildings, including airports, shopping malls, grocery stores, retail shops, buses, movie theaters, banks, convention facilities, and all government buildings and facilities. There is no smoking in restaurants, bars, and nightclubs. Most bed-and-breakfasts prohibit smoking indoors, and more and more hotels and resorts are becoming nonsmoking even in public areas. Also, there is no smoking within 20 feet of a doorway, window, or ventilation intake (so no hanging around outside a bar to smoke—you must go 20 ft. away).

Taxes The United States has no value-added tax (VAT) or other indirect tax at the national level. Every state, county, and city may levy its own local tax on all purchases, including hotel and restaurant checks and airline tickets. These taxes will not appear on price tags.

Hawaii state general excise tax is 4%. The tax you'll pay on a hotel room is currently 11.25%, though after much political hand wringing, the Hawaii State Legislature voted (and overrode the governor's veto) to increase the hotel tax by 1% in July 2009 (to 12.25%), and another 1% in July 2010 (to 13.25%). In addition to the taxes noted above, the City and County of Honolulu (which is the entire island of Oahu) adds an additional .5% on anything purchased there (including a hotel room). These taxes will not appear on price tags.

Telephones See "Staying Connected," p. 27.

Time The continental United States is divided into **four time zones:** Eastern Standard Time (EST), Central Standard Time (CST), Mountain Standard Time (MST), and Pacific Standard Time (PST). Alaska and Hawaii have their own zones. For example, when it's 9am in Los Angeles (PST), it's 7am in Honolulu (HST),10am in Denver (MST),

11am in Chicago (CST), noon in New York City (EST), 5pm in London (GMT), and 2am the next day in Sydney.

Daylight saving time is in effect from 1am on the second Sunday in March to 1am on the first Sunday in November, except in Arizona, Hawaii, the U.S. Virgin Islands, and Puerto Rico. Daylight saving time moves the clock 1 hour ahead of standard time.

Tipping   Tips are a very important part of certain workers' income, and gratuities are the standard way of showing appreciation for services provided. (Tipping is certainly not compulsory if the service is poor!) In hotels, tip **bellhops** at least $1 per bag ($2–$3 if you have a lot of luggage) and tip the **chamber staff** $1 to $2 per day (more if you've left a disaster area for him or her to clean up). Tip the **doorman** or **concierge** only if he or she has provided you with some specific service (for example, calling a cab for you or obtaining difficult-to-get theater tickets). Tip the **valet-parking attendant** $1 every time you get your car.

In restaurants, bars, and nightclubs, tip service staff and bartenders 15% to 20% of the check, tip checkroom attendants $1 per garment, and tip valet-parking attendants $1 per vehicle.

As for other service personnel, tip **cab drivers** 15% of the fare; tip **skycaps** at airports at least $1 per bag ($2–$3 if you have a lot of luggage); and tip **hairdressers** and **barbers** 15% to 20%.

Toilets   You won't find public toilets or "restrooms" on the streets in most U.S. cities but they can be found in hotel lobbies, bars, restaurants, museums, department stores, railway and bus stations, and service stations. Large hotels and fast-food restaurants are often the best bet for clean facilities. Restaurants and bars in resorts or heavily visited areas may reserve their restrooms for patrons.

Visas   For information about U.S. visas go to **http://travel.state.gov** and click on "Visas." Or go to one of the following websites:

Australian citizens can obtain up-to-date visa information from the **U.S. Embassy Canberra,** Moonah Place, Yarralumla, ACT 2600 (© **02/ 6214-5600**) or by checking the U.S. Diplomatic Mission's website at **http://usembassy-australia.state.gov/consular**.

British subjects can obtain up-to-date visa information by calling the **U.S. Embassy Visa Information Line** (© **0891/200-290**) or by visiting the "Visas to the U.S." section of the American Embassy London's website at **www.usembassy.org.uk**.

Irish citizens can obtain up-to-date visa information through the **Embassy of the USA Dublin,** 42 Elgin Rd., Dublin 4, Ireland (© **353/1- 668-8777;** or by checking the "Visas to the U.S." section of the website at **http://dublin.usembassy.gov**).

Citizens of **New Zealand** can obtain up-to-date visa information by contacting the **U.S. Embassy New Zealand,** 29 Fitzherbert Terrace, Thorndon, Wellington (© **644/472-2068**), or get the information directly from the website at **http://wellington.usembassy.gov**.

Visitor Information For information about traveling in Hawaii, contact the **Hawaii Visitors & Convention Bureau (HVCB),** Waikiki Business Plaza, 2270 Kalakaua Ave., Suite 801, Honolulu, HI 96815 (© **800/ GO-HAWAII** or 808/923-1811; www.gohawaii.com). The bureau publishes the helpful *Accommodations and Car Rental Guide* and supplies free brochures, maps, and *Islands of Aloha* magazine, the official HVCB magazine. For information about working and living in Hawaii, contact the **Chamber of Commerce of Hawaii,** 1132 Bishop St., Suite 402, Honolulu, HI 96813 (© **808/545-4300;** www.cochawaii.com).

Information on Hawaii's Parks Hawaii has several national parks and historical sites. The Big Island has four: **Hawaii Volcanoes National Park,** P.O. Box 52, Hawaii National Park, HI 96718 (© 808/985-6000); **Puuhonua O Honaunau National Historical Park,** P.O. Box 129, Honaunau, HI 96726 (© 808/328-2326); **Puukohola Heiau National Historic Site,** P.O. Box 44340, Kawaihae, HI 96743 (© 808/882-7218); and **Kaloko-Honokohau National Historical Park,** 72–4786 Kanalani St., Kailua-Kona, HI 96740 (© 808/329-6881).

To find out more about Hawaii's state parks, contact the **Hawaii State Department of Land and Natural Resources,** 1151 Punchbowl St., No. 130, Honolulu, HI 96813 (© **808/587-0300;** www.hawaii. gov). The office can provide you with information on hiking and camping at the parks and will send you free topographic trail maps.

Hawaii on the Web Listed below are some of the most useful Hawaii websites.

- Hawaii Visitors & Convention Bureau: www.gohawaii.com
- Hawaii State Vacation Planner: www.hshawaii.com
- The Hawaiian Language Website: www.geocities.com/~olelo
- Planet Hawaii: www.planet-hawaii.com
- Big Island's Kohala Coast Resort Association: www.kohala coastresorts.com
- Big Island Visitors Bureau: www.bigisland.org

Weather For conditions call © **808/961-5582.** For marine forecasts, call © **808/935-9883.**

WHERE TO STAY

Before you reach for the phone to reserve your accommodations, remember that the Big Island is really big; see "The Island in Brief" (p. 5) to decide where to base yourself. Also, be sure to add Hawaii's 13.41% in taxes to your final bill. In the listings below, all rooms come with a full private bathroom (with tub or shower) and free parking unless otherwise noted.

For additional information on bed-and-breakfasts, contact the Hawaii Island B&B Association, P.O. Box 1890, Honokaa, HI 96727 (no phone; www.stayhawaii. com). If you would like to go "on the road," contact Island RV & Safari Activities (© 800/406-4555 or 808/334-0464; www.islandrv.com). It offers weekly rentals of a 22-foot class-C motor home, which sleeps up to four, for $2,200. Included in the package are airport pickup, all linens, barbecue grill, all park registration fee permits, your last night in a hotel (Royal Kona Resort), and help with planning your itinerary and booking activities.

THE KONA COAST
In & Around Kailua-Kona
VERY EXPENSIVE

Four Seasons Resort Hualalai at Historic Kaupulehu ★★★ ☺ This is a great place to relax in the lap of luxury. Low-rise clusters of oceanview villas nestle between the sea and the greens of a new golf course. The Four Seasons has no concrete corridors and no massive central building—it looks like a two-story town-house project, surrounding three seaside swimming pools and a snorkeling pond. Guest rooms are furnished in Pacific tropical style: light gold walls, hand-knotted rugs over clay-colored slate, and rattan-and-bamboo settees. The ground-level rooms have

Where to Stay on the Kona Coast

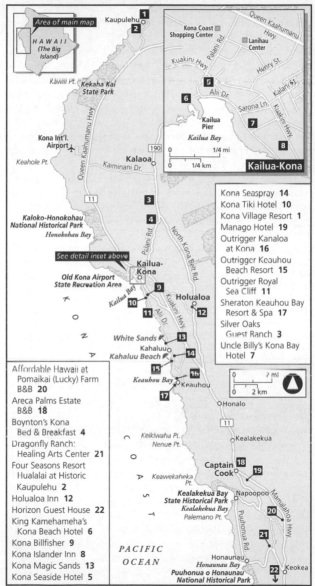

Area of main map

HAWAII
(The Big Island)

Kaupulehu **1**
2

Kona Coast Shopping Center

Lanihau Center

Queen Kaahumanu Hwy.

Palani Rd.

Kuakini Hwy.

Henry St.

Kalani St.

5

6

Alii Dr.

Sarona Ln.

Kuakini Hwy.

Kailua Pier

Kailua Bay

7

8

0   1/4 mi
0   1/4 km

Kailua-Kona

Kāwili Pt.

Kekaha Kai State Park

Kona Int'l. Airport

Keahole Pt.

Queen Kaahumanu Hwy.

Kalaoa

Kaiminani Dr.

190

11

Kaloko-Honokohau National Historical Park

Honokohau Bay

Palani Rd.

North Kona Belt Rd.

3

4

See detail inset above

Kailua-Kona

Old Kona Airport State Recreation Area

Kailua Bay

9

10

Holualoa

11

Alii Dr.

Kuakini Hwy.

12

White Sands

13

Kahaluu

Kahaluu Beach

14

15

Keauhou Bay

16

Keauhou

17

Honalo

11

K.

O

N

A

P

Kelkiwaha Pt.

Nenue Pt.

Kealakekua

Captain Cook

18

19

Keawekaheka Pt.

Napoopoo

Mamalahoa Hwy.

Kealakekua Bay State Historical Park

Kealakekua Bay

Palemano Pt.

Puuhonua Rd.

20

21

PACIFIC OCEAN

Honaunau

Honaunau Bay

Puuhonua o Honaunau National Historical Park

Keokea

22

0   2 mi
0   2 km

Kona Seaspray **14**
Kona Tiki Hotel **10**
Kona Village Resort **1**
Manago Hotel **19**
Outrigger Kanaloa at Kona **16**
Outrigger Keauhou Beach Resort **15**
Outrigger Royal Sea Cliff **11**
Sheraton Keauhou Bay Resort & Spa **17**
Silver Oaks Guest Ranch **3**
Uncle Billy's Kona Bay Hotel **7**

Affordable Hawaii at Pomaikai (Lucky) Farm B&B **20**
Areca Palms Estate B&B **18**
Boynton's Kona Bed & Breakfast **4**
Dragonfly Ranch: Healing Arts Center **21**
Four Seasons Resort Hualalai at Historic Kaupulehu **2**
Holualoa Inn **12**
Horizon Guest House **22**
King Kamehameha's Kona Beach Hotel **6**
Kona Billfisher **9**
Kona Islander Inn **8**
Kona Magic Sands **13**
Kona Seaside Hotel **5**

bathrooms with private outdoor gardens—surrounded by black-lava rock and a bamboo roof—so you can shower under the tropical sun or nighttime stars. All units have new flatscreen TVs.

If you can afford it, this is the place to be pampered—sit back and relax as the pool attendants bring you ice-cold water, chilled towels, and fresh-fruit kabobs. Other pluses include a Hawaiian history and cultural interpretive center, complimentary scuba lessons, a complimentary valet, twice-daily maid service, and a multilingual concierge. The spa has been selected by *Condé Nast Traveler* magazine as the world's best resort spa. One of the five pools is a saltwater pond carved out of black-lava rock with reef fish swimming about. The new Lava Lounge offers exotic martinis, entertainment, and the best view for watching the sun sink into the Pacific.

Your kids will be pampered, too—the complimentary Kids for All Seasons program features plenty of activities to keep the little ones busy. The resort also offers children's menus in all restaurants, a game room, videos, complimentary infant gear (cribs, highchairs, and so on), and more.

72-100 Kaupulehu Dr., Kailua-Kona, HI 96745. www.fourseasons.com/hualalai. © **888/340-5662** or 808/325-8000. Fax 808/325-8053. 243 units. $625–$1,450 double; from $1,525 suite. Extra person $170. Children 17 and under stay free in parent's room (maximum occupancy is 3 people; couples with more than 1 child must get 2 rooms). AE, DC, DISC, MC, V. Valet parking $20 per day. **Amenities:** 3 restaurants (including Pahu i'a, p. 70, and Beach Tree Bar & Grill, p. 70); 2 bars (w/nightly entertainment ranging from contemporary Hawaiian to pianist); babysitting; complimentary year-round children's program; concierge; 18-hole Jack Nicklaus signature golf course exclusively for guests and residents; complete fitness center; 6 whirlpools; 5 exquisite outdoor pools (including a giant infinity pool and a lap pool); room service; award-winning spa; 8 tennis courts (4 lit for night play); watersports equipment rentals. *In room:* A/C, TV/DVD, fridge, hair dryer, wired or Wi-Fi ($14 per day).

Kona Village Resort ★ ☺

This oceanside Polynesian village, which had begun to fall into disrepair in the past few years, was recently sold (to computer magnate Michael Dell), and it appears that the new owners are pouring much-needed funds into maintenance of this fabulous resort. Since 1965, those seeking a great escape have crossed the black-lava fields to find refuge at this exclusive, one-of-a-kind haven by the sea with its wonderful dark-sand beach. Unfortunately, long-time guests of the Village have noted a remarkable decline in the once-sterling aloha service. Veteran employees still have that gracious welcoming attitude, but the newer employees (who are quickly becoming a majority) don't seem able to match the high standards that made the resort famous. Dining service is rushed and, in some cases, practically nonexistent for a luxury resort.

But yes, that blissful languor still settles in as you surrender to the peaceful, low-key atmosphere here. The resort resembles an eclectic Polynesian village, with historic sites and beaches. Make sure you request one of the "renovated" thatched-roof, Island-style bungalows—and, if money is no object, ask for one of my favorite bungalows, the Lava Tahitians, each of which has a hot tub on the deck overlooking the ocean. The Village is no longer located on a secluded cove (guests at the nearby Four Seasons can now walk the beach) and will likely get even more crowded—houses and condos are being built. On the plus side, however: The room rate includes breakfast, lunch, and dinner (unless you choose the "breakfast only" option)—the luau here is fabulous—plus all snorkeling equipment, other beach toys, and scheduled activities throughout the day for kids and teens (there's even a special dinner seating for kids so parents can have a quiet meal alone).

Note: The Kona Village Resort sustained damage to many of their individual hales (huts) as a result of the 2011 tsunami and at press time remains closed. Please contact them in advance of your visit to get updates on repairs and the anticipated date of reopening.

P.O. Box 1299, Kailua-Kona, HI 96745. www.konavillage.com. ℭ **800/367-5290** or 808/325-5555. Fax 808/325-5124. 125 units. $330–$1,230 double. Extra person $250 per adult (13 and up), $185 per child 10–12, $140 per child 5–9. Children 4 and under stay free in parent's room. Packages available. Rates include all meals (including luau) for 2 adults (except for the "Bed & Breakfast" package); tennis, watersports, and walking tours. AE, DC, MC, V. **Amenities:** 2 restaurants (plus Wed and Fri luau, p. 171); 3 bars (w/live entertainment most nights); baby-sitting; extensive children's program (especially in summer, when it extends past dinnertime); concierge; fitness room; Internet; 2 Jacuzzis; 2 outdoor pools; tennis courts; complimentary use of watersports equipment. *In room:* Fridge, hair dryer, no phone.

MODERATE

King Kamehameha's Kona Beach Hotel The location is terrific: downtown Kailua-Kona, right on the ocean. Recent renovations have provided a clean, new look throughout the entire hotel and room upgrades that include LCD flatscreen TVs. Ask for a room with a view of either the Kailua Pier or the sparkling Kailua Bay. The hotel's own small gold-sand beach is right out the front door. The restaurant is forgettable, but you're within walking distance of dozens of other options. The hotel sustained a bit of damage in the 2011 tsunami, mostly in the way of water and mud damage in the lobby area and shops. Though both areas are currently closed for clean-up, they should be back to normal by the time you read this.

75–5660 Palani Rd., Kailua-Kona, HI 96740. www.konabeachhotel.com. ℭ **800/367-2111** or 808/329-2911. Fax 808/922-8061. 460 units. $119–$172 up to 4 people. Check website for discounts; 3rd night free. AE, DC, DISC, MC, V. Parking $10.

Amenities: Restaurant; outdoor bar w/Hawaiian entertainment; Jacuzzi; new outdoor infinity pool; room service; 4 tennis courts; watersports equipment rentals. *In room:* A/C, TV, fridge, hair dryer, Wi-Fi (free).

Outrigger Royal Sea Cliff ☺ Families will love these luxuriously appointed apartments and their affordable rates. The architecturally striking, five-story white buildings that make up this resort/condo complex, 2 miles from Kailua-Kona, are stepped back from the ocean for maximum views and privacy. (The downside is that there's no ocean swimming here, but the waves are near enough to lull you to sleep, and there's a decent swimming beach about a mile away.) Atrium gardens and hanging bougainvillea soften the look. The spacious units are furnished in tropical rattan with a full kitchen, a washer/dryer, and a large, sunny lanai. There are barbecue and picnic facilities for oceanfront dining.

75-6040 Alii Dr., Kailua-Kona, HI 96740. www.outrigger.com. ℂ **800/688-7444** or 808/329-8021. Fax 808/326-1887. 148 units. $129 studio double; $149–$219 1-bedroom apt for 4; $165–$249 2-bedroom apt for 6. AE, DC, DISC, MC, V. **Amenities:** Jacuzzi; 2 outdoor pools; complimentary tennis courts; Wi-Fi in lobby (free). *In room:* A/C, TV, fridge, hair dryer, kitchen, washer/dryer.

Silver Oaks Guest Ranch ★★ 🏠 Book this place! This is a true "guest ranch," consisting of two cottages spread over a 10-acre working ranch complete with friendly horses (no riding, just petting), the cutest Nigerian dwarf goats, chickens, and wild turkeys. The ranch sits at 1,300 feet, where the temperatures are in the 70s (low to mid-20s Celsius) year-round. The views are spectacular, some 40 miles of coastline from the ocean to Mauna Loa, yet the place is just 5 miles from the airport and 5 miles from downtown Kailua-Kona. Hosts Amy and Rick Decker have impeccable taste, and each unit is uniquely decorated. You'll get breakfast items (cereal, milk, yogurt, coffee, fruit, and bread) for your first day. They have a closet full of beach gear for guests, not to mention books, videos, binoculars, and even a couple of backpacks.

75-1027 Henry St., Ste. 310, Kailua-Kona, HI 96740. www.silveroaksranch.com. ℂ **808/325-2000.** Fax 808/325-2200. 3 units, plus additional space available for large groups. $125–$200 double. Extra person $20. 5-night minimum. MC, V. **Amenities:** Jacuzzi; outdoor pool. *In room:* TV/VCR, fridge, Internet (free), kitchen or kitchenette.

INEXPENSIVE

Boynton's Kona Bed & Breakfast ★ ☺ Just 3 miles from Kailua-Kona, but up in the cooler, rolling hills, is this quaint two-bedroom B&B, perfect for a family vacation. The house is perched at 1,000 feet in a quiet country neighborhood; guests can enjoy views of the coastline from the lanai. A private entrance leads into the full kitchen, which is stocked with breakfast fixings (including eggs, cereals, muffins, and juice). You have a choice of a two-bedroom unit, with complete kitchen and a hot tub outdoors, or a one-bedroom unit, with a small kitchenette and spacious lanai outside.

The two-bedroom unit has one bedroom that looks out on tropical greenery, while the other has an ocean view. The second unit, which has just one bedroom and is perfect for a couple, is located next door. This one-bedroom unit has a large lanai (with a dining table and a terrific panoramic ocean view), a sleeper bed in the living room, and a small kitchenette (refrigerator, electric tea-pot, coffeemaker, and a microwave), great for a couple who wants to eat out but would like a hot cup of coffee or tea in the morning. There's a king-size bed in the separate bedroom. Hosts Peter and Tracy Boynton have lovingly created a little bit of heaven here. The beach is just a 5-minute drive away.

744920-A Palani Rd., Kailua-Kona, HI 96740. www.konabandb.com. ℂ **808/329-4178.** Fax 808/326-1510. 2 units. $90 1-bedroom; $120 2-bedroom. Extra person $15. 3-night minimum. No credit cards. **Amenities:** Hot tub. *In room:* TV, fridge, hair dryer, Internet (free), kitchenette (1-bedroom), kitchen (2-bedroom).

Kona Billfisher ☺ The pluses here: It's within walking distance of downtown Kailua-Kona, and the big, blue Pacific is just across the street. (The ocean here is not good for swimming or snorkeling, but there's an on-site pool, and you can swim at the Kailua Pier, just a mile away.) The property is very well maintained. Each unit comes with a full kitchen and a balcony, and features new furnishings and king-size beds. The one-bedroom units have sliding-glass doors that allow you to close off the living room and make it into another private bedroom, so for the price of a one-bedroom unit, you can have a two-bedroom—a real deal and a great setup for families. Other on-site facilities include a barbecue area.

Alii Dr. (across from the Royal Kona Resort), Kailua-Kona, HI 96740. Reservations c/o Hawaii Resort Management, P.O. Box 39, Kailua-Kona, HI 96745. www.kona hawaii.com. ℂ **800/244-4752** or 808/329-3333. Fax 808/326-4137. 60 units. High season $150 1-bedroom; $165 2-bedroom; low season $115 1-bedroom, $135 2-bedroom. Cleaning fee $35–$45. 3-night minimum. DC, DISC, MC, V. **Amenities:** Outdoor pool. *In room:* TV, fridge, kitchen.

Kona Islander Inn 🔑 This is the most affordable place to stay in Kailua-Kona. These plantation-style, three-story buildings are surrounded by lush palm-tree-lined gardens with torch-lit pathways that make it hard to believe you're smack-dab in the middle of downtown. The central location—across the street from the historic Kona Inn Shops—is convenient but can be noisy. Built in 1962, the complex is showing some signs of age, but the units were recently outfitted with new appliances, new bedspreads and curtains, and a fresh coat of paint. The studios are small, but extras such as lanais and kitchenettes outfitted with microwaves, minifridges, and coffeemakers make up for the lack of space.

75-5776 Kuakini Hwy. (south of Hualalai Rd.), Kailua-Kona, HI 96740. Reservations c/o Hawaii Resort Management, P.O. Box 39, Kailua-Kona, HI 96745. www.konahawaii.com. *C* **800/244-4752** or 808/329-3333. Fax 808/326-4137. 80 units. $80–$115 double. DC, DISC, MC, V. **Amenities:** Hot tub; outdoor pool. *In room:* A/C, TV, fridge, kitchenette.

Kona Magic Sands ★ 🏊

If you want to stay right on the ocean without spending a fortune, this is the place to do it—it's one of the best oceanfront deals you'll find on a Kona condo, and the only one with a beach for swimming and snorkeling right next door. Every unit in this older complex has a lanai that steps out over the ocean and sunset views that you'll dream about long after you return home. These studio units aren't luxurious; they're small (two people max) and cozy, great for people who want to be lulled to sleep by the sound of the waves crashing on the shore. Each consists of one long, narrow room with a small kitchen at one end and the lanai at the other, with a living room/dining room/bedroom combo in between.

77-6452 Alii Dr. (next to Magic Sands Beach Park), Kailua-Kona, HI 96740. Reservations c/o Hawaii Resort Management, P.O. Box 39, Kailua-Kona, HI 96745. www.konahawaii.com. *C* **800/244-4752** or 808/329-3333. Fax 808/326-4137. 37 units, all with shower only. $115–$160 double. Cleaning fee $85. 3-night minimum. DC, DISC, MC, V. **Amenities:** Excellent restaurant; bar; oceanfront outdoor pool. *In room:* TV, fridge, Internet (free), kitchen.

Kona Seaside Hotel

The best deal at this budget hotel is the room-and-car package; it's cheaper than the rack rates. Located in the heart of Kailua-Kona, the Kona Seaside is just steps away from Kailua Bay and Kailua-Kona's shopping, restaurants, and historic sites. The rooms are large and comfy (even if they don't have fancy soaps and extra amenities), but they can be noisy (ask for one away from the road). You may want to splurge on one of the 14 units with kitchenettes.

75-5646 Palani Rd. (at Kuakini Hwy.), Kailua-Kona, HI 96740. www.sand-seaside.com. *C* **800/560-5558** or 808/329-2455. Fax 808/329-6157. 225 units. $82–$130 double. Extra person $15. Children 11 and under stay free in parent's room. Check the website for specials starting at $88. AE, DC, MC, V. Parking $5. **Amenities:** Restaurant; bar; 2 small outdoor pools. *In room:* A/C, TV, fridge, kitchenette (in some units).

Kona Tiki Hotel ★★ 🏨

It's hard to believe that places like this still exist. The Kona Tiki, located right on the ocean, away from the hustle and bustle of downtown Kailua-Kona, is one of the best budget deals in Hawaii. All of the rooms are tastefully decorated and feature queen-size beds, ceiling fans, and private lanais overlooking the water. Although it's called a hotel, this small, family-run operation is more like a large B&B, with lots of aloha and plenty of friendly conversation at the morning breakfast buffet around the pool. The staff is helpful in planning activities. There are no TVs or phones in the rooms (there's a pay phone in the lobby). If a double with a kitchenette is available, grab it—the extra few bucks will save you a bundle in food costs. Book way in advance.

75-5968 Alii Dr. (about a mile from downtown Kailua-Kona), Kailua Kona, HI 96740. www.konatiki.com. © **808/329-1425.** Fax 808/327-9402. 15 units. $75–$89 double; $99 double w/kitchenette. Extra person $12 per adult, $6 per child 2-12. Rates include continental breakfast. 3-night minimum. No credit cards. **Amenities:** Outdoor pool. *In room:* Fridge, kitchenette (in some units), no phone.

Uncle Billy's Kona Bay Hotel   An institution in Kona, Uncle Billy's is where visitors from the other islands stay. A thatched roof hangs over the lobby area, and a Polynesian longhouse restaurant is next door. The rooms are old but comfortable and come with large lanais and minifridges. This budget hotel is a good place to sleep, but don't expect new carpeting or fancy soap in the bathroom. It can be noisy at night when big groups book in; avoid Labor Day weekend, when all the canoe paddlers in the state want to stay here and rehash the race into the wee morning hours.

75-5739 Alii Dr., Kailua-Kona, HI 96740. www.unclebilly.com. © **800/367-5102** or 808/961-5818. Fax 808/935-7903. 139 units. $79–$129 double. Extra person $20. Children 18 and under stay free in parent's room. Check the website for specials. AE, DC, DISC, MC, V. **Amenities:** Outdoor pool; watersports equipment rentals. *In room:* A/C, TV, fridge, hair dryer.

Upcountry Kona: Holualoa
EXPENSIVE

Holualoa Inn ★★ 🎁   The quiet, secluded setting of this B&B—30 pastoral acres just off the main drag of the artsy village of Holualoa, 1,350 feet above Kailua-Kona—provides stunning panoramic views of the entire coast. Recently sold to Sandy Hazen, a local Kona coffee farmer, this contemporary 7,000-square-foot Hawaiian home has six private suites and window-walls that roll back to embrace the gardens and views. Sandy rejuvenated the guest rooms with new furnishings, upgraded bathrooms, and lauhala matting on the ceilings. Plus, the inn now has a chef cooking your gourmet breakfast. Cows graze on the bucolic pastures below the garden Jacuzzi and pool, and the 30-acre estate includes 3,000 coffee trees, which are the source of the morning brew. The inn offers a gas grill for a romantic dinner beside the pool, a telescope for stargazing, and a billiard table. It's a 15-minute drive down the hill to busy Kailua-Kona and about

20 minutes to the beach, but the pool has a stunning view of Kailua-Kona and the sparkling Pacific below.

76–5932 Mamalahoa Hwy. (P.O. Box 222), Holualoa, HI 96725. www.holualoainn. com. ⓒ **800/392-1812** or 808/324-1121. Fax 808/322-2472. 6 units, 1 with shower only. $260–$375 double. Rates include full breakfast. AE, DC, DISC, MC, V. On Mamalahoa Hwy., just after the Holualoa post office, look for Paul's Place General Store; the next driveway is the inn. Children must be 13 or older. **Amenities:** Jacuzzi; huge outdoor pool; guest kitchenette; Wi-Fi (free). *In room:* Hair dryer, no phone.

Keauhou

VERY EXPENSIVE

Sheraton Keauhou Bay Resort & Spa ★ ☺
There has been a huge drop in rates at this resort at the ocean's edge. Prices now are cheaper than they were in 2005, when the Sheraton spent $70 million in renovations, and opened the Sheraton Keauhou Bay Resort. The complete overhaul of this 1970s resort is remarkable: Walls were torn out in the lobby and the main dining room to allow access to the incredible view of Keauhou Bay, and the 420-square-foot rooms were completely redone to bring them into the 21st century. (The best addition to the rooms: Sheraton's Sweet Sleeper Bed, with a cushy mattress top, a featherweight duvet, and five pillows to choose from.) The next biggest change to the resort is the mammoth freshwater pool, tucked in around the tropical gardens and splashing waterfalls, with its own small manmade beach, the island's largest water slide, bubbling whirlpool spas, and a children's play area. Speaking of kids, there's a children's center and seasonal program on the property and plenty to keep the little ones occupied (water activities, cultural games, arts and crafts, video games, and so on). Plus, the Sheraton has a golf course next door, on-site tennis courts, and a shopping center (with restaurants) close by.

78–128 Ehukai St., Kailua-Kona, HI 96740. www.sheratonkeauhou.com. ⓒ **888/488-3535** or 808/930-4900. Fax 808/930-4800. 522 units. $169–$259 double; from $485 suite. Extra person $60. Children 18 and under stay free in parent's room using existing bedding. Starwood members get reduced rates. Resort fee $15 per day, includes self-parking, Internet, local calls, Kona Trolley. AE, DC, DISC, MC, V. Valet parking $16. **Amenities:** 3 restaurants (luau once a week, p. 173); bar; babysitting; seasonal children's program; concierge; 36-hole golf course nearby w/preferred guest rate; fitness center; whirlpool; multilevel pool w/200-ft. water slide; room service; spa; 2 tennis courts; *In room:* A/C, TV, fridge, hair dryer, Wi-Fi (free).

EXPENSIVE

Outrigger Kanaloa at Kona ★★ ☺
These big, comfortable, well-managed, and spacious vacation condos, on 16 landscaped

acres, border the rocky coast beside Keauhou Bay, 6 miles south of Kailua-Kona. They're exceptional units, ideal for families, with comforts such as huge bathrooms with whirlpool bathtubs, dressing rooms, and bidets at prices lower than they have been for years. In addition, the spacious lanais, tropical decor, and many appliances make for free and easy living. It's easy to stock up on supplies at the supermarket and at the mall just up the hill. Guests receive discounted golf rates at a nearby country club.

78-261 Manukai St., Kailua-Kona, HI 96740. www.outrigger.com. ⟨℃⟩ **800/959-5662** or 808/322-9625. Fax 808/322-3818. 76 units. $179–$195 1-bedroom apt. (sleeps up to 4); $199–$339 2-bedroom apt. (up to 6). AE, DC, DISC, MC, V. **Amenities:** Babysitting; concierge; 3 Jacuzzis; 3 outdoor pools (1 for adults only); 2 tennis courts (lit for night play). *In room:* TV, fridge, hair dryer, Internet (free), kitchen.

Outrigger Keauhou Beach Resort ★ 🏷 Located on 10 acres, this former Ohana Keauhou Beach Hotel, still owned by the same company, has been upgraded to the more upscale Outrigger brand. The setting is perfect, on a large reef system (where sea turtles come ashore for a brief nap) and next door to one of Kona's best white-sand beaches, Kahuluu. Lush tropical gardens of native plants and flowers surround the hotel, and it's just a mile from the Kona Country Club's 36 holes of golf. The rooms are small (you could fit a crib in there, but a family of four should get two rooms); the oceanview units are well worth the extra money. The main dining room serves fresh local produce, meats, and fish, and you also have the option of other restaurants and shopping at the nearby Keauhou Shopping Center, just a 2-minute drive away. Rates are much cheaper here than at the nearby Sheraton Keauhou (reviewed above).

78-6740 Alii Dr., Kailua-Kona, HI 96740. www.outrigger.com. ⟨℃⟩ **800/959-5662** or 808/322-3441. Fax 808/322-3117. 309 units. $149–$225 double; from $350 suite. Extra person $50. AE, DC, DISC, MC, V. Parking $7 per day. **Amenities:** Restaurant; bar; year-round children's program; concierge; 36-hole golf course nearby; fitness center; whirlpool; outdoor pool; room service; spa; 6 tennis courts (2 lit for night play). *In room:* A/C, TV, fridge, hair dryer, Internet (free).

MODERATE

Kona Seaspray ★ 🏷 The Kona Seaspray has a couple of great things going for it: location and price. It's just across from the Kahaluu Beach Park, possibly the best snorkeling area in Kona. The rates are a great deal when you consider that the one-bedroom apartments easily sleep four and the two-bedroom units can sleep six. It's under new ownership, and all units are undergoing renovations that include upgraded furniture and new carpets. Every unit has a full kitchen, lanai, and fabulous ocean view. Golf and tennis are nearby; there's also a barbecue area.

This is the place to book if you are going to spend a lot of time lounging around, or if you need the extra space.

78–6671 Alii Dr., Kailua-Kona, HI 96740. Reservations c/o Johnson Resort Properties, 78–6665 Alii Dr., Kailua-Kona, HI 96740. www.konaseaspray.com. © **808/ 322-2403.** Fax 808/322-0105. 12 units. $150–$175 1-bedroom; $165–$190 2-bedroom/2-bathroom. Extra person $20. Cleaning fee $65–$90. 3-night minimum. AE, DISC, MC, V. **Amenities:** Whirlpool hot tub; gorgeous outdoor pool w/ waterfall. *In room:* TV/VCR, full-size fridge, hair dryer, full kitchen, Wi-Fi (free).

South Kona
EXPENSIVE

Horizon Guest House ★★ 🏠 If you're planning to stay in South Kona, get on the phone right now and book this place—it's the Hawaiian hideaway of your dreams. Host Clem Classen spent 2 years researching the elements of a perfect B&B, and the Horizon Guest House is the result. Its 40 acres of pastureland are located at an altitude of 1,100 feet. You can see 25 miles of coastline, from Kealakekua to just about South Point, yet you cannot see another structure or hear any sounds of civilization. The carefully thought out individual units (all under one roof but positioned at an angle to one another so you don't see any other units) are filled with incredible Hawaiian furnishings, including hand-quilted Hawaiian bedspreads, and boast private lanais with coastline views. The property features barbecue facilities, gardens everywhere, an outdoor shower, and plenty of beach toys. Clem whips up a gourmet breakfast in the main house, which also features a media room with library, video collection, TV (which you can take to your room if you use headphones so you won't disturb other guests), DVD player, VCR, and cordless phone. At first glance, the rates may seem high, but once you're ensconced on the unique property, I think you'll agree they're worth every penny.

P.O. Box 268, Honaunau, HI 96726. www.horizonguesthouse.com. © **888/328- 8301** or 808/328-2540. Fax 808/328-8707. 4 units. $250–$350 double based on 1–3 nights. Rates include full gourmet breakfast. MC, V. Located 21 miles south of Kailua-Kona on Hwy. 11, just before mile marker 100. Children must be 14 or older. **Amenities:** Jacuzzi perfectly placed to watch the sunset behind Kealakekua Bay; large outdoor pool worthy of a big resort; Wi-Fi (free). *In room:* Fridge, hair dryer, no phone.

INEXPENSIVE

Affordable Hawaii at Pomaikai (Lucky) Farm Bed & Breakfast 🏷 True to its name, Affordable Hawaii offers an inexpensive perch from which to explore the South Kona Coast. Come share the century-old 4-acre farm, which is overflowing with macadamia nuts, coffee, avocados as big as footballs, tropical fruits, and even *jaboticaba,* an exotic fruit that makes a zingy jam and local wine. The least expensive room is inside the old farm-house (at $80 a night, this is a deal). The Greenhouse wing has two rooms with wooden floors, big windows, and private entrances. The most unusual accommodation is the old coffee barn, updated into a rustic room for two with a raised queen-size bed, a fabulous view of the coastline, and an outdoor shower. Guests can use a common kitchen with a refrigerator, microwave, hot plate, and barbecue grill.

83-5465 Mamalahoa Hwy. (south of Kailua-Kona, after mile marker 107), Captain Cook, HI 96704. www.luckyfarm.com. ℭ **800/325-6427** or 808/328-2112. Fax 808/328-2112. 4 units. $80–$140 double. Extra person $10, $5 per child 5 and under. Rates include full farm breakfast. 2-night minimum. AE, DISC, MC, V. **Amenities:** Wi-Fi (free). *In room:* No phone.

Areca Palms Estate Bed & Breakfast ★ 🎒

Everything about this upcountry B&B is impeccable: the landscaping, the furnishings, the fresh flowers in every room—even breakfast is served with attention to every detail. This charming cedar home, surrounded by immaculate parklike landscaping, sits above the Captain Cook–Kealakekua area, close to beaches, shopping, and restaurants. Guests enjoy watching the sun sink into the ocean from the large lanai or gazing at the starry sky as they soak in the hot tub. Hosts Janice and Steve Glass serve memorable break-fasts (orange-oatmeal quiche, tropical stuffed French toast, tree-ripened banana cakes), offer daily maid service, provide guests with beach equipment, and gladly help with reservations for activities and dinner.

P.O. Box 489, Captain Cook, HI 96704. www.konabedandbreakfast.com. ℭ **800/545-4390** or 808/323-2276. Fax 808/323-3749. 4 units. $115–$145 double. Extra person $30. Rates include full breakfast. 2-night minimum. MC, V. From Hwy. 11, make a left at the Pacific Island Tire dealer (after mile marker 111) and follow the signs. **Amenities:** Outdoor Jacuzzi. *In room:* TV, hair dryer, no phone, Wi-Fi (free).

Dragonfly Ranch: Healing Arts Center

Some may find the Dragonfly Ranch too rustic. But if you want to enjoy Hawaii's tropical outdoors and you're thrilled by the island's most unique architecture—structures that bring the outdoors inside—this may be the place for you. Cabins range from one room (with screens only, no drapes) to suites; you might describe the style as "early hippie." Breakfast includes healthy hot cereal such as amaranth, quinoa, and oatmeal with assorted toppings (toasted pecans, sun-flower seeds, walnuts, raisins, and golden flaxseed); fresh home-grown organic fruit (the sought-after "apple" bananas and "strawberry" papayas); wheat-free granola and waffles; and sprouted grain bread. The location is ideal, with Puuhonua O Honaunau National Historical Park right down the road and five bays offering great swimming and diving just minutes away. The place itself, with freestanding cabins tucked away on 2 acres of fruit trees and exotic flowers, truly is a tropical fantasy.

P.O. Box 675 (19 miles south of Kailua-Kona on Hwy. 160), Honaunau, HI 96726. www.dragonflyranch.com. © **808/328-2159.** Fax 808/328-9570. 5 units, all with private bathroom, 1 with shower only. $100–$250 double. Extra person $20. Rates include continental breakfast. 3-night minimum. MC, V. From Hwy. 11, turn onto Hwy. 160 (the road to Puuhonua O Honaunau National Historical Park), between mile markers 103 and 104; after 1½ miles, look for the Dragonfly Ranch mailbox. **Amenities:** Babysitting; yoga studio and fitness room; spa; watersports equipment rentals. *In room:* DVD, fridge, hair dryer, kitchenette (in some units), Wi-Fi (free).

Manago Hotel ⚲   If you want to experience the history and culture of the 50th state, the Manago Hotel may be the place for you. This living relic is still operated by the third generation of the same Japanese family that opened it in 1917. It offers clean accommodations, tasty home cooking, and generous helpings of aloha, all at budget prices. The older rooms (with community bathrooms) are ultraspartan—strictly for desperate budget travelers. The rooms with private bathrooms in the new wing are still pretty sparse (freshly painted walls with no decoration and no TV), but they're spotlessly clean and surrounded by Japanese gardens with a koi pond. The rates increase as you go up; the third-floor units have the most spectacular views of the Kona coastline. Adventuresome travelers might want to try the Japanese rooms with tatami mats to sleep on and *furo* (deep hot tubs) in each room to soak in. By the end of your stay, you may leave with new friends—the Manago family is very friendly.

P.O. Box 145, Captain Cook, HI 96704. www.managohotel.com. © **808/323-2642.** Fax 808/323-3451. 63 units, some with shared bathroom. $36 double with shared bathroom; $59–$64 double with private bathroom; $78 double Japanese room with small *furo* tub and private bathroom. Extra person $3. DISC, MC, V. **Amenities:** Restaurant (Manago Hotel Restaurant, p. 79); bar. *In room:* No phone.

THE KOHALA COAST
Very Expensive

Hapuna Beach Prince Hotel ★★   If you've ever dreamed of staying in a luxury "Prince" hotel, now is your chance, as rates have dropped considerably this year. One of the best locations on the Kohala Coast, this property is nestled behind the magnificent white sands of Hapuna Beach. Accommodations are comfortable, all attuned to the fabulous ocean view and the sea breezes. Although the rooms are small for a luxury hotel, the sprawling grounds make up for it (some guests, however, complain about the

Where to Stay & Dine in North Kohala & Waimea

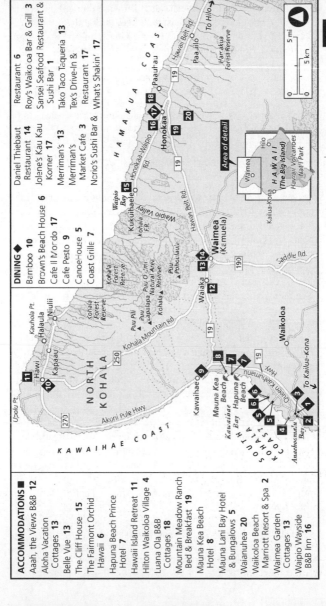

ACCOMMODATIONS ■

Aaah, the Views B&B **12**
Aloha Vacation Cottages **13**
Belle Vue **13**
The Cliff House **15**
The Fairmont Orchid Hawaii **6**
Hapuna Beach Prince Hotel **7**
Hawaii Island Retreat **11**
Hilton Waikoloa Village **4**
Luana Ola B&B Cottages **18**
Mountain Meadow Ranch Bed & Breakfast **19**
Mauna Kea Beach Hotel **8**
Mauna Lani Bay Hotel & Bungalows **5**
Waianuhea **20**
Waikoloa Beach Marriott Resort & Spa **2**
Waimea Garden Cottages **13**
Waipio Wayside B&B Inn **16**

DINING ◆

Bamboo **10**
Brown's Beach House **6**
Cafe Il M'or'do **17**
Cafe Pesto **9**
Canoe House **5**
Coast Grille **7**
Daniel Thiebaut Restaurant **14**
Jolene's Kau Kau Korner **17**
Merriman's **13**
Merriman's Market Cafe **3**
Ncrio's Sushi Bar & Restaurant **6**
Roy's Waiko oa Bar & Grill **3**
Sansei Seafood Restaurant & Sushi Bar **1**
Tako Taco Taqueria **13**
Tex's Drive-In & Restaurant **17**
What's Shakin' **17**

long walk from the lobby to their rooms). Service is friendly and caring. There is also a wealth of amenities on the property, from the 18-hole championship golf course (designed by Arnold Palmer and Ed Seay, and reserved for guests and residents) to the state-of-the-art fitness center and world-class Paul Brown Salon & Spa, one of the state's top salons. The atmosphere here is slightly more formal than most Hawaii resorts on the Kohala Coast; guests, many from Japan, dress up here, some in the latest Tokyo fashions.

At the Mauna Kea Resort, 62-100 Kaunaoa Dr., Kohala Coast, HI 96743. www.princeresortshawaii.com. ✆ **800/882-6060** or 808/880-1111. Fax 808/880-3112. 350 units. $195–$700 double; from $499 suite. Extra person $60. Children 17 and under stay free in parent's room using existing bedding. AE, DC, MC, V. Parking $20 valet, $15 self. **Amenities:** 3 restaurants (including the Coast Grille, p. 80); 2 bars (including an open-air beachfront bar w/live evening entertainment); babysitting; year-round Keiki Club children's program; concierge; golf course; fitness center; Jacuzzi; huge outdoor pool; room service; spa; 13 tennis courts; watersports equipment rentals. *In room:* A/C, TV, fridge, hair dryer, Wi-Fi ($10).

Mauna Kea Beach Hotel ★★★ The phoenix has risen! Last renovated in 2006 after the earthquake, management has brought this wonderful icon into the 21st century. They took three hotel rooms and converted them into just two hotel rooms with spacious bathrooms (with a shower with a view in the deluxe units, huge soaking tubs, and a separate sink/dressing area with two separate sinks). Also added in the rooms: a giant walk-in closet, 44-inch flatscreen TV, lots of plugs to charge your computer, an iPod docking station, one-switch light controls both at the bed and at the entry door, and a coffeemaker.

This resort dates from the early 1960s. Laurance S. Rockefeller was sailing around Hawaii when he spotted a perfect crescent of gold sand and dropped anchor. In 1965, he built the Mauna Kea on the spot. Since then, several luxury hotels have been added to the area, but Mauna Kea's beach out front tops them all, and the loyal old-money guests keep coming back to savor the relaxed, clubby ambience, remote setting, world-class golf, and old Hawaii ways. Rooms are huge by today's standards, with breathtaking views from the large lanais—plus the hotel is positioned to catch the cooling trade winds. The two championship golf courses—the famous Mauna Kea course, designed by Robert Trent Jones, Sr., and the Hapuna course, designed by Arnold Palmer—are both award winners.

At the Mauna Kea Resort, 62-100 Mauna Kea Beach Dr., Kohala Coast, HI 96743. www.princeresortshawaii.com. ✆ **866/977-4589** or 808/882-7222. Fax 808/880-3112. 310 units. $299–$950 double; from $680 suite. Extra person $75. AE, DC, MC, V. Parking $15. **Amenities:** 3 restaurants; 3 bars w/live music; babysitting; children's program; concierge; 2 championship golf courses; excellent fitness center; Jacuzzi; large outdoor pool; room service; 13-court oceanside tennis complex; watersports equipment rentals. *In room:* A/C, TV, fridge, hair dryer, Wi-Fi ($15).

Mauna Lani Bay Hotel & Bungalows ★★ ☺

Burned out? In need of tranquility and gorgeous surroundings? Look no further. Sandy beaches and lava tide pools are the focus of this serene seaside resort, where gracious hospitality is dispensed in a historic setting. From the lounge chairs on the pristine beach to the turn-down service at night, everything here is done impeccably. Louvered doors open onto the plush guest rooms, which are outfitted in natural tones with teak accents, each with a lanai. They're arranged to capture maximum ocean views, and they surround interior atrium gardens and pools in which endangered baby sea turtles are raised. A shoreline trail leads across the whole 3,200-acre resort, giving you an intimate glimpse into the ancient past, when people lived in lava caves and tended the large complex of fish ponds.

The hotel offers a very complete children's program, plus kid-friendly restaurants, but in addition, this is simply a great place for kids to explore. The saltwater stream that meanders through the hotel and onto the property outside is filled with reef fish and even a shark. The fish ponds are a great educational experience for *keiki*, and the beach has plenty of room for the youngsters to run and play. Next door to the resort are ancient Hawaiian petroglyph fields, where older kids can learn about Hawaii's past.

The Sports & Fitness Club (one of the best on the island) was just renovated, and the Shops at Mauna Lani recently opened with great retail-therapy opportunities and several food options.

At the Mauna Lani Resort, 68-1400 Mauna Lani Dr., Kohala Coast, HI 96743. www. maunalani.com. ✆ **800/367-2323** or 808/885-6622. Fax 808/885-1484. 342 units. $395–$825 double; from $995 suite; $3,300–$3,900 bungalow (sleeps up to 4). Extra person $75. AE, DC, DISC, MC, V. **Amenities:** 3 excellent restaurants (including CanoeHouse, p. 80) with live music Tues–Sat; bar (w/live music Fri–Sat); babysitting; bike rentals; concierge; year-round children's program; 2 celebrated 18-hole championship golf courses; full-service fitness facility; Jacuzzi; large outdoor pool; room service; range of massage treatments at the spa; 10 Plexipave tennis courts; watersports equipment rentals. *In room:* A/C, TV, CD player, fridge, hair dryer, Internet (free).

Waikoloa Beach Marriott Resort & Spa ★

This resort has always had one outstanding attribute: an excellent location on Anaehoomalu Bay (or A-Bay, as the locals call it), one of the best ocean-sports bays on the Kohala Coast. The gentle sloping beach has everything: swimming, snorkeling, diving, kayaking, windsurfing, and even old royal fish ponds. Now Marriott has made big, big changes here. It has gutted all the guest rooms (back down to the bare concrete) and redesigned them, adding 27-inch flatscreen TVs, putting in glass lanai railings (which actually glow at sunset), and topping everything off with Marriott's very comfy Revive beds. The property still isn't as posh as other luxury hotels along the Kohala Coast, but it also isn't nearly as expensive. The size and layout of the guest rooms remain the same—perfectly nice, but not luxurious. Families might want to book the deluxe units, which are oversize. An adults-only infinity pool was added in 2006, and the Mandara Spa was expanded to 5,000 square feet on two levels. The main dining room, Hawaii Calls, was also expanded, with a new patio area and a new menu. Guests may use the two championship golf courses at the adjacent Hilton Waikoloa Village.

69–275 Waikoloa Beach Dr., Waikoloa, HI 96738. www.marriotthawaii.com. © **888/ 236-2427** or 808/886-6789. Fax 808/866-3601. 555 units. $199–$384 double; from $500 suite. Extra person $45. Children 17 and under stay free in parent's room. Daily $20 resort fee for overnight self-parking, half-day snorkel rental for 2, free local calls. AE, DC, DISC, MC, V. Valet parking $33. **Amenities:** 2 restaurants; bar w/nightly live entertainment; luau Wed and Sun; babysitting; concierge; year-round children's program; fitness center; Jacuzzi; outdoor pools (including a huge pool w/water slide and separate children's pool); room service; full-service Mandara Spa; 2 tennis courts; watersports equipment rentals; Hawaiian cultural activities, including petroglyphs tour. *In room:* A/C, TV, fridge, hair dryer, Internet ($15 per day).

Expensive

The Fairmont Orchid Hawaii ★★★ ☺ Located on 32 acres of oceanfront property, the Orchid is the place for watersports nuts, cultural explorers, families with children, or anyone who just wants to lie back and soak up the sun. This elegant beach resort takes full advantage of the spectacular ocean views and historic sites on its grounds. The sports facilities here are extensive, and there's an excellent Hawaiiana program: The "beach boys" demonstrate how to do everything from creating drums from the trunks of coconut trees to paddling a Hawaiian canoe to strumming a ukulele.

All rooms in this luxury hotel underwent complete renovation in 2006 (to the tune of $9.3 million) and sport new carpets, paint, artwork, lanai furniture, and amenities. Every unit has a big lanai, sitting area, and marble bathroom with double vanity and separate shower. I recommend spending a few dollars more to book a room on the Fairmont Gold Floor, which offers personalized service, complimentary Internet access, a lounge (serving continental breakfast, finger sandwiches in the afternoon, and appetizers in the evening), and exquisite ocean views. The Spa Without Walls allows you to book a massage just about anywhere on the property—overlooking the ocean, nestled deep in the lush vegetation, or in the privacy of your room.

The Orchid's four restaurants are all wonderful, with a casual, relaxed atmosphere. The award-winning Norio's Sushi Bar & Restaurant has expanded, with three sushi chefs chopping, rolling, and performing magic at the sushi bar. The recently opened luau and Polynesian revue ("Gathering of the Kings," p. 173) is making a big splash, with everything from fire-knife dancing performances to culinary creations from Samoa, Tahiti, and New Zealand. The Keiki Aloha program, for kids 5 to 12, features watersports, Hawaiian cultural activities, and other supervised adventures. Some special money-saving family packages are also available.

I applaud the Fairmont Orchid for dropping the obnoxious "resort fee" and allowing guests to pay for the extra services they want. *Hot tip:* Before you arrive, sign up online for the Fairmont President's Club (which is free)—you'll get lots of benefits, including free Internet access.

At the Mauna Lani Resort, 1 N. Kaniku Dr., Kohala Coast, HI 96743. www.fairmont.com/orchid. ✆ **800/845-9905** or 808/885-2000. Fax 808/885-5778. 540 units. $369–$619 double; $589–$669 Gold Floor double; from $789 suite. Extra person $75. Children 17 and under stay free in parent's room. AE, DC, DISC, MC, V. Valet parking $22; self-parking $17. **Amenities:** 4 restaurants (including Norio's Sushi Bar & Restaurant, p. 81, and Brown's Beach House, p. 79); 5 bars (w/evening entertainment in the Paniolo Lounge); luau and Polynesian revue (p. 173); babysitting; bike rentals; year-round children's program; concierge; concierge-level rooms; 2 championship golf courses; well-equipped fitness center; 2 lava-rock whirlpools; large outdoor pool; room service; outstanding spa; 10 award-winning Plexipave tennis courts (7 lit for night play); watersports equipment rentals. *In room:* A/C, TV, hair dryer, Internet (free), minibar.

Hawaii Island Retreat ★★★ 🎁 Hidden in the rolling hills of North Kohala is a 50-acre palatial estate, overlooking the ocean. It's the perfect spot to relax and rejuvenate. Created by the local town doctor and his wife, who created the "Spa Without Walls" (above) and is skilled in Hawaiian healing arts, the property offers accommodations in an ecofriendly environment. Included are a sumptuous boutique hotel and luxury yurts. You'll also find a full spa with yoga and fitness classes. An opulent breakfast is included. The entire property is self-sufficient, down to the organic food grown on the property. The large rooms in the main hotel are decorated with turn-of-the-20th-century Hawaiian furniture and have private lanais. The individual yurts, nestled in an iron grove, are surprisingly spacious with a private toilet (showers are shared). The yurts are located next door to the spa massage treatment area, fitness center, sauna, and infinity pool. For those on a budget, the yurts allow more affordable accommodations, with all the amenities, including breakfast, spa, and fitness classes. All-inclusive, custom packages (meals, spa treatments, and fitness classes) are available. This is the place to come if you are looking for a vacation to simply relax and restore your energy. The property is honeycombed with hiking trails down to the ocean and the atmosphere is steeped in Hawaiian culture.

54-250 Maluhia Rd., P.O. Box 189, Hawi, HI 96719. www.hawaiiislandretreat.com. ℂ **808/889-6336.** 10 units in hotel; 7 yurts. $275–$450 hotel double; $150 yurt double. Rates include large breakfast. DISC, MC, V. **Amenities:** Outdoor pool; spa; Wi-Fi (free). *In room:* CD player.

Hilton Waikoloa Village ★   This hotel is a fantasy world all its own, perfect for those who love Vegas and Disneyland. Its high-rise towers are connected by silver-bullet trams, boats, and museum-like walkways lined with $7 million in Asian/Pacific reproductions. The kids will love it, but Mom and Dad may get a little weary waiting for the tram or boat to take them to breakfast (sometimes a 20-min. ordeal or a mile-long walk). The 62 acres feature tropical gardens, cascading waterfalls, exotic wildlife, exaggerated architecture, a 175-foot water slide twisting into a 1-acre pool, hidden grottoes, and manmade lagoons, including a dolphin lagoon (where you can swim with the dolphins for a fee).

The contemporary guest rooms are spacious and luxurious, with built-in platform beds, lanais, and loads of amenities, from spacious dressing areas to a second phone line in all units. All rooms and bathrooms have recently undergone renovations from top to bottom, including new drapes, new beds and bedding, bigger televisions, and new carpet and tile. With nine restaurants to choose from, you'll never lack for culinary options, and golfers can try out the two championship golf courses, one designed by Robert Trent Jones, Jr., and the other by Tom Weiskopf.

Even if you aren't staying here, drop by for the Kohala Sports Club & Spa, one of the best spas on the Kohala Coast, with 25,000 square feet of treatment rooms, saunas, whirlpools, and a host of treatments, including acupuncture and Eastern medicine practices—there's even an astrologer on staff.

69-425 Waikoloa Beach Dr., Waikoloa, HI 96738. www.hiltonwaikoloavillage. com. ℂ **800/HILTONS** or 808/886-1234. Fax 808/886-2900. 1,240 units. $199–$284 double; $305–$339 tower deluxe double; from $549 suite; $309–$599 double cabana. Extra person $50. Children 18 and under stay free in parent's room. AE, DC, DISC, MC, V. Valet parking $21; self-parking $15. **Amenities:** 7 restaurants; luau; 9 bars (many w/entertainment); babysitting; bike rentals; fabulous children's program; concierge; concierge-level rooms; 2 18-hole golf courses; Jacuzzi; 3 huge outdoor pools (w/waterfalls, slides, whirlpools, and an adults-only pool); room service; excellent spa w/cardio machines,

MODERATE

Puakea Ranch ★★ 🏠 If you're looking for a really special vacation stay that will remain in your memory long after your tan has faded, these luxury vacation rental homes will do the trick. They sit on the historic pastures (from 1870) of the Puakea Ranch, where plantation workers, cowboys, and their families lived. Located at 400 feet above sea level (with temperatures hovering about 85°F/29°C year-round and gentle trades keeping everything cool), these enchanting cabins (ranging from studios to three bed rooms) all have ocean views and are listed on the state's Register of Historic Places. The homes all have full, modern kitchens, charming Japanese-style outdoor bathhouses, swimming pools, and herb gardens. The quaint towns of Hawi and Kapaau are just 2 miles away, and the beautiful beaches of the Kohala coast are reached in just a 15 minute drive. For a truly relaxing, private vacation, I'd recommend nestling into your own private historic home on this ecofriendly ranch and decompressing.

56-2864 Akoni Pule Hwy., Hawi. Reservations: 65-1126 Puu Opelu Rd., Kamuela, 96743. www.puakearanch.com. © **808/315-0805.** 4 units. $225-$525 double. Minimum stay 2 nights. AE, DISC, MC, V. **Amenities:** Swimming pool. *In room:* TV, fridge, hair dryer, full kitchen.

WAIMEA

Note: You'll find Waimea accommodations on the map on p. 49.

Moderate

Aaah, the Views Bed & Breakfast ★ 🍃 This quiet B&B, just 15 minutes from the fabulous beaches of the Kohala Coast and 5 minutes from the cowboy town of Waimea, lives up to its name—each of the two units has huge picture windows from which you can watch the sun rise or set, or gaze out over green pastureland to the slopes of Mauna Kea. One unit is a studio apartment, complete with kitchen. The second unit is a two-bedroom, one bathroom with a kitchenette that can sleep up to six people. New owners Erika and Derek Stuart recently took over this B&B and have added a new deck to the streamside property. Rooms have a phone with free long distance to the mainland.

P.O. Box 6593, Kamuela, HI 96743. www.aaahtheviews.com. © **808/885-3455.** Fax 808/885-4031. 2 units. $165-$195 double. Extra person $20. Rates include continental breakfast. Prefer 2-night minimum. MC, V. *In room:* TV/VCR, fridge, hair dryer, kitchenette, Wi-Fi (free).

Waimea Garden Cottages ★★ 🎁 Imagine rolling hills on pastoral ranch land. Then add a babbling stream and two cozy Hawaiian cottages. Complete the picture with mountain views, and you have Waimea Garden Cottages. One unit has the feel of an old English country cottage, with oak floors, a fireplace, and French doors opening onto a spacious brick patio. The other is a remodeled century-old Hawaiian washhouse, filled with antiques, eucalyptus-wood floors, and a full kitchen. Extra touches keep guests returning again and again: plush English robes, sandalwood soaps in the bathroom, mints next to the bed, and fresh flowers throughout. Hosts Barbara and Charlie Campbell live on the spacious property. They have added a studio (with kitchenette), attached to the main house with its own entrance.

P.O. Box 520 (off Mamalahoa Hwy., 2 miles west of Waimea town center), Kamuela, HI 96743. www.waimeagardens.com. ⓒ **808/885-8550.** Fax 808/885-0473. 3 units. $150–$180 double. Extra person $50 12 years and older, $25 for children. Rates include breakfast treats in the refrigerator. 3-night minimum. No credit cards. *In room:* TV/VCR, fridge, hair dryer, kitchen, whirlpool bathtub (in 1 unit), fireplace (in 1 unit), Wi-Fi (free).

Inexpensive

Aloha Vacation Cottages ★ 🎁 You'll find these two rental units in a residential area in the cool climate of Waimea. The small, intimate guesthouse has a full kitchen, a separate bedroom, a washer/dryer, and all the comforts of home, including a selection of pillows and a mattress with an adjustable "comfort level" on each side. The larger stand-alone cottage has all the same amenities, plus more space. Guests are greeted with a fruit basket; barbecue facilities are available. The cottages are on the "dry" side of Waimea, about a 10- to 15-minute drive to the beach and just a few minutes to the restaurants of Waimea.

P.O. Box 1395, Kamuela, HI 96743. www.alohavacationcottages.com. ⓒ **877/875-1722** or 808/885-6535. 2 units. $120–$150 double. Extra person $20. 5-night minimum. Credit cards through PayPal. *In room:* TV/VCR, computer with Internet (free), hair dryer, beach gear.

Belle Vue ★ This two-story vacation rental has a truly beautiful view. Sitting in the hills overlooking Waimea and surrounded by manicured gardens, the charming home is just 15 minutes from the Kohala Coast beaches. The penthouse unit is a large cathedral-ceilinged studio apartment with a kitchenette, huge bedroom, luxurious bathroom, and view of Mauna Loa and Mauna Kea mountains down to the Pacific Ocean. The one-bedroom apartment has a kitchenette and a sofa bed. Each unit has a separate entrance. The rates include breakfast fixings (toast, juice, fruit, cereal, coffee) inside the kitchenettes.

1351 Konokohau Rd., off Opelo Rd. (P.O. Box 1295), Kamuela, HI 96743. www.
hawaii-bellevue.com. (℃) **800/772-5044** or (℃)/fax 808/885-7732. 2 units.
$95–$175 double. Extra person $25. Rates include breakfast fixings inside the
kitchenettes. 3-night minimum. MC, V. *In room:* TV, fridge, hair dryer, kitchenette, Wi-Fi (free).

THE HAMAKUA COAST

In addition to those listed below, another B&B in this area, in Ahua-
loa, a mountain community a short drive from Waipio, is **Mountain
Meadow Ranch Bed & Breakfast,** 46–3895 Kapuna Rd., Honokaa, HI 96727 ((℃) **808/775-9376;** www.mountainmeadowranch.
com), offering both a private cottage ($150 for four) and rooms in a
house ($115 double).

Note: You'll find the following accommodations on the map on
p. 49.

Expensive

Waianuhea ★★ 🎁 Located in the rural rolling hills above
Honokaa, totally off the grid, and nestled in 7 beautifully landscaped acres (with a lily pond, fruit trees, a vegetable garden, and
a bucolic horse pasture) is this oasis of luxury and relaxation. Just
off a narrow country road, the two-story inn features five posh
guest rooms with soaking tubs, gas or wood stoves, phones, and
flatscreen satellite TVs, all on photovoltaic solar power. Splurge a
little and ask for the Malamalama suite, with a cherrywood sleigh
bed, extra large soaking tub, glass-enclosed shower, and separate
living room. The inn's sumptuous main room has highly polished
wood floors, a rock fireplace, and custom Italian sofas, while the
Great Room has wraparound glass windows with multicolored
glass balloons hanging from the ceiling. Other amenities include
nightly wine tasting (featuring different wines every month) with
gourmet hors d'oeuvres, a guest kitchenette stocked with a range
of goodies (enough to make a meal), and beverages at surprisingly
reasonable prices. Complete multicourse gourmet breakfasts are
served every morning.

45-3503 Kahana Dr. (P.O. Box 185), Honokaa, HI 96727. www.waianuhea.com.
(℃) **888/775-2577** or 808/775-1118. Fax 888/296-6302. 5 units. $210–$400
double. Rates include full breakfast. AE, MC, V. **Amenities:** Outdoor hot tub;
guest kitchenette. *In room:* TV/DVD, hair dryer.

Moderate

The Cliff House ★★ 🎁 Perched on the cliffs above the ocean
is this romantic two-bedroom getaway, surrounded by horse pastures and million-dollar views. A large deck takes in the ocean
vista, where whales frolic offshore in winter. Impeccably decorated

(the owner also owns Waipio Valley Artworks), the unit features a very well-equipped kitchen with access to a barbecue, two large bedrooms, and a full bathroom. Lots of little touches make this property stand out from the others: an answering machine for the phone, a pair of binoculars, a chess set, and even an umbrella for the rain squalls. Four people could comfortably share this unit. Also available is the slightly smaller house next door, two bedrooms, one bath for $165 double.

P.O. Box 5070, Kukuihaele, HI 96727. www.cliffhousehawaii.com. © **800/492-4746** or 808/775-0005. Fax 808/775-0058. 1 unit. $199 double. Extra person $35. 3-night minimum. MC, V. *In room:* TV/VCR, CD player, fridge, hair dryer, Internet (free), kitchen, washer/dryer.

Inexpensive

Luana Ola B&B Cottages ★ 🎁 These off-the-beaten-path, plantation-style, open-room cottages hearken back to the romantic 1940s. Furnished in rattan and wicker, each features a kitchenette and sleeps up to four. One unit has a spectacular ocean view; while the ocean view from the other unit isn't as panoramic, a satellite TV helps make up for it. Hostess Marsha Tokareff leaves coffee in your kitchen so you can get up at your leisure. The cottages are within walking distance to Honokaa town, yet far enough away to feel the peace and quiet of this bucolic area.

P.O. Box 1967, Honokaa, HI 96727. www.island-hawaii.com. © **800/357-7727** or 808/775-1150. 2 units. $115 double. Extra person $15. 2-night minimum. MC, V. *In room:* TV, CD player, fridge, hair dryer, kitchenette, Wi-Fi (free).

Waipio Wayside Bed & Breakfast Inn ★★ 🎁 Jackie Horne's restored Hamakua Sugar supervisor's home, built in 1938, sits nestled among fruit trees, surrounded by sweet-smelling ginger, fragile orchids, and blooming birds-of-paradise. The comfortable house, done in old Hawaii style, abounds with thoughtful touches, such as the help-yourself tea-and-cookies bar with 26 different kinds of tea. A sunny lanai with hammocks overlooks a yard lush with banana, lemon, lime, tangerine, and avocado trees; the cliffside gazebo has views of the ocean 600 feet below. There are five vintage rooms to choose from: My favorite is the master bedroom suite (dubbed the Birds Eye Room), with double doors that open onto the deck; I also love the Library Room, which has an ocean view, hundreds of books, and a skylight in the shower. There's a shared living room with a TV (including VCR and DVD player). Jackie's friendly hospitality and excellent breakfasts round out the experience.

P.O. Box 840, Honokaa, HI 96727. www.waipiowayside.com. © **800/833-8849** or 808/775-0275. 5 units. $99–$190 double. Extra person $25. Rates include full organic tropical breakfast with coffee, fruit (sunrise papayas, mangoes, tangerines), granola, yogurt, and muffins. MC, V. Located on Hwy. 240, 2 miles from the Honokaa post office; look on the right for a long white picket fence and sign on the ocean side of the road; the 2nd driveway is the parking lot. **Amenities:** Concierge; TV/VCR/DVD in living room; Wi-Fi (free).

HILO

Just outside Hilo is a terrific bed-and-breakfast called **Lihi Kai,** 30 Kahoa St., Hilo, HI 96720 (☏ **808/935-7865**), a beautifully designed house with mahogany floors, perched on the edge of a cliff with a wide-angle view of Hilo Bay. Double rooms start at $78 a night.

Note: You'll find the following accommodations on the "Hilo" map on p. 60.

Expensive

The Palms Cliff House Inn ★★ 🎁   This place is gorgeous, but a little pricey for what you get. You'd do better to stay at the Mauna Kea Beach Resort, which has a beautiful sand beach out front, swimming pool, golfing, and a host of eating opportunities. You'll find no sand beach, swimming pool, or the like here. This inn is a 15-minute drive north of Hilo town, at Honomu (where Akaka Falls is located). Perched on the side of a cliff, the grand old Victorian-style inn is surrounded by manicured lawns and macadamia-nut, lemon, banana, lime, orange, avocado, papaya, star fruit, bread fruit, grapefruit, and mango trees. Eight oversize suites, filled with antiques and equipped with DVD players, fireplaces, and private lanais, all overlook the ocean. Four rooms have private Jacuzzis; other extras on the property include yoga classes, hula lessons, high tea, and private massages and other spa treatments. A gourmet hot breakfast (entrees range from banana/mac-nut pancakes to asparagus/sweet-potato quiche) is served on the wraparound lanai overlooking the rolling surf. A stay here is a magnificent getaway, but very pricey.

P.O. Box 189, Honomu, 96728. www.palmscliffhouse.com. ☏ **866/963-6076** or 808/963-6076. Fax 808/963-6316. 8 units. $299–$449 double. Rates include full gourmet breakfast. AE, DC, DISC, MC, V. **Amenities:** Hot tub. *In room:* A/C (in upper units), TV/DVD, fridge, hair dryer, Jacuzzi (in some units).

Moderate

Shipman House Bed & Breakfast Inn ★★ 🎁   Built in 1900, the Shipman House is on both the national and state registers of historic places. This Victorian mansion has been totally restored by Barbara Andersen, the great-granddaughter of the original owner, and her husband, Gary. Despite the home's historic appearance, Barbara has made sure that its conveniences are strictly 21st

Hilo

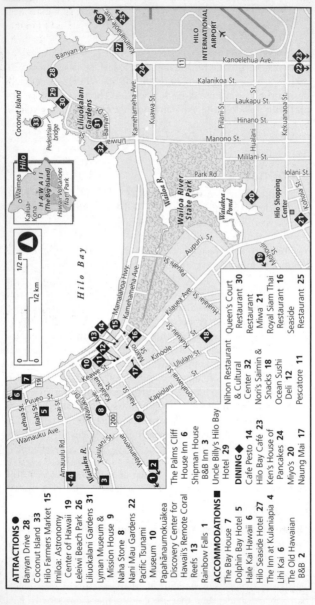

ATTRACTIONS ●
Banyan Drive **28**
Coconut Island **33**
Hilo Farmers Market **15**
Imiloa: Astronomy
  Center of Hawaii **19**
Leleiwi Beach Park **26**
Liliuokalani Gardens **31**
Lyman Museum &
  Mission House **9**
Naha Stone **8**
Nani Mau Gardens **22**
Pacific Tsunami
  Museum **10**
Papahānaumokuākea
  Discovery Center for
  Hawaii's Remote Coral
  Reefs **13**
Rainbow Falls **1**

ACCOMMODATIONS ■
The Bay House **7**
Dolphin Bay Hotel **5**
Hale Kai Hawaii **6**
Hilo Seaside Hotel **27**
The Inn at Kulaniapia **4**
Lihi Kai **6**
The Old Hawaiian
  B&B **2**

The Palms Cliff
  House Inn **6**
Shipman House
  B&B Inn **3**
Uncle Billy's Hilo Bay
  Hotel **29**

DINING ◆
Cafe Pesto **14**
Hilo Bay Café **23**
Ken's House of
  Pancakes **24**
Miyo's **20**
Naung Mai **17**

Nihon Restaurant
  & Cultural
  Center **32**
Nori's Saimin &
  Snacks **18**
Ocean Sushi
  Deli **12**
Pescatore **11**

Queen's Court
  Restaurant **30**
Restaurant
  Miwa **21**
Royal Siam Thai
  Restaurant **16**
Seaside
  Restaurant **25**

century, including full bathrooms with all the amenities. All five guest bedrooms are large, with 10- to 12-foot ceilings and touches such as heirloom furnishings and hand-woven lauhala mats. Wake up to a large continental breakfast buffet (with fresh fruit from the garden). On Wednesdays evenings, guests can join in with the hula class practicing on the lanai. The owners have recently added lei making and other cultural activities.

131 Kaiulani St., Hilo, HI 96720. www.hilo-hawaii.com. ⓒ **800/627-8447** or 808/934-8002. Fax 808/934-8002. 5 units. $219–$249 double. Extra person $35. Rates include continental breakfast. 2-night minimum. AE, MC, V. From Hwy. 19, take Waianuenue Ave.; turn right on Kaiulani St. and go 1 block over the wooden bridge; look for the large house on the left. *In room:* Small fridge, no phone, Wi-Fi (free).

Inexpensive

The Bay House ★ 🛏 Overlooking Hilo Bay, this B&B offers immaculate rooms (each with oak floors, king-size bed, sofa, private bathroom, and oceanview lanai) at reasonable prices. A continental breakfast of tropical fruit, pastries, and Kona coffee is set out every morning in a common area (which also has a refrigerator, toaster, and microwave for guests' use); you can take all you want to eat back to your lanai and watch the sun rise over Hilo Bay. In the evening, relax in the cliffside Jacuzzi as the stars come out.

42 Pukihae St., Hilo, HI 96720. www.bayhousehawaii.com. ⓒ **888/235-8195** or ⓒ/fax 808/961-6311. 3 units. $150 double (no 3rd person in units). Rates include continental breakfast. AE, MC, V. **Amenities:** Hot tub. *In room:* TV, hair dryer, Wi-Fi (free).

Dolphin Bay Hotel ★ 🍴 This two-story, motel-like building, 4 blocks from downtown, is a clean, family run property that offers good value in a quiet garden setting. Ripe star fruit hang from the trees, flowers abound, and there's a junglelike trail by a stream. The tidy concrete-block apartments are small and often breezeless, but they're equipped with table fans and jalousie windows. Rooms are brightly painted and outfitted with rattan furniture and Hawaiian prints. There are no phones in the units, but there's one in the lobby. You're welcome to all the papayas and bananas you can eat.

333 Iliahi St., Hilo, HI 96720. www.dolphinbayhilo.com. ⓒ **808/935-1466.** Fax 808/935-1523. 18 units. $109–$129 studio double; $159 1-bedroom apt. double; $169 2-bedroom apt. double. Extra person $10. Savings for multiple nights. From Hwy. 19, turn mauka (toward the mountains) on Hwy. 200 (Waianuenue St.), and then right on Puueo St.; go over the bridge and turn left on Iliahi St. MC, V. **Amenities:** Concierge. *In room:* TV, fridge, hair dryer (on request), Internet (free), kitchenette, no phone.

Hale Kai Hawaii ★ 🎁   An eye-popping view of the ocean runs the entire length of this house; you can sit on the wide deck and watch the surfers slide down the waves. All guest rooms have that fabulous ocean view through sliding-glass doors. There's one suite, with a living room, kitchenette, and separate bedroom. Guests have access to a pool, hot tub, and small common area with fridge, telephone, and library. Breakfast is a treat, with entrees such as homemade mac-nut waffles or double-cheese soufflé. New owners Maria Macias and Ricardo Zepeda have breathed new life into this B&B. The rooms are now all painted in vibrant tropical colors, Maria has improved the landscaping, and they've installed privacy barriers between each room.

111 Honolii Pali, Hilo, HI 96720. www.halekaihawaii.com. ⓒ **808/935-6330.** Fax 808/935-8439. 4 units. $150–$155 double; $165 suite. Extra person $30. Rates include gourmet breakfast. 2-night minimum. MC, V. **Amenities:** Jacuzzi; ocean-front outdoor pool; Wi-Fi (free). *In room:* TV, no phone.

Hilo Seaside Hotel   This family-operated hotel is located across Hilo Bay on historic Banyan Drive. Surrounded by lush tropical gardens and a spring pond filled with Japanese carp, this place isn't fancy, but it's great for those on a budget. The location is terrific for exploring East Hawaii: It's a 45-minute scenic drive to Hawaii Volcanoes National Park, a few minutes by car to downtown, and close to a 9-hole golf course and tennis courts.

126 Banyan Dr. (off Hwy. 19), Hilo, HI 96720. www.hiloseasidehotel.com. ⓒ **800/560-5557** or 808/935-0821. Fax 808/969-9195. 135 units. $76–$130 double. Extra person $15. AE, DISC, MC, V. **Amenities:** Restaurant; bar; 9-hole golf course nearby; outdoor pool. *In room:* A/C, TV, fridge, hair dryer (in some units or on request).

The Inn at Kulaniapia Falls ★ 🎁   The view from this off-the-beaten-track inn is worth the price alone: the 120-foot Kulaniapia Waterfall in one direction and the entire town of Hilo sprawled out 850 feet below in another direction. This is *the* place for a romantic getaway. In addition to luxury accommodations in the well-appointed rooms (with balconies), you'll enjoy a royal breakfast with egg dishes, fresh fruit grown on the 22-acre property, and just-baked breads. Wander along the 2-mile pathways that follow the Waiau River (check out the exotic bamboo garden) or swim at the base of the waterfall in the 300-foot pond. In addition to the Inn, they've added a couple of very beautiful guesthouses. It's just 15 minutes from Hilo, but you'll feel a zillion miles away from everything in the peaceful surroundings of a 2,000-acre macadamia-nut grove.

P.O. Box 11338, Hilo, HI 96720. www.waterfall.net. ⓒ **808/935-6789.** 10 units. $129–$149 rooms in Inn double; $200 cottage double. Extra person $25. Rates include full breakfast. AE, MC, V. **Amenities:** Hot tub; Internet (free). *In room:* TV (in some rooms).

The Old Hawaiian Bed & Breakfast 🏷 Bargain hunters, take note: This old plantation house from the 1930s has been renovated and offers great room rates that include breakfast. Located on the Wailuku River, the house features a large lanai, where guests have use of a phone, refrigerator, and microwave. The rooms range from tiny to large (the latter with its own sitting area, sunken bathtub, and separate shower). All have their own private entrances and private bathrooms. Hosts Stewart and Lory Hunter prepare a beautiful breakfast of fruit cup, fruit smoothie, juice, coffee or tea, and two types of homemade bread (you'll want seconds of Lory's mac-nut scones). The Hunters happily help guests with sightseeing plans, too.

1492 Wailuku Dr., Hilo, HI 96720. www.thebigislandvacation.com. 📞 **877/961-2816** or 808/961-2816. 3 units. $80–$110 double. Extra person $10. 2-night minimum. MC, V. *In room:* Hair dryer, Wi-Fi (free).

Uncle Billy's Hilo Bay Hotel Uncle Billy's is one of the least expensive places to stay along Hilo's hotel row, Banyan Drive. This oceanfront budget hotel boasts a dynamite location. You enter via a tiny lobby, gussied-up Polynesian style; it's slightly overdone, with sagging fishnets and *tapa* (bark cloth) on the walls. The guest rooms are simple: bed, TV, phone, closet, and bathroom—that's about it. The walls seem paper thin, and it can get very noisy at night (you may want to bring earplugs), but at these rates, you're still getting your money's worth.

87 Banyan Dr. (off Hwy. 19), Hilo, HI 96720. www.unclebilly.com. 📞 **800/367-5102** or 808/935-0861. Fax 808/935-7903. 144 units. $104–$129 double; $119 studio with kitchenette. Extra person $20. Children 18 and under stay free in parent's room. Check the website for specials starting at $73, car/room packages, and senior rates. Rates include continental breakfast buffet. AE, DC, DISC, MC, V. **Amenities:** Restaurant; bar w/live Hawaiian music, hula Fri and Sun nights; oceanfront pool. *In room:* A/C, TV, fridge (in some units), hair dryer (in some units), kitchenette (in some units).

HAWAII VOLCANOES NATIONAL PARK

As a result of Hawaii Volcanoes being officially designated a national park in 1916, a village has popped up at its front door. Volcano Village isn't so much a town as a wide spot in Old Volcano Road, with two general stores, a handful of restaurants, a post office, a coffee shop, a new firehouse, and a winery.

Except for Volcano House (see below), which is within the national park, all of the accommodations in this section are in

Where to Stay & Dine in the Volcano Area

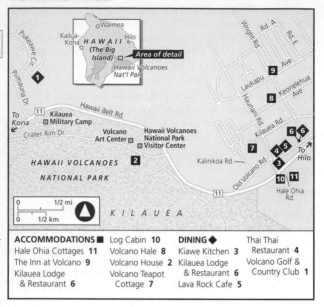

ACCOMMODATIONS ■

Hale Ohia Cottages **11**
The Inn at Volcano **9**
Kilauea Lodge
 & Restaurant **6**

Log Cabin **10**
Volcano Hale **8**
Volcano House **2**
Volcano Teapot
 Cottage **7**

DINING ◆

Kiawe Kitchen **3**
Kilauea Lodge
 & Restaurant **6**
Lava Rock Cafe **5**

Thai Thai
 Restaurant **4**
Volcano Golf &
 Country Club **1**

Volcano Village. It gets cool here at night—Volcano Village is located at 3,700 feet—so a fireplace might be an attractive amenity. It also rains a lot in Volcano—100 inches a year—which makes everything grow *Jack and the Beanstalk* style.

I recommend spending at least 3 days to really see and enjoy the park. The best way to do this is to rent a cottage or house, and the best rental agency is **Hawaii Volcano Vacations ★★**, P.O. Box 913, Volcano, HI 96785 (© **800/709-0907** or 808/967-7271; www.hawaiivolcanovacations.com). Manager Joey Gutierrez selects only the top cottages, cabins, and houses in Volcano and makes sure they're perfect for you. Her reasonably priced units range from $99 to $200, and each one is outfitted with a full kitchen, plus an outdoor grill, cooler, flashlight, Wi-Fi, umbrella, and fresh flowers for your arrival. Many of them are great options for families traveling with kids.

Expensive

The Inn at Volcano Formerly called Chalet Kilauea, this is the most expensive B&B in Volcano. It has a storybook, enchanting quality to it. The least expensive room is decorated in memorabilia from the owners' extensive travels to eastern and southern Africa. Other units include the Jade Room (with collectibles from the Far East), the Continental Suite (with Victorian decor), the Treehouse Suite, and a separate cabin located next door to the Inn. I found some rooms, although exquisitely decorated, not very practical for things like hanging clothes, storing toiletries, and so on.

P.O. Box 998, Volcano, HI 96785. www.volcano-hawaii.com. (⊘ **800/937-7786** or 808/967-7786. Fax 808/967-8660. 6 units. $105–$399 double. A buffet continental breakfast is $6 extra. Extra person $25. AE, DISC, MC, V. **Amenities:** Hot tub; 3 of the rooms share a fridge, microwave, and coffeemaker on the porch. *In room:* TV/DVD, fridge (in some units), Wi-Fi (free).

Moderate

The **Volcano Teapot Cottage** (⊘ **808/967-7112;** www.volcano teapot.com) is a quaint 1914 two-bedroom cottage, decorated with one-of-a-kind antiques, and complete with hot tub in the forest out back ($195 double).

Kilauea Lodge & Restaurant ★   This popular roadside lodge, built in 1938 as a YMCA camp, sits on 10 wooded and landscaped acres. Its rooms offer heating systems and hot-towel warmers, beautiful art on the walls, fresh flowers, and, in some, fireplaces. In addition to the Lodge, there are two cottages available: a 1929 two-bedroom cottage with a fireplace and a full kitchen, just a couple of blocks down the street, and a two-bedroom with full kitchen on the sixth fairway of the Volcano Golf Course. A full gourmet breakfast is served to guests at the restaurant.

P.O. Box 116 (1 block off Hwy. 11 on Old Volcano Rd.), Volcano, HI 96785. www.kilauealodge.com. (⊘ **808/967-7366.** Fax 808/967-7367. 14 units. $170–$185 double room; $200–$220 cottage. Extra person $20 (ages 2 and older). Rates include full breakfast. AE, MC, V. **Amenities:** Restaurant (p. 93); hot tub. *In room:* No phone.

Inexpensive

On the way to the park is **Bed & Breakfast Mountain View** (⊘ **888/698-9896** or 808/968-6868; www.bbmtview.com), a 7,000-square-foot home overlooking a 10,000-square-foot fish pond with a teahouse, spa, and patio; rooms start at $90 (2-night minimum). The **Log Cabin** (⊘ **808/735-9191;** www.crubinstein.com/cabin.html) is a century-old ohia-log cabin for the young at heart ($125 for two, $150 for four, and $200 for six).

Hale Ohia Cottages ★ 🎁   Take a step back in time to the 1930s. Here you'll have a choice of suites, each with private entrance. There are also four guest cottages, ranging from one bedroom to three. The surrounding botanical gardens contribute to the overall tranquil ambience of the estate. They were groomed in the 1930s by a resident Japanese gardener, who worked with the natural volcanic terrain but gently tamed the flora into soothing shapes and designs. The lush grounds are just a mile from Hawaii Volcanoes National Park. The latest addition is a romantic, cozy cottage with fireplace, hot tub, and unusual bedroom made from a 1930s redwood water tank.

P.O. Box 758 (Hale Ohia Rd., off Hwy. 11), Volcano, HI 96785. www.haleohia.com. *C* **800/455-3803** or 808/967-7986. Fax 808/985-8887. 10 units. $109–$189 double. Extra person $25. Rates include continental breakfast. MC, V. *In room:* Fridge, hair dryer, no phone, Wi-Fi (some rooms; free).

Volcano Hale 🗲 If you're on a tight budget, check into this charming, 1912 historic home offering comfortable, clean, quiet rooms, all with shared bathrooms. The restored house sits on beautifully landscaped grounds and has new carpeting throughout, plus new furnishings in the common area. The bedrooms are tiny but clean and inviting. The common rooms include a living room with TV/VCR, a reading room, and a sunroom.

P.O. Box 998 (19–4178 Wright Rd., off Hwy. 11), Volcano, HI 96785. www.volcano-hawaii.com. *C* **800/937-7786** or 808/967-7786. Fax 808/967-8660. 6 units, none with private bathroom. $60–$89 double. Extra person $25. AE, DC, DISC, MC, V. From Hwy. 11, turn north onto Wright Rd.; go 1 mile to the Inn at Volcano on the right, where you'll check in. **Amenities:** Free Wi-Fi at the office. *In room:* No phone.

Volcano House As we went to press, the Volcano House was closed for renovations; it is expected to open by the end of 2011. Call to make sure it is reopened and for new rates. It is one of the greatest locations in Hawaii—inside the boundaries of the national park—and perched on the edge of an active volcano. This mountain lodge, which evolved out of a grass lean-to in 1865, is Hawaii's oldest visitor accommodations. It stands on the edge of Halemaumau's bubbling crater, and although the view of the crater is still an awesome sight, don't expect the Ritz here—rooms are very plain and heated with volcanic steam. *Tip:* Book only if you can get a room facing the volcano; if they're filled, don't bother—you can do better elsewhere.

P.O. Box 53, Hawaii Volcanoes National Park, HI 96718. www.volcanohousehotel. com. *C* **808/967-7321.** Fax 808/967-8429. 42 units. $55–$250 double. Extra person $25. Plus one-time $10 park entrance fee. AE, DC, DISC, MC, V. **Amenities:** Restaurant w/great view; bar.

SOUTH POINT

Bougainvillea Bed & Breakfast ★ 🎁 Don and Martie Jean Nitsche bought this 3-acre property in the Hawaiian Rancho subdivision of Ocean View and had a *Field of Dreams* experience: They decided that if they built a bed-and-breakfast, people would come. Where some people saw just lava, the Nitsches saw the ancient Hawaiian path that went from the mountain to the sea. So they built. And out of the lava came gardens—colorful bougainvillea, a pineapple patch, and a fish pond to add to the pool and hot tub. Word got out. Martie's breakfast—her secret-recipe banana and mac-nut pancakes, sausage, fruit, and coffee—drew people from all over. Things got so good, they had to add more rooms (all with their own private entrances) and expand the living room (complete with TV, VCR, and video library) and dining room. Guests usually take their breakfast plates out to the lanai, which boasts ocean views. Or they wander over to the pavilion, located next to the pool, which has a big barbecue area (with a kitchenette), a games area (darts, Ping-Pong, and so on), satellite TV, some exercise equipment, even a horseshoe pit. You can borrow snorkeling gear, beach mats, coolers, and other beach equipment.

P.O. Box 6045, Ocean View, HI 96737. www.bougainvilleabedandbreakfast.com. © **800/688-1763** or 808/929-7089. Fax 808/929-7089. 4 units. $89 double. Extra person $15. Rates include full breakfast. AE, DC, DISC, MC, V. **Amenities:** Concierge; games area; hot tub; kitchenette w/microwave in pavilion; satellite TV; big outdoor pool. *In room:* TV/VCR, hair dryer, no phone, Wi-Fi (free).

Macadamia Meadows Farm Bed & Breakfast ★ ☺ Near the southernmost point in the United States and just 45 minutes from Hawaii Volcanoes National Park lies one of the Big Island's most welcoming B&Bs. It's located on an 8-acre working macadamia-nut farm, in a great place for stargazing, and the warmth and hospitality of host Charlene Cowan is unsurpassed. Because the owner has children herself, the entire property is very kid friendly. In addition to exploring the groves of mac-nut trees, children can swim in the pool or play tennis. Charlene also has puzzles, games, and other rainy-day items to entertain youngsters. All rooms have private entrances and are immaculately clean; two of the units can be reserved together as a two-bedroom suite. Ask Charlene about the free orchid tours.

94-6263 Kamaoa Rd., Waiohinu, HI 96772. Reservations c/o P.O. Box 756, Naalehu, HI 96772. www.macadamiameadows.com. © **888/929-8118** or 808/ 929-8097. Fax 808/929-8097. 5 units. $119–$149 double. Extra person $15 per adult, $10 per child 17 and under. Rates include continental breakfast. 2-night minimum. DISC, MC, V. **Amenities:** Resort-size outdoor pool; tennis courts. *In room:* TV, fridge, no phone.

South Point Banyan Tree House ★ 📖 Couples looking for an exotic place to nest should try this tree house nestled inside a huge Chinese banyan tree. The cottage comes complete with a see-through roof that lets the outside in, plus a comfy, just-for-two hot tub on the wraparound deck. Inside there's a queen-size bed and a kitchen with microwave and two-burner stove. The scent of ginger brings you sweet dreams at night, and the twitter of birds greets you in the morning.

At Hwy. 11 and Pinao St., Waiohinu, HI 96772. www.southpointbth.com. ℂ **808/ 217-2504.** 1 unit. $100 double. Cleaning fee $50. 2-night minimum. No credit cards. **Amenities:** Hot tub; outside grill. *In room:* TV/VCR, CD player, fridge, kitchen, Wi-Fi (free).

WHERE TO EAT

So many restaurants, so little time. What's a traveler to do? The Big Island's delicious dilemma is its daunting size and abundant offerings. Its gastronomic environment— the fruitful marriage of creative chefs, good soil, and rich cultural traditions—has made this island as much a culinary destination as a recreational one. And from the Kona Coffee Festival to the Aloha Festival's Poke Recipe Contest, the Big Island is host to extraordinary world-renowned culinary events.

The Big Island's volcanic soil produces fine tomatoes, lettuces, beets, beans, fruits, and basic herbs and vegetables that were once difficult to find locally. Southeast Asian fruit, such as mangosteen and rambutan, are beginning to appear in markets, along with the sweet white pineapple that is by now a well-established Big Island crop. Along with the lamb and beef from Big Island ranches and seafood from local fishermen, this fresh produce forms the backbone of ethnic cookery and Hawaii Regional Cuisine.

Kailua-Kona is teeming with restaurants for all pocketbooks, while the haute cuisine of the island is concentrated in the Kohala Coast resorts. Waimea, also known as Kamuela, is a thriving upcountry community, a haven for yuppies, techies, and retirees who love a good bite to eat. In Hawi, North Kohala, expect bakeries, neighborhood diners, and one tropical-chic restaurant that's worth a special trip. In Hilo in East Hawaii, you'll find pockets of trendiness among the precious old Japanese and ethnic restaurants that provide honest, tasty, and affordable meals in unpretentious surroundings.

In the listings below, reservations are not necessary unless noted. *Warning:* Big Island restaurants, especially along the Kona Coast, seem to have a chronic shortage of waitstaff. Come prepared for a leisurely meal; sit and enjoy the warm moonlit night, sip a tasty libation, and realize time is relative here.

THE KONA COAST
In & Around Kailua-Kona, Holualoa & Keauhou

Note: Pahu i'a and Beach Tree Bar & Grill are located north of Kailua-Kona in the Four Seasons Resort Hualalai, 6 miles north of the Kona Airport and just south of the Kohala Coast.

VERY EXPENSIVE

Pahu i'a ★★★ CONTEMPORARY PACIFIC RIM   You can't find a better oceanfront location on the Big Island (maybe in the entire state)—Pahu i'a sits just feet from the lapping waves. A small bridge of natural logs leads to this enchanting oceanfront dining room, where views on three sides expand on the aquatic theme (*pahu i'a* is Hawaiian for "aquarium," and there's a large one at the entrance). The cuisine highlights fresh produce and seafood from the island—and even from the resort's own aquaculture ponds, which teem with shrimp and moi (threadfin), a rich Island fish. The day begins with the coast's most elegant breakfast buffet, featuring excellent omelets, meats, fresh fruit, and regional specialties. At dinner, part of the menu changes daily and always includes several fresh seafood preparations; crispy-skin opakapaka meunière; veal Oscar; dry-aged prime New York steak; and Hawaiian whole lobster thermidor. On Saturday, the Surf, Sand, and Stars feast offers an array of buffet-style items from fresh fish to grilled New York sirloin. From ambience to execution to presentation, Pahu i'a is top-drawer.

At the Four Seasons Resort Hualalai, Queen Kaahumanu Hwy., Kaupulehu-Kona. ✆ **808/325-8000.** Reservations recommended. Breakfast buffet $34; dinner main courses $32–$69. Surf, Sand, and Stars buffet $85 adults, $43 kids 5–12. AE, DC, DISC, MC, V. Daily 6:30–11:30am (buffet 7–11am) and 6–9:30pm (6–9pm Apr–Sept).

EXPENSIVE

Beach Tree Bar & Grill ★ CALIFORNIA WITH ITALIAN INFLUENCE   Here's an example of outstanding cuisine in a perfect setting—without being fancy, fussy, or prohibitively expensive. The bar on the sand is a sunset paradise, and the sandwiches, seafood, and grilled items at the casual outdoor restaurant (a few feet from the bar) are in a class of their own—simple, excellent, fresh local produce, seafood, poultry, and meat imaginatively prepared with strong Italian influences. The menu, which varies,

Where to Eat on the Kona Coast

Los Habaneros **12**
Lulu's **9**
Manago Hotel
  Restaurant **16**
Pahu i'a **1**
Quinn's Almost
  by the Sea **3**
Teshima's **13**

Aloha Angel Cafe **14**
Ba-Le Sandwich Shop **2**
Beach Tree Bar & Grill **1**
Big Island Grill **5**
Boston Basil's **4**
The Coffee Shack **17**
Huggo's **7**
Island Lava Java **8**
Jackie Rey's Ohana
  Grill **10**
Keei Cafe **15**
Kenichi Pacific **12**
Kona Inn Restaurant **6**
La Bourgogne **11**

includes items such as seafood paella, scallops with corn puree, wild shrimp scampi with baby spinach, lobster ravioli, or braised short ribs with carrot puree. An added attraction is entertainment from 6 to 9pm nightly.

At the Four Seasons Resort Hualalai, Queen Kaahumanu Hwy., Kaupulehu-Kona. ✆ **808/325-8000.** Main courses $13–$24 lunch, $18–$59 dinner. AE, DC, DISC, MC, V. Daily 11:30am–8:30pm.

Huggo's ★ PACIFIC RIM/SEAFOOD At the main Huggo's dining room, fresh seafood remains the signature, as does the coral-strewn beach with tide pools just beyond the wooden deck. The tables are so close to the water, you can see the entire curve of Kailua Bay. Feast on sautéed mahi-mahi, steamed clams, seared ahi, or *imu*-style chicken cooked in ti leaves. At lunch, specialties include kalua-chicken quesadillas, brick-oven pizzas, and sandwiches ranging from hot turkey to prime rib and fresh fish.

Huggo's on the Rocks ★ is a thatched-bar fantasy that's *really* on the rocks. This mound of thatch, rock, and grassy-sandy ground, right next to Huggo's, is a sunset-lover's nirvana. At sundown, this place is packed with people sipping mai tais and noshing on salads, poke, sandwiches, plate lunches, sashimi, and fish and chips. At lunchtime, the new menu ranges from a spicy grilled mahi-mahi taco plate to a huge burger with barbecue sauce. From 6 to 11am, this same location turns into the **Java on the Rocks** ★★ espresso bar, which is *not* to be missed—sip Kona coffee, enjoy your eggs, and watch the waves roll onto the shore.

75-5828 Kahakai Rd., Kailua-Kona. ✆ **808/329-1493.** www.huggos.com. Reservations recommended. Main courses $9–$15 lunch, $23–$38 dinner. AE, MC, V. Daily 6–11am, 11:30am–5:30pm, and 5:30–10pm.

Kona Inn Restaurant ★ AMERICAN/SEAFOOD This is touristy, but it can be a very pleasant experience, especially when the sun is setting. The wide-ranging menu and fresh seafood in the open-air oceanfront setting will remind you why you have come to Kailua-Kona. The large, open room and panoramic view of the Kailua shoreline are the most attractive features, especially for sunset cocktails and appetizers. It's a huge menu—everything from nachos and chicken Caesar salad to sandwiches, pasta, stir-fried dishes, and the highlight: the fresh fish served Cajun style or broiled and basted in lemon butter. Watch for the daily specials on the less expensive Cafe Grill menu (coconut shrimp, stuffed mushrooms, fish and chips, and so on).

At the Kona Inn Shopping Village, 75-5744 Alii Dr., Kailua-Kona. ✆ **808/329-4455.** www.konainnrestaurant.com. Reservations recommended for dinner. Main courses $18–$45; Cafe Grill $7–$18. AE, MC, V. Dinner menu winter daily 5–9pm; summer daily 5:30–9pm. Cafe Grill menu daily 11am–9pm.

A tasty TOUR

Kona Joe Coffee Farm & Chocolate Company, 79–7346 Mamalahoa Hwy., between mile markers 113 and 114, in Kealakekua (© **808/322-2100;** www.konajoe.com), home of the world's first trellised coffee farm, offers guided tours at its 20-acre estate in the "Gold Belt of Kona Coffee."

The tours begin with an excursion through the well-manicured fields of the unique coffee plants on a patented trellis technology developed by Joe Alban. When he began farming in 1997, Alban wanted a unique, top-of-the-line coffee, so he turned to his brother, John, who is a graduate of the viticulture and oenology program at University of California, Davis. Joe planted 5 acres of coffee in the traditional way and 5 acres of trellised coffee. The trellised coffee had a harvest of 35% more berries, which produced a sweeter, fuller-bodied coffee. With lots of pruning and uniform sun exposure, Kona Joe coffee was awarded the "Best New Roasted Coffee" blue ribbon by the Specialty Coffee Association in 2001, and a local newspaper gave Kona Joe the "People's Choice Award for Best Coffee" in 2006.

In the 10,000-square-foot visitor center on the plantation, the tour continues with live demonstrations on roasting, sorting, brewing, and panning. At the end, you'll get a sample of Kona Joe Coffee in your own coffee mug and the chocolate-covered coffee beans (yum, yum!) also sold here. Tours are given daily from 9am to 4pm and cost $15 adults and $7.50 children.

3

La Bourgogne ★★ 🎁 CLASSIC FRENCH   An intimate spot with 10 tables, La Bourgogne serves classic French fare with simple, skillful elegance. Baked brie in puff pastry is a tasty treat, and the fresh Maine lobster salad, served on a bed of greens with mango slices and passion-fruit vinaigrette, is a master stroke. Other offerings include classic onion soup, fresh catch of the day, *osso buco,* and scallops sautéed in olive oil, tomato, basil, and garlic. The roast duck breast with raspberries and pine nuts is exactly the kind of dish that characterizes La Bourgogne—done to perfection, presented attractively, and with an unbeatable match of flavors and textures. Classically trained chef Ron Gallaher expresses his allegiance to *la cuisine Française* down to the last morsel of flourless chocolate cake and lemon tartlet.

77-6400 Nalani St. (3 miles south of Kailua-Kona), Kailua-Kona. © **808/329-6711.** Reservations recommended. Main courses $34–$40. AE, DC, DISC, MC, V. Tues–Sat 6–10pm.

MODERATE

Jackie Rey's Ohana Grill ★★ 🍴 ECLECTIC   This off-the-beaten-path eatery is hard to categorize: part sports bar, part family restaurant, part music/dancing (salsa, country and western), part neighborhood cafe. No matter what you call it, you'll get great food at wallet-pleasing prices. Locals pile in at lunch for burgers, fish tacos, and mac-nut basil chicken sandwiches. On weekdays, a happy-hour crowd downs a few brews and pupu (appetizers). Starting at 5pm, families with kids in tow show up for the delicious seared wasabi tuna, Pacific Rim bouillabaisse, seafood pasta, and beef short ribs with a *ko-chu-jang* glaze.

75-5995 Kuakini Hwy., Kailua-Kona. 📞 **808/327-0209.** www.jackiereys.com. Reservations recommended for dinner. Main courses $10–$17 lunch, $15–$30 dinner; pupu menu $6.50–$18. AE, DISC, MC, V. Mon–Fri 11am–9pm; Sat–Sun 5–9pm.

Kenichi Pacific ★★★ 🍴 PACIFIC RIM/SUSHI   Hidden in the Keauhou Shopping Center is this gem of a restaurant, decorated in muted tones and with understated furnishings, featuring both Pacific Rim fusion cuisine and a sushi bar. The fantastic food and efficient service will leave you smiling. The appetizer menu is so tempting (ginger-marinated squid, blackened tuna, Dungeness crab cakes, fresh lobster summer rolls), you might just want to graze from one dish to the next. Entrees include fresh catch of the day, macadamia-crusted lamb accompanied by taro risotto, ono *tataki*, lemon-grass ahi, and bamboo salmon. If you love duck, don't miss Kenichi's duck confit, which has Chinese five-spice cured duck leg with celeriac purée, *ali'i* mushrooms, pea tendrils, red-pepper coulis, and balsamic reduction. Leave room for the warm flourless molten cake with Kona coffee-chip ice cream.

At the Keauhou Shopping Center, 78-6831 Alii Dr., Keauhou. 📞 **808/322-6400.** www.kenichirestaurants.com. Reservations recommended for dinner. Main courses $19–$30. AE, DC, DISC, MC, V. Tues–Fri 11:30am–1:30pm; daily 5–9:30pm.

INEXPENSIVE

Ba-Le Sandwich Shop 🏷 FRENCH-VIETNAMESE SANDWICHES/BAKERY   This statewide chain specializes in "fast" French-Vietnamese sandwiches, Vietnamese rice and noodle entrees, and bakery items. It's a nondescript place in a local shopping center, but with great deals such as sandwiches on homemade French rolls from just $4. This family-run restaurant is the perfect place to stop before heading for the beach.

At the Kona Coast Shopping Center, 74-5588 Palani Rd., Kailua-Kona. 📞 **808/327-1212.** Entrees $10–$15; sandwiches $5–$8. MC, V. Mon–Sat 10am–9pm; Sun 11am–7pm.

Big Island Grill 🎁 AMERICAN   One of the best-kept secrets among local residents is the Big Island Grill, where you get huge servings of home cooking at 1970s prices. The place is always packed, from the first cup of coffee at breakfast to the last bite of dessert at night. In 2007, Chef Bruce Gould sold the restaurant to family that has kept the staff and recipes of this localized American cuisine. This is a place to take the family for dinner (excellent fresh salmon, generous salads, and the world's tastiest mashed potatoes) without having to go into debt. ***Warning:*** You'll likely have to wait (no reservations), and once you finally land a table, service can sometimes be slow. Relax, it's Hawaii.

75-5702 Kuakini Hwy., Kailua-Kona. ⓒ **808/326-1153.** Reservations not accepted. Main courses breakfast $4.75–$17, lunch $8–$20, dinner $8.75–$23. AE, DISC, MC, V. Mon–Sat 7am–9pm.

Boston Basil's ★ PIZZA/ITALIAN   Long-time pizzeria Basil's became Boston Basil's in 2007 and grew up. Yes, it still has delicious pizza, but its Italian food now shines. Two dining rooms seat 100 in a garlic-infused atmosphere where prices are low, considering the location across the street from the ocean on Alii Drive. Shrimp pesto and the original barbecue-chicken pizza are longstanding favorites, as is the artichoke-olive-caper version, a Greek-Italian hybrid. The menu has recently expanded to include sandwiches and burgers. Very popular with the 20 something crowd as well as hungry visitors drawn in by the wonderful aroma wafting out into the street.

75-5707 Alii Dr., Kailua-Kona. ⓒ **808/326-7836.** www.bostonbasils.com. Individual pizzas $14–$18; main courses $9–$24. MC, V. Daily 9am–9pm.

Island Lava Java ★ 🍴 AMERICAN   Perched directly across the street from the ocean with an unimpaired view of the water activities in Kailua Bay, this inexpensive outdoor coffee shop started as a small espresso joint with a few pastries a few years ago. Eventually it added lunch and then dinner. Today Lava Java is the "in" place to sip espresso drinks, chow down on good food, and enjoy the ocean view. A handful of tables ring the small shop outside, and a few more tiny tables are located inside. The breakfast menu features stacks of pancakes and eggs in various preparations, such as in a massive omelet, wrapped in a tortilla, or on an English muffin or bagel. The lunch menu is big on sandwiches, burgers, and salads. Dinners can be small (sandwiches or salads) or big (New York steak with all the trimmings, veggie lasagna, fresh fish). Be sure to come with a laid-back attitude; service can be slow, but the price and the view more than make up for it.

75–5799 Alii Dr., Kailua-Kona. ✆ **808/327-2161.** www.islandlavajava.com. Breakfast items $5–$12; lunch items $10–$15; dinner items $15–$25. AE, DISC, MC, V. Daily 6:30am–9:30pm.

Los Habaneros 🖐 MEXICAN There's no leisurely dining at this small eatery—just great, fast Mexican food at budget prices. You order at one counter and pick up at another. Habaneros starts off the day with huevos rancheros and other egg dishes, such as a chorizo-egg burrito. Lunch and dinner items include burritos (the fish with black beans is my favorite), soft and hard tacos (the veggie is surprisingly tasty and filling), nachos, tostadas, quesadillas, enchiladas, and daily specials, such as Friday night's shrimp Vallarta.

At the Keauhou Shopping Center, 78–6831 Alii Dr., Keauhou. ✆ **808/324-HOTT.** All items under $12. MC, V. Mon–Sat 9am–9pm.

Lulu's AMERICAN As is often the case with popular joints, Lulu's has fallen prey to the deadly sin of self-importance. Service is brisk and can be downright rude. The place is casual, noisy, and corny (black-velvet paintings at the entrance), but it's undeniably popular, with open-air dining, ocean views, and a sports-bar atmosphere. Other elements include Capiz-shell lamps, clamshell sconces, and hula-girl replicas. The offerings include appetizers, sandwiches, salads, burgers, fresh-fish tacos, and fresh fish and meats in the evening. *Hint:* Check out their $5 breakfast menu.

At the Coconut Grove Market Place, 75–5819 Alii Dr., Kailua-Kona. ✆ **808/331-2633.** www.lulushawaii.com. Reservations not accepted. Main courses $5–$10 breakfast, $10–$16 lunch and dinner. AE, DC, DISC, MC, V. Daily 8am–10pm. Bar until 2am.

Quinn's Almost by the Sea ★ STEAK/SEAFOOD Latenight noshers, take note: This is one of the few places you can grab a bite in Kona after 9pm. Quinn's, located at the northern gateway to town, has a nautical/sports-bar atmosphere and offers casual alfresco dining on a garden lanai, with an air-conditioned, nonsmoking area also available. The menu is surf-and-turf basic: burgers, sandwiches, and a limited dinner menu of dependably good fresh fish, filet mignon, and a few shrimp dishes. There are eight burger selections and, when available, fresh ahi or ono sandwiches.

75–5655A Palani Rd., Kailua-Kona. ✆ **808/329-3822.** Main courses $12–$25. DISC, MC, V. Daily 11am–11pm.

South Kona
MODERATE
Aloha Theatre Cafe ISLAND The former Aloha Cafe is under new management, but it has kept the trademark large servings,

heroic burgers and sandwiches, and a home-style menu for vegetarians and carnivores alike. Breakfast and lunch are served on the veranda that wraps around the old Aloha Theatre, with sweeping views down from the coffee fields to the shoreline. Dinner is served in the tiny dining room (which, sadly, has no view); space is limited, so phone ahead to ensure that you get a table. The cheaper daytime staples include omelets, burritos, tostadas, quesadillas, and home-baked goods (breakfast is served all day). Most of the produce is organic, and fresh-squeezed orange juice and fresh-fruit smoothies are served daily. Sandwiches, from turkey to tofu-avocado and a wonderful fresh ahi, are heaped with vegetables on tasty whole-wheat buns. Unfortunately, dinner is only served when an event (community theater or dance performance) is happening at the Aloha Theatre.

79-7384 Mamalahoa Hwy. (Hwy. 11), Kainaliu. ⓒ **808/322-3383.** www.alohatheatre cafe.com. Reservations recommended for event-night dinner. Main courses $7–$15 breakfast, $10–$15 lunch. AE, MC, V. Daily 7:30am–2:30pm (dinner 5–7pm when an event is scheduled for the Aloha Theatre).

Keei Cafe ♨ MEDITERRANEAN/LATIN AMERICAN/ISLAND When this bistro cafe opened in a former fish market in Keei, it was fabulous in every respect—delicious food at frugal prices, friendly service, and quirky decor. The restaurant became so popular it moved a few years ago to a new location with hardwood floors, first-class artwork, and a view of the coast. It got really big, really fast, and can't seem to keep up with the rapid growth. The first thing that went was seating people on time. On my last visit, I waited more than an hour for a 7:30pm reservation (the staff was unapologetic). Now the food, once the draw, is no longer dependably good. I'm including the restaurant in this guide because it's so popular, but I can no longer recommend it—not only because of the not-up-to-par food and the slow service, but more because of the cavalier attitude: The owners are making money (right now) and don't really care how they treat their clientele.

79-7511 Mamalahoa Hwy. (Hwy. 11, by mile marker 113), Kalakekua. ⓒ **808/322-9992.** Main courses $9–$13 lunch, $16–$26 dinner. No credit cards. Tues–Fri 11am–2pm and 5–9pm; Sat 5–9pm.

INEXPENSIVE

The Coffee Shack ★★ ☺ COFFEEHOUSE/DELI Great food, crisp air, and a sweeping ocean view make the Coffee Shack one of South Kona's great finds. It's an informal place with counter service, pool chairs, and white trellises on the deck, which is framed by ferns, palms, and banana and avocado trees. The fare is equally inviting: French toast made with homemade luau bread, lemon bars and carrot cake, and eggs Benedict with

KONA COFFEE craze!

Coffeehouses are booming on the Big Island—this is, after all, the home of Kona coffee, with dozens of vendors competing for your loyalty and dollars.

Most of the farms are concentrated in the North and South Kona districts, where coffee remains a viable industry. Notable among them is the **Kona Blue Sky Coffee Company,** in Holualoa (✆ 877/322-1700 or 808/322-1700; www.konablueskycoffee. com), which handles its own beans exclusively. The Christian Twigg-Smith family and staff grow, handpick, sun-dry, roast, grind, and sell their coffee on a 400-acre estate. You can buy coffee on the farm itself and see the operation from field to final product. You can also find Blue Sky at the Waikoloa Beach Marriott Resort and at KTA Super Stores in Kailua-Kona and Keauhou. Open Monday through Saturday 9am to 4pm.

Also in Holualoa, 10 minutes above Kailua-Kona, **Holualoa Kona Coffee Company** (✆ 800/334-0348 or 808/322-9937; www.konalea.com) purveys organic Kona from its own farm and other growers. Not only can you buy premium, unadulterated Kona coffee here, but you can also witness the hulling, sorting, roasting, and packaging of beans on a farm tour Monday through Friday from 7:30am to 4pm.

Some other coffees to watch for: **Bong Brothers** (✆ 808/328-9289; www.bongbrothers.com) thrives with its coffees, roadside fruit stand, and natural-foods deli that sells smoothies and healthful foods. Aficionados know that **Langenstein Farms** (✆ 808/328-8356; www.konafarmscoffee.com), a name associated with quality and integrity, distributes excellent Kona coffee and distinctively tasty macadamia nuts in the town of Honaunau. There are also great tours of the farm; just call ahead to set one up. **Rooster Farms,** also in Honaunau (✆ 808/328-9173; www.roosterfarms.com), enjoys an excellent reputation for the quality of its organic coffee beans.

A good bet in Hilo is **Bears' Coffee,** 106 Keawe St. (✆ 808/935-0708), the quintessential sidewalk coffeehouse and a local stalwart. Regulars love to start their day here, with coffee and specialties such as souffléd eggs, cooked light and fluffy in the espresso machine and served in a croissant. It's a great lunchtime spot as well.

a delectable hollandaise. At lunch, you'll find an assortment of imported beers, excellent sandwiches on home-baked breads, and fresh, hearty salads made with organic lettuces. Let the kids order peanut-butter-and-jelly or grilled-cheese sandwiches while you head for the smoked Alaskan salmon sandwich or the hot, authentic Reuben.

Hwy. 11, 1 mile south of Captain Cook. ✆ **808/328-9555.** www.coffeeshack.com. Most items under $11; pizzas $11–$14. DISC, MC, V. Daily 7:30am–3pm.

Manago Hotel Restaurant ◢ AMERICAN The dining room of the decades-old Manago Hotel is a local legend, greatly loved for its unpretentious, tasty food at bargain prices. At breakfast, $6 buys you eggs, bacon, papaya, rice, and coffee. At lunch or dinner, you can dine on a 12-ounce T-bone, fried ahi, opelu, or the house specialty, pork chops—the restaurant serves nearly 1,500 pounds monthly. When the akule or opelu are running, count on a rush by the regular customers. This place is nothing fancy, and lots of things are fried, but the local folks would riot if anything were to change after so many years.

At the Manago Hotel, Hwy. 11, Captain Cook. ✆ **808/323-2642.** Reservations recommended for dinner. Main courses $8–$15. DISC, MC, V. Tues–Sun 7–9am, 11am–2pm, and 5–7:30pm.

Teshima's JAPANESE/AMERICAN This is local style all the way. Shizuko Teshima has a strong following among those who have made her miso soup and sukiyaki an integral part of their lives. The early morning crowd starts gathering for omelets or Japanese breakfasts (soup, rice, and fish) while it's still dark outside. As the day progresses, the orders pour in for shrimp tempura and sukiyaki. By dinner, no. 3 *teishoku* trays—miso soup, sashimi, sukiyaki, shrimp, pickles, and other delights—are streaming out of the kitchen. Other combinations include steak and shrimp tempura, beef teriyaki and shrimp tempura, and the deep-sea trio of shrimp tempura, fried fish, and sashimi.

Hwy. 11, Honalo. ✆ **808/322-9140.** Reservations recommended. Complete dinners $24 and under. No credit cards. Daily 6:30am–1:45pm and 5–9pm.

THE KOHALA COAST

Note: You'll find the following restaurants on "Where to Stay & Dine in North Kohala & Waimea" map (p. 49).

Very Expensive

Brown's Beach House ★★ BIG ISLAND The nearby lagoon takes on the pink-orange glow of sunset, while torches flicker among the coconut trees. With white tablecloths, candles, and seating near the lagoon, this is a spectacular setting, complemented by a menu that keeps getting better by the year. The chef de cuisine, Thepthikone Keosavang, from Dubai, serves Big Island cuisine with a flair that includes unusual dishes such as grilled walu with lemon balm emulsion, Szechuan-spiced filet with cabernet reduction, crab-crusted mahi-mahi with mango coulis, and prosciutto-wrapped pork tenderloin with a sweet potato and taro mash. Next door is **Brown's Deli,** with freshly made breads, pastries, and espresso coffees for breakfast, and pizza, salads, and sandwiches for lunch and dinner.

At the Fairmont Orchid, Mauna Lani Resort, 1 N. Kaniku Dr. © **808/885-2000.** www.fairmont.com/orchid. Reservations recommended for dinner. Main courses $9–$15 deli, $32–$50 dinner. AE, DC, DISC, MC, V. Deli daily 6:30am–5pm. Beach House daily 5:30–8:30pm.

CanoeHouse ★★ HAWAII REGIONAL   The setting is as gorgeous as ever, but this is not the same restaurant as it was when Alan Wong was the chef and the food coming out of the kitchen was nothing short of extraordinary. However, Wong didn't take the ambience with him, and the legendary sunset views remain, along with a koa canoe hanging from the ceiling in the open-air dining room. (*Tip:* Reserve a table outside and go at sunset to get the real flavor of this incredible setting.) The menu, which changes seasonally, includes great fish items (prawns, scallops, clams and mussels in a spicy coconut broth, and fresh fish cooked a variety of ways such as moi with a tamari glaze and avocado cream), meats (Mongolian-barbecued rack of lamb, and pan-roasted chicken with pineapple and fingerling potatoes), and even vegetarian items. Save room for dessert.

At the Mauna Lani Bay Hotel & Bungalows, Mauna Lani Resort, 68-1400 Mauna Lani Dr. © **808/881-7911.** www.maunalani.com. Reservations recommended. Main courses $34–$40. AE, DC, DISC, MC, V. Tues–Sat 6–9pm.

Coast Grille ★★ STEAK/SEAFOOD/HAWAII REGIONAL   It's a 3-minute walk from the main lobby to the open-air Grille, but the view along the way is nothing to complain about and will help you work up an appetite. The split-level dining room has banquettes and wicker furniture, open-air seating, and an oyster bar that's famous. The extensive seafood selection includes poke, clams, and fresh oysters from all over the world, as well as fresh seafood from local waters, served in multicultural preparations.

At the Hapuna Beach Prince Hotel, Mauna Kea Resort, 62-100 Kaunaoa Dr. © **808/882-5810.** www.hapunabeachprincehotel.com. Reservations recommended. Main courses $20–$40. AE, DISC, MC, V. Wed–Thurs and Sat 5:30–9pm.

Manta & Pavilion Wine Bar ★★★ HAWAIIAN REGIONAL The view alone (either through the floor-to-ceiling windows or outside on the terrace) is enough to draw you into Mauna Kea Beach Hotel's casual-but-elegant restaurant. That ocean view is just the beginning; the added value here is the incredible cuisine of executive chef George Gomes and the attraction of their Enomatic wine system (which allows them to pour one glass at a time). This is "the" place to have breakfast on a sunny deck overlooking the ocean as lazy waves roll in. Choose either the breakfast buffet ($32) with numerous items (including made-to-order omelets and waffles) or the a la carte menu—try the homemade Portuguese sweet bread French toast with wild poha jam ($17) or the Hamakua three-egg omelet with feta cheese, spinach, mushrooms, and olives ($24). The atmosphere changes when the sun sets for dinner. A huge variety of wines by the glass are offered via the Enomatic wine system. Dinner, which Chef Gomes calls Kohala Cuisine, features fresh ingredients found within a 20-mile radius of the restaurant, ranging from Big Island grass-fed beef to locally raised rack of lamb to just-caught Hawaiian fish. Personally, I could make a meal on the creative appetizers such as Hawaii Island goat cheese ravioli with local lobster and smoked bacon ($15), Hawaiian shrimp tempura with local fern shoots, green papaya, and chili water aioli ($16), or roasted organic baby beets ($13).

Mauna Kea Beach Hotel, 62-100 Mauna Kea Beach Dr., Kohala Coast. ✆ **808/ 882-5810.** www.princeresortshawaii.com/mauna-kea-beach-hotel/big-island-restaurants.php. Reservations recommended. Main courses dinner $35–$45; breakfast $16–$26; Sun brunch $48 adults, $24 children 11 and under. AE, DISC, MC, V. Daily 6:30–11am; Tues–Sat 6–9pm; Sun brunch 11:30am–2pm.

Monettes ★★★ FISH AND STEAK The Mauna Kea's top restaurant was designed by the Monette brothers, owners of the award winning Flagstaff House Restaurant in Boulder, Colorado, in the mode of the new, "modern" steakhouse. Luxury dining, with eye-popping ocean views, and outstanding service describe this top-notch restaurant, a must for any foodie. The a la carte menu changes daily, but always features fresh Island fish (such as potato-crusted mahi-mahi or prosciutto-wrapped ono), a variety of steaks, and some creative dishes such as short ribs in a coconut brown ale or pineapple-braised port cheeks.

Mauna Kea Beach Hotel, 62-100 Mauna Kea Beach Dr., Kohala Coast. ✆ **808/ 443-2853.** www.princeresortshawaii.com/mauna-kea-beach-hotel/hawaii-fine-dining.php. Reservations a must. Main courses $25–$56. AE, DISC, MC, V. Thurs–Mon 5:30–10pm.

Expensive

Norio's Sushi Bar & Restaurant ★ JAPANESE/SUSHI This new upscale sushi bar and restaurant at the Fairmont Orchid features master sushi chef Norio Yamamoto, who trained in Tokyo and most recently worked at the sushi bar at The Ritz-Carlton Kapalua on Maui. His menu reflects a reverence for traditional Japanese delicacies such as sushi and tempura dishes, plus a few signature items such as *kushi* katsu (a panko-fried pork loin and onion skewer served with sesame-katsu sauce) and sukiyaki (thinly sliced beef and vegetables). Also on the menu are a selection of sakes, Japanese beers, and green teas. Sushi lovers can sit at the newly expanded 15-seat sushi bar to watch the master and his team of three at work.

At the Fairmont Orchid, Mauna Lani Resort, 1 N. Kaniku Dr. © **808/885-2000.** www.fairmont.com/orchid. Reservations recommended. Main courses $27–$44. AE, DC, DISC, MC, V. Thurs–Mon 5:30–9pm.

Roy's Waikoloa Bar & Grill ★★★ PACIFIC RIM/EURO-ASIAN   Don't let the resort-mall location fool you—Roy's Waikoloa has several distinctive and inviting features, such as a golf-course view, large windows overlooking a 10-acre lake, and the East-West cuisine and upbeat service that are Roy Yamaguchi signatures. This is a clone of his Oahu restaurant, offering favorites such as Szechuan baby back ribs, blackened Island ahi, hibachi-style salmon, and six other types of fresh fish prepared charred, steamed, or seared, and topped with exotic sauces such as shiitake-miso and gingered lime-chili butter. Yamaguchi's tireless exploration of local ingredients and world traditions produces food that keeps him at Hawaii's culinary cutting edge. ***Be warned:*** Roy's is always packed (make reservations) and noisy, but the food is always great and the service is excellent. The menu changes daily.

At Kings' Shops, Waikoloa Beach Resort, 69–250 Waikoloa Beach Dr. © **808/ 886-4321.** www.roysrestaurant.com. Reservations recommended. Main courses $26–$45. AE, DC, DISC, MC, V. Daily 5–9:30pm.

Sansei Seafood Restaurant & Sushi Bar ★★★ SUSHI/PACIFIC RIM   In 2007, award-winning chef D. K. Kodama opened a branch of his popular Sansei (also on Maui and Oahu) on the Big Island. The very classy restaurant offers an extensive menu of Japanese and East-West delicacies. Part fusion, part Hawaii regional cuisine, Sansei is tirelessly creative, with a menu that scores higher with adventurous palates than with purists (although there are endless traditional choices as well). Options include panko-crusted ahi sashimi, miso garlic prawns, noodle dishes, Asian shrimp cakes, and sauces that surprise, in creative combinations such as ginger-lime chile butter and cilantro pesto. But there's simpler fare as well, such as shrimp tempura, noodles, and wok-tossed upcountry vegetables. Desserts are not to be missed. If it's autumn, don't pass up the Granny Smith apple tart with vanilla ice cream and homemade caramel sauce. In other seasons, opt for tempura-fried ice cream with chocolate sauce. There's karaoke on Friday nights from 10pm to

1am. ***Money-saving tip:*** Eat early: Specials such as a 50% discount are offered Sunday and Monday from 5 to 6pm.

At Queens' MarketPlace, Waikoloa Beach Resort, 69-191 Waikoloa Beach Dr. ℂ **808/886-6286.** www.sanseihawaii.com. Reservations recommended. Main courses $16–$48; sushi $5–$17. AE, DISC, MC, V. Daily 5:30-10pm (Fri–Sat karaoke and sushi until 1am).

Moderate

Cafe Pesto ★★ MEDITERRANEAN/ITALIAN Fans drive miles for the gourmet pizzas, calzones, and fresh organic greens grown from Kealakekua to Kamuela. The herb-infused Italian pies are adorned with lobster from the aquaculture farms on Keahole Point, shiitake mushrooms from a few miles mauka (inland), and fresh fish, shrimp, and crab. Seared poke with spinach, Santa Fe chicken pasta, and local seafood risotto are other favorites.

At the Kawaihae Shopping Center, at Kawaihae Harbor, Pule Hwy. and Kawaihae Rd. ℂ **808/882-1071.** www.cafepesto.com. Main courses $11–$17 lunch, $18–$35 dinner; $9–$21 pizza. AE, DC, DISC, MC, V. Daily 11am–9pm.

Merriman's Market Cafe ★ MEDITERRANEAN/DELI Peter Merriman, who has long reigned as king of Hawaii Regional Cuisine with Merriman's restaurant in Waimea (p. 85), has opened this tiny "market cafe" featuring cuisines of the Mediterranean made with fresh local produce, house-made sausages, artisan-style breads, and great cheese and wines. This is a fun place for lunch or a light dinner. The 3,000-square-foot restaurant and deli features full-service indoor and outdoor dining in a casual atmosphere. Lunch ranges from salads to sandwiches; dinner features small-plate dishes, pizzas, and entrees from grilled fish to large salads.

At Kings' Shops, Waikoloa Beach Resort, 69-250 Waikoloa Beach Dr. ℂ **808/886-1700.** www.merrimanshawaii.com. Main courses $10–$16 lunch specials, $14–$29 all day. AE, MC, V. Daily 11am–2pm and 5–9pm.

NORTH KOHALA

Note: You'll find the following restaurants on "Where to Stay & Dine in North Kohala & Waimea" map (p. 49).

Moderate

Bamboo ★★ 🍴 PACIFIC RIM Serving fresh fish and Asian specialties in a historic building, Hawaii's self-professed "tropical saloon" is a major attraction on the island's northern coastline. The exotic interior is a nod to nostalgia, with high wicker chairs from Waikiki's historic Moana Hotel, works by local artists, and old Matson liner menus accenting the bamboo-lined walls. The fare,

Tropical Dreams of Ice Cream

Tropical Dreams ice cream has spread all over the island but got its start in North Kohala. Across the street from Bamboo, **Kohala Coffee Mill and Tropical Dreams Ice Cream,** Hwy. 270, Hawi (**(C) 808/889-5577**), serves upscale ice creams along with sandwiches, pastries, and a selection of Island coffees. The Tahitian vanilla and litchi ice creams are local legends. Jams, jellies, herb vinegars, Hawaiian honey, herbal salts, and macadamia-nut oils are among the gift items for sale. It's open Monday through Friday from 6am to 6pm, and Saturday and Sunday from 7am to 5:30pm. For other Tropical Dreams outlets, check www.tropicaldreams icecream.com.

Island favorites in sophisticated presentations, is a match for all this style: *imu*-smoked pork quesadillas, fish prepared several ways, sesame-nori-crusted or tequila-lime shrimp, and selections of pork, beef, and chicken. There are even some local faves, such as fried noodles served vegetarian, with chicken, or with shrimp. Produce from nearby gardens and fish fresh off the chef's own hook are among the highlights. Hawaiian music wafts through Bamboo from 6:30pm to closing on weekends.

Hwy. 270, Hawi. **(C) 808/889-5555.** www.bamboorestaurant.info. Reservations recommended. Main courses $10–$20 lunch, $10–$35 dinner (full- and half-size portions available at dinner). MC, V. Tues–Sat 11:30am–2:30pm and 6–8pm; Sun brunch 11:30am–2:30pm.

WAIMEA

Note: You'll find the following restaurants on "Where to Stay & Dine in North Kohala & Waimea" map (p. 49).

Expensive

Daniel Thiebaut Restaurant ★★ FRENCH/ASIAN   Come here for Sunday brunch. This restaurant features Big Island products (Kamuela Pride beef, Kahua Ranch lettuces, Hirabara Farms field greens, herbs and greens from Adaptations in South Kona) as interpreted by the French-trained Thiebaut, formerly executive chef at Mauna Kea Beach Resort. Brunch is just as fabulous as the fancy Kohala resorts at half the price. Dinner highlights include Hunan-style rack of lamb, wok-fried scallops, vegetarian specials (such as crispy avocado spring rolls with a smoked-tomato coulis), and fresh fish. The recently remodeled restaurant is full of intimate enclaves and has a gaily lit plantation-style veranda. In recent years, unfortunately, the quality of this once-sterling restaurant has varied wildly. If Chef Daniel is in, you will most likely get an excellent meal, but if he is not cooking that night, service may suffer. My other complaints are the alarming rise in prices and simultaneous decrease in the amount of food on your plate.

At the Historic Yellow Building, 65-1259 Kawaihae Rd. © **808/887-2200.** www.danielthiebaut.com. Reservations recommended. Main courses $15–$40 dinner; Sun brunch $24, children 8 and under are free. AE, DISC, MC, V. Daily 3:30–9pm; Sun brunch 10am–1:30pm.

Merriman's ★★ HAWAII REGIONAL   Merriman's is peerless. Although founder/owner/chef Peter Merriman now commutes between the Big Island and Maui, where he runs the Hula Grill, he manages to maintain the sizzle that has made Merriman's a premier Hawaii attraction. Order anything from Chinese short ribs to grilled shrimp and asparagus for lunch; at dinner, choose from the signature wok-charred ahi, Szechuan pepper–rubbed New York steak, lamb from nearby Kahua Ranch, and a noteworthy vegetarian selection. Among my favorites are the Caesar salad with sashimi, baked local goat cheese in pastry, and the steamed opakapaka with macadamia-nut spaetzle and pineapple cinnamon sauce. Kalua-pig quesadillas and the famous platters of seafood and meats are among the many reasons this is still the best, and busiest, dining spot in Waimea. They are offering small and large portions at dinner.

At the Opelo Plaza, Hwy. 19. © **808/885-6822.** www.merrimanshawaii.com. Reservations recommended. Main courses $10–$18 lunch, $23–$47 dinner (market prices for ranch lamb and ahi). AE, MC, V. Mon–Fri 11:30am–1:30pm; daily 5:30–9:30pm.

Inexpensive

Tako Taco Taqueria HEALTHY MEXICAN   Once a tiny hole-in-the-wall with the most delicious (and healthy) Mexican food, Tako Taco recently moved to the other side of Waimea into bigger quarters and added margaritas, beer, and wine to the menu. Alas, the food is not what it once was. There's plenty of room to eat in, or you can take out. Most items fall between $9 and $12. There are plenty of vegetarian selections as well. If the Mexican wedding cookies or chocolate-chip cookies are available, grab one (they're huge and only 85¢–$1.50 each). They are adding a brewery to the operation.

64-1066 Mamalahoa Hwy. © **808/887-1717.** All items $17 and under. AE, MC, V. Mon–Fri 11am–9pm; Sat 11am–8:30pm; Sun noon–8pm.

THE HAMAKUA COAST
Inexpensive

Cafe II Mondo ★ PIZZA/ESPRESSO BAR   A tiny cafe with a big spirit has taken over the Andrade Building in the heart of Honokaa. Tropical watercolors and local art, the irresistible aromas of garlic sauces and pizzas, and a 1924 koa bar meld gracefully in Sergio and Dena Ramirez's tribute to the Old World. A classical and flamenco guitarist, Sergio occasionally plays solo guitar in his restaurant while contented diners tuck into the stone-oven-baked pizzas. Try the Sergio—pesto pizza with marinated artichokes and mushrooms—or one of the calzones. Sandwiches come cradled in fresh baked French, onion, or rosemary buns. There's fresh soup daily, roasted chicken, and other specials; all greens are local and organic. Now serving Tropical Dreams ice cream (see box on p. 84). Live music Friday nights.

Mamane St., Honokaa. ℭ **808/775-7711.** www.cafeilmondo.com. Pizzas $12–$23; sandwiches $7–$9. No credit cards. Mon–Sat 11am–8pm.

Jolene's Kau Kau Korner AMERICAN/LOCAL   This place is nothing fancy, but it's homey and friendly, with eight tables and windows overlooking a scene much like an old Western town but for the cars. Choose from saimin, stir-fried tempeh with vegetables, sandwiches (including a good vegetarian tempeh burger), plate lunches (mahi-mahi, fried chicken, shrimp, beef stew), and familiar selections of local food.

At Mamane St. and Lehua, Honokaa. ℭ **808/775-9498.** Plate lunches $9–$22. No credit cards. Daily 10:30am–3:30pm; Mon and Wed 3:30–8pm.

Simply Natural ★ 🍴 HEALTH FOOD/SANDWICH SHOP   Simply Natural is a superb find on Honokaa's main street. I love this charming deli with its friendly staff, wholesome food, and vintage interior. It offers a counter and a few small tables with bright tablecloths and fresh anthuriums. Don't be fooled by the unpretentiousness of the place. The wholesome menu features flavorful items (saimin bowls, tuna melts) and breakfast delights that include taro-banana pancakes. Top it off with premium ice cream by Hilo Homemade (another favorite) or a smoothie. The mango-pineapple-banana-strawberry version is sublime.

Mamane St., Honokaa. ℭ **808/775-0119.** www.hawaiisimplynatural.com. Deli items $5–$9. No credit cards. Mon–Sat 8am–3:30pm.

Tex Drive-In & Restaurant AMERICAN/LOCAL   When Ada Pulin-Lamme bought the old Tex Drive-In, she made significant changes, such as improving upon an ages-old recipe for Portuguese *malasadas,* a cakelike doughnut without a hole. Tex

SHAH, PRASHANT PRAKASH

Unclaim : 7/5/2021

Held date   : 6/24/2021
Pickup location : Cedar Mill Library

Title   : Frommer's portable the Big Isl
and of Hawaii.
Call number   : 919.691 FRO 2012
Item barcode   : 33614046917174
Assigned branch : Beaverton City Library

Notes:

sells tens of thousands of these sugar-rolled morsels a month, including ones filled with pineapple/papaya preserves, pepper jelly, or Bavarian cream. The menu has a local flavor and features ethnic specialties: Korean chicken, teriyaki meat, kalua pork with cabbage, Filipino specials, and a new addition, Tex wraps served with homemade sweet-potato chips. With its gift shop and visitor center, Tex is a roadside attraction and a local hangout; residents have been gathering here over early morning coffee and breakfast for decades.

Hwy. 19, Honokaa. ⓒ **808/775-0598.** Main courses $4–$12. MC, V. Daily 6am–8pm.

What's Shakin' ★ 🍴 HEALTH FOOD   Look for the cheerful, yellow-and-white plantation-style wooden house with a green roof, 2 miles north of the Hawaii Tropical Botanical Garden. Many of the bananas and papayas from Patsy and Tim Withers's 20-acre farm end up here, in fresh-fruit smoothies such as the Papaya Paradise, an ambrosial blend of pineapples, coconuts, papayas, and bananas. If you're in the mood for something more substantial, try the chicken tamale with homemade salsa, the fish wrap with their home-grown avocado, or one of the burgers. There are several lunch specials daily, and every plate arrives with fresh fruit and a green salad topped with Patsy's Oriental sesame dressing. You can sit outdoors in the garden and enjoy the staggering ocean view.

27-999 Old Mamalahoa Hwy. (on the 4-mile scenic drive), Pepeekeo. ⓒ **808/ 964-3080.** Most items under $10; smoothies $6.50. MC, V. Daily 10am–5pm.

HILO

Note: You'll find the following restaurants on the "Hilo" map on p. 60.

Expensive

Pescatore ★ SOUTHERN ITALIAN   In a town of ethnic eateries and casual mom-and-pop diners, this is a special-occasion restaurant, dressier and pricier than most Hilo choices. It's ornate, especially for Hilo, with gilded frames on antique paintings, chairs of vintage velvet, koa walls, and a tile floor. The fresh catch is offered in several preparations, including reduced-cream and Parmesan or capers and wine. The paper-thin ahi carpaccio is garnished with capers, red onion, garlic, lemon, olive oil, and shaved Parmesan—and it's superb. Chicken, veal, and fish Marsala; a rich and garlicky scampi Alfredo; and the *fra diavolo* (a spicy seafood marinara) are among the dinner offerings, which come with soup or salad. Lighter fare, such as simple pasta marinara and chicken Parmesan, prevails at lunch. Breakfast is terrific, too.

A lunch **FOR ALL FIVE SENSES**

Hidden in the tall eucalyptus trees outside the old plantation community of Paauilo lies the **Hawaiian Vanilla Company,** on Paauilo Mauka Road (© **877/771-1771;** www.hawaiianvanilla. com). Located next to a gulch, surrounded by wild coffee, guava, loquat, and avocado trees, the company hosts one of the truly sensuous experiences on the Big Island—a multicourse Vanilla Luncheon. Before you even enter the huge Vanilla Gallery and Kitchen, you will be embraced by the heavenly sent of vanilla. You'll see vanilla orchid vines and, if you're truly lucky, the elusive blossoms. One of the real treats is listening to owner Jim Reddekopp's presentation (and video) on how vanilla is grown, how it's used in the meal you will be eating, and just about everything else you ever wanted to know about this magical orchid and bean. The four-course, 2-hour **Hawaiian Vanilla Luncheon** is held most Wednesdays, Thursdays, and Fridays from 12:30 to 2:30pm (reservations required); the cost is $39 and worth every penny. Check out the retail store, where myriad vanilla products, from beans and extracts to teas and lotions are for sale. You can also arrange to do a **Vanilla Tasting,** which occurs Monday to Saturday at 10:30am and lasts until 11:15am; the cost is $25 per person (reservations required).

235 Keawe St. © **808/969-9090.** Reservations recommended for dinner. Main courses $6–$16 lunch, $16–$40 dinner. AE, DC, DISC, MC, V. Mon–Sat 11am–2pm and 5:30–9pm; Sun 10am–2pm and 5:30–9pm.

Moderate

Hilo Bay Café ★★ 🍴 PACIFIC RIM *Foodie alert:* In the midst of a suburban shopping mall is this upscale, elegant eatery. It was created by the people from the Island Naturals Market & Deli, located on the other side of the shopping center. When you enter, the cascade of orchids on the marble bar is the first thing you see. Mellow jazz wafts from speakers, and plush chairs at low tables fill out the room. The creative menu ranges from spanako-pita with spinach and three cheeses to sautéed fresh catch to macadamia-nut praline scallops with capellini and beurre blanc. Lunch features salads (such as seared ahi Caesar), sandwiches (think Kalua pork with Swiss cheese and caramelized onions), and entrees (such as flaky-crust vegetarian potpie, slow-cooked pork barbecue ribs, and crispy fish and chips). There are also a terrific wine list and great martinis. Don't miss eating here.

At the Waiakea Center, 315 Makaala St. © **808/935-4939.** www.hilobaycafe. com. Reservations recommended for dinner. Main courses $9.50-$16 lunch, $10-$30 dinner. AE, DISC, MC, V. Mon-Sat 11am-9pm; Sun 5-9pm.

Nihon Restaurant & Cultural Center ★ 🎁 JAPANESE   This restaurant offers a beautiful view of Hilo Bay on one side and the soothing green sprawl of Liliuokalani Gardens on the other. This is a magnificent part of Hilo that's often overlooked because of its distance from the central business district. The menu features steak-and-seafood combination dinners and selections from the sushi bar, including the innovative poke and lomi-salmon hand rolls. The Businessman's Lunch, a terrific deal, comes with sushi, potato salad, soup, vegetables, and two choices from the following: butterfish, shrimp tempura, sashimi, chicken, and other morsels. This isn't inexpensive dining, but the value is sky-high, with a presentation that matches the serenity of the room and its stunning view of the bay.

123 Lihiwai St., overlooking Liliuokalani Gardens and Hilo Bay. © **808/969-1133.** Reservations recommended. Main courses $12-$20 lunch, $16-$26 dinner; combination dinners $22. AE, DC, DISC, MC, V. Mon-Sat 11am-1:15pm and 5-8pm.

Ocean Sushi Deli ★ 🎁 SUSHI   At Hilo's nexus of affordable sushi, local-style specials stretch purist boundaries but are so much fun: lomi salmon, oyster nigiri, opihi nigiri, unagi-avocado hand roll, ahi-poke roll, and special new rolls that use thin sheets of tofu skins and cooked egg. For traditionalists, there are ample shrimp, salmon, hamachi, clam, and other sushi delights—a long menu of them, including handy ready-to-cook sukiyaki and shabu-shabu sets.

250 Keawe St. © **808/961-6625.** Sushi boxes $4.75-$13; sushi family platters $20-$50. MC, V. Mon-Sat 10:30am-2pm and 5-9pm.

Queen's Court Restaurant AMERICAN/BUFFET   Many of those with a "not me!" attitude toward buffets have been disarmed by the Hilo Hawaiian's generous and well-rounded offerings at budget-friendly prices. A la carte menu items are offered Saturday through Thursday, but it's the Hawaiian, seafood buffet on the weekends that draw throngs of local families.

At the Hilo Hawaiian Hotel, 71 Banyan Dr. © **808/935-9361.** www.castleresorts. com. Reservations recommended. Fri seafood buffet $36. Main courses $10-$22. AE, DC, DISC, MC, V. Daily 6:30-9:15am; Sat-Thurs 5:30-8pm; Fri 5:30-9pm.

Restaurant Miwa ★ JAPANESE/SUSHI   Come to the Hilo Shopping Center to discover sensational seafood in a quintessential neighborhood sushi bar. This self-contained slice of Japan is a pleasant surprise in an otherwise unremarkable mall. Shabu-shabu

BET YOU can't eat JUST ONE

Hawaii Island Gourmet Products, which, under the brand Atebara Chips, has been making potato, taro, and shrimp chips in Hilo for 70 years, recently added a couple of new products that you just cannot miss: sweet-potato chips and the delicious taro chips, and regular potato chips covered in chocolate (the first-place winner at the Taste of Hilo). You can find them at most stores and major resorts on the Big Island, or contact the company directly (☏ **808/969-9600;** www.hawaiichips.com). *Warning:* As we say in Hawaii, these chips are so *ono* (delicious), you will be mail-ordering more when you get home.

(you cook your own ingredients in a heavy pot), tempura, fresh catch, and a full sushi selection are among the offerings. At dinner, you can splurge on the steak and lobster combination without dressing up. The haupia (coconut pudding) cream-cheese pie is a Miwa signature but is not offered daily; blueberry cream cheese is the alternative.

At the Hilo Shopping Center, 1261 Kilauea Ave. ☏ **808/961-4454.** Reservations recommended. Main courses $9–$21 lunch (most items $10–$15), $12–$40 dinner. AE, DC, DISC, MC, V. Mon–Thurs 11am–2pm and 5–9pm; Fri–Sat 11am–2pm and 5–9:30pm; Sun 5–9pm.

Seaside Restaurant ★★ STEAK/SEAFOOD   This is a casual local favorite, a Hilo signature with a character all its own. The restaurant has large windows overlooking glassy ponds—from which your dinner of mullet and *aholehole* (a silvery mountain bass) is fished out shortly before you arrive (you can't get much fresher than that!). Colin Nakagawa and his family cook the fish in two unadorned styles: fried or steamed in ti leaves with lemon juice and onions. Daily specials include steamed opakapaka, onaga (snapper), steak and lobster, *paniolo*-style prime rib, salmon encrusted with a nori-wasabi sprinkle, New York steak, and shrimp. Very fresh sushi is available daily. *Note:* If you want fish from the pond, *you must call ahead.* The outdoor tables are fabulous at dusk, when the light reflects on the water with an otherworldly glow.

1790 Kalanianaole Ave. ☏ **808/935-8825.** www.seasiderestaurant.com. Reservations recommended. Main courses $14–$33. AE, DC, MC, V. Tues–Thurs 5–8:30pm; Fri–Sat 5–9pm.

Inexpensive

Cafe Pesto ★★ PIZZA/PACIFIC RIM   Cafe Pesto's Italian brick oven burns many bushels of ohia and kiawe wood to turn out its toothsome pizzas, topped with fresh organic herbs and Island-grown produce. It's difficult to resist the wild-mushroom-and-artichoke pizza or the chipotle-and-tomato-drenched Southwestern. But go with the Pepperoni Classico, dripping with pepperoni, Italian sausage, and salami—it won't disappoint. Some of my other favorites are the Milolii, a crab-shrimp-mushroom sandwich with basil pesto; the chili-grilled shrimp pizza; and the flash-seared poke and spinach salad. The restaurant's high-ceilinged 1912 room looks out over Hilo's bay.

At the S. Hata Bldg., 308 Kamehameha Ave. ✆ **808/969-6640.** www.cafepesto. com. Pizzas $9–$21; main courses $11–$17 lunch, $19–$27 dinner. AE, DC, DISC, MC, V. Sun–Thurs 11am–9pm; Fri–Sat 11am–10pm.

Ken's House of Pancakes AMERICAN/LOCAL   The only 24-hour coffee shop on the Big Island, Ken's fulfills basic dining needs simply and efficiently, with a good dose of local color. Lighter servings and a concession toward health-conscious meals and salads have been added to the menu, a clever antidote to the numerous pies available. Omelets, pancakes, French toast made with Portuguese sweet bread, saimin, sandwiches, and soup stream out of the busy kitchen. Other affordable selections include fried chicken, steak, prime rib, and grilled fish. Tuesday is taco night, Wednesday is prime-rib night, Thursday is Hawaiian-plate night, and Sunday is all-you-can-eat-spaghetti night. Very local, very Hilo.

1730 Kamehameha Ave. ✆ **808/935-8711.** Most items under $11. AE, DC, DISC, MC, V. Daily 24 hr.

Miyo's JAPANESE   Often cited by local publications as the island's best Japanese restaurant, Miyo's offers home-cooked, healthy food (no MSG) served in an open-air room on Wailoa Pond, where curving footpaths and greenery fill the horizon. Sliding shoji doors bordering the dining area are left open so you can take in the view, which includes Mauna Kea on clear days. The sesame chicken (deep-fried and boneless with a spine-tingling sesame sauce) is a bestseller, but the entire menu is appealing. For vegetarians, there are specials such as vegetable tempura, vegetarian shabu-shabu (cooked in a chafing dish at your table, then dipped in a special sauce), and noodle and seaweed dishes. Other choices include mouthwatering sashimi, beef teriyaki, fried oysters, tempura, ahi *donburi* (seasoned and steamed in a bowl of rice), sukiyaki, and generous combination dinners. All orders are served with rice, soup, and pickled vegetables. The miso soup is a wonder, and the ahi-tempura plate is one of Hilo's best buys. Special diets (low sodium, sugarless) are cheerfully accommodated.

At the Waiakea Villas Hotel, 400 Hualani St. ℂ **808/935-2273.** Lunch main courses $7–$14, combinations $12–$15; dinner main courses $9–$17, combinations $13–$19. MC, V. Mon–Sat 11am–2pm and 5:30–8:30pm.

Naung Mai 🗡 THAI   This quintessential hole in the wall has gained an extra room, but even with 26 seats, it fills up quickly. In a short time, Naung Mai has gained the respect of Hilo residents for its curries and pad Thai—and for its use of fresh local ingredients. The flavors are assertive, the produce comes straight from the Hilo Farmers Market, and the prices are good. The four curries—green, red, yellow, and Mussaman—go with the jasmine, brown, white, and sticky rice. The pad Thai rice noodles, served with tofu and fresh vegetables, come with a choice of chicken, pork, or shrimp, and are sprinkled with fresh peanuts. You can order your curry Thai-spicy (incendiary) or American-spicy (moderately hot), but even mild, the flavors are outstanding. Chefs Sukanya Heideman and Siriporn Elkins also make wonderful spring rolls and a Tom Yum spicy soup that is legendary. Lunch specials are a steal. Naung Mai is obscured behind the Garden Exchange, so it may take some seeking out.

86 Kilauea Ave. ℂ **808/934-7540.** www.naungmaithai.com. Reservations recommended. Main dishes $11–$16. MC, V. Daily 11am–9pm.

Nori's Saimin & Snacks ★ 🎒 SAIMIN/NOODLES   Like Naung Mai, Nori's requires some searching out, but it's worth it. Unmarked and not visible from the street, it's located across from the Hilo Lanes bowling alley, down a short driveway into an obscure parking lot. You'll wonder what you're doing here, but stroll into the tiny noodle house with the neon sign of chopsticks and a bowl, grab a plywood booth or Formica table, and prepare to enjoy the best saimin on the island. Saimin comes fried or in a savory homemade broth—the key to its success—with various embellishments, from seaweed to wonton dumplings. Ramen, soba, udon, and *mundoo* (a Korean noodle soup) are among the 16 varieties of noodle soups. The barbecued chicken and beef sticks are smoky and marvelous. Plate lunches (teriyaki beef, ahi, Korean short ribs) and sandwiches give diners ample choices from morning to late night, though noodles are the stars. The "big plate" dinners feature ahi, barbecued beef, fried noodles, kalbi ribs, and salad—not for junior appetites. The desserts at Nori's are also legendary, with the signature haupia and sweet-potato pies flying out the door almost as fast as the famous chocolate-*mochi* cookies and cakes.

688 Kinoole St. ℂ **808/935-9133.** Most items under $16; "big plate" dinners for 2 $22. AE, DC, MC, V. Mon–Thurs 10:30am–11pm; Fri–Sat 10:30am–midnight; Sun 10:30am–10pm.

Royal Siam Thai Restaurant ★ THAI   A popular neighborhood restaurant, the Royal Siam serves consistently good Thai curries in a simple room just off the sidewalk. Fresh herbs and vegetables from the owner's gardens add an extra zip to the platters of noodles, soups, curries, and specialties, which pour out of the kitchen in clouds of spicy fragrance. The Buddha Rama, a wonderful concoction of spinach, chicken, and peanut sauce, is a scene-stealer and a personal favorite. The Thai garlic chicken, in sweet basil with garlic and coconut milk, is equally superb.

70 Mamo St. ℂ **808/961-6100.** Main courses $9–$14. AE, DC, DISC, MC, V. Mon–Sat 11am–2pm and 5–8:30pm; Sun 5–8pm.

HAWAII VOLCANOES NATIONAL PARK

Note: You'll find the following restaurants on the "Where to Stay & Dine in the Volcano Area" map on p. 64.

Expensive

Kiawe Kitchen PIZZA/MEDITERRANEAN   Although it has a somewhat limited menu, this small eatery is a great place to stop for hot soup or a fresh salad after viewing the volcano; it has recently added a full bar. The pizza is excellent (all fresh ingredients) but pricey; I recommend the *insalata caprese* and a bowl of soup for lunch. Dinners include lamb (both rack and shank), pasta dishes, a vegetarian item, and usually beef. The menu changes daily (whatever they can get fresh that day). There's an interesting beer list (all from Hawaii) and yummy espresso drinks (including Kona coffees). You can eat on the lanai or inside the restaurant.

19-4005 Haunani Rd. (off Hwy. 11, Volcano Village exit). ℂ **808/967-7711.** Main courses $11–$15 lunch, $18–$34 dinner. MC, V. Daily 11–2:30pm and 5:30–8:30pm.

Kilauea Lodge & Restaurant ★ CONTINENTAL   Diners travel long distances to escape from the crisp upland air into the warmth of this high-ceilinged lodge. The decor is a cross between chalet-cozy and volcano-rugged; the sofa in front of the 1938 fireplace is especially inviting when a fire is roaring. The European cooking is a fine culinary act. Favorites include the fresh catch, hasenpfeffer, potato-leek soup (all flavor and no cream), and Alsatian soup. All dinners come with soup or salad and a loaf of freshly baked bread.

19-3948 Old Volcano Rd. (1 block off Hwy. 11, Volcano Village exit). ℂ **808/967-7366.** www.kilauealodge.com. Reservations recommended. Main courses $6.50–$14 breakfast, $7.50–$13 lunch, $20–$47 dinner. AE, MC, V. Daily 7:30am–2pm and 5–9pm; Sun brunch 10am–2pm.

Inexpensive

Lava Rock Cafe ★ ECLECTIC/LOCAL   Volcano Village's newest favorite spot is a cheerful, airy oasis with tables and booths indoors and semi-outdoors, under a clear corrugated-plastic ceiling. The cross-cultural menu includes everything from chow fun to fajitas. The choices include three-egg omelets and pancakes with wonderful housemade lilikoi butter, teriyaki beef and chicken, fresh catch, T-bone steak, steak-and-shrimp combos, and serious desserts (such as mango cheesecake). The lunchtime winners are the "seismic sandwiches" (which the cafe will pack for hikers), chili, quarter-pound burgers, salads, plate lunches, and "volcanic" heavies such as southern-fried chicken and grilled meats.

19-3972 Old Volcano Rd. (1 block off Hwy. 11, Volcano Village exit), next to Kilauea Kreations. © **808/967-8526.** Main courses $6.50–$10 breakfast, $8–$10 lunch, $7–$23 dinner. MC, V. Sun 7:30am–4pm; Mon 7:30am–5pm; Tues–Sat 7:30am–9pm.

Thai Thai Restaurant THAI   Volcano's first Thai restaurant adds warming curries to the chill of upcountry life. The menu features spicy curries (five types, rich with coconut milk and spices), satays, coconut-rich soups, noodles and rice, and sweet-and-sour stir-fries of fish, vegetables, beef, cashew chicken, and garlic shrimp. A big hit is the green-papaya salad made with tomatoes, crunchy green beans, green onions, and a heap of raw and roasted peanuts—a full symphony of color, aroma, texture, and flavor.

Lava Flow & Lunch

The Puna District's scruffy, offbeat town of Pahoa is still rough around the edges, but a tiny handful of good-quality restaurants and stylish shops have popped up of late. At this writing, the Puna District offered the island's easiest access to Kilauea's current lava flow, which was spilling into the ocean at the end of the road in Kalapana. National park officials have set up a temporary viewing area to accommodate visitors. If lava viewing leaves you a bit peckish and in the mood for something different, here is a tip: Nestled among Pahoa's rustic storefronts is **Paolo's Bistro,** 333 Old Government Rd. (© **808/965-7033**). This charming Italian bistro—complete with lace curtains and checkered tablecloths—offers smoothly attentive service and a limited but high-quality menu of homemade pastas and other Tuscan-style favorites, plus a sweetly simple Italian-style dessert. Come bearing your own bottle of wine; the BYOB policy helps keep your bill down.

19-4084 Old Volcano Rd. (1 block off Hwy. 11, Volcano Village exit). © **808/967-7969.** Main courses $13–$25. AE, DISC, MC, V. Thurs–Tues 11:30am–9pm; Wed 11:30am–4pm.

Volcano Golf & Country Club AMERICAN/LOCAL   One of the first two eateries in the area, this golf-course clubhouse has a reputation as a low-key purveyor of local specialties. The food ranges from okay to good, while the room—looking out over a fairway—is cordial. It's not as clichéd as it sounds, especially when the mists are rolling in and the greens and grays assume an eye-popping intensity; I've even seen nene geese from my table. In the typically cool Volcano air, local favorites such as chicken or pork katsu, kalua pork sandwiches, and hamburgers become especially comforting. Also featured are Portuguese bean soup and teriyaki beef or chicken.

Pii Mauna Dr., off Hwy. 11 (mile marker 30). © **808/967-8228.** www.volcano golfshop.com. Reservations recommended for large groups. Breakfast items under $10; lunch items under $13. AE, DC, DISC, MC, V. Mon–Thurs 11am–3pm; Fri–Sun 8am–3pm.

SOUTH POINT/NAALEHU

South Side Shaka Restaurant ☺ AMERICAN/LOCAL   You can't miss the Shaka sign from the highway. This welcome addition to the Naalehu restaurant scene has white tile floors, long tables, an espresso machine, and a friendly, casual atmosphere. The serviceable menu of plate lunches and American fare will seem like gourmet cuisine after a long drive through the Kau Desert. The servings are humongous, and the prices kind to your wallet. Locals come for the plate lunches, sandwiches (the Shaka burger is very popular), and honey-dipped fried chicken, and for the fresh catch at dinner—grilled, deep-fried, or prepared in a special panko crust. In fact, the new owner, a former fish wholesaler, is now focusing more on fresh fish.

95-5673 Mamalahoa Hwy. (Hwy. 11), Naalehu. © **808/929-7404.** Main courses $4–$13 breakfast, $7–$15 lunch, $9–$20 dinner. MC, V. Daily 7am–9pm.

FUN ON & OFF THE BEACH

This is why you've come to Hawaii—the sun, the sand, and the surf. In this chapter, we'll tell you about the best beaches, a range of ocean activities on the Big Island, and our favorite places and outfitters for these marine adventures. Also in this chapter are things to do on dry land, including the best spots for hiking and camping and the greatest golf courses.

4

BEACHES

Too young geologically to have many great beaches, the Big Island instead has a collection of unusual ones: brand-new black-sand beaches, green-sand beaches, salt-and-pepper beaches, and even a rare (for this island) white-sand beach.

The Kona Coast
KAHALUU BEACH PARK ★★
This is the most popular beach on the Kona Coast; these reef-protected lagoons attract 1,000 people a day almost year-round. Kahaluu is the best all-around beach on Alii Drive, with coconut trees lining a narrow salt-and-pepper sand shore that gently slopes to turquoise pools. The schools of brilliantly colored tropical fish that weave in and out of the reef make this a great place to snorkel. In summer, it's also an ideal spot for children and beginning snorkelers; the water is so shallow that you can just stand up if you feel uncomfortable. But in winter, there's a rip current when the high surf rolls in; look for the lifeguard warnings. Kahaluu isn't the biggest beach on the island, but it's one of the best equipped, with off-road parking, beach-gear rentals, a covered pavilion,

restrooms, barbecue pits, and a food concession. It gets crowded, so come early to stake out a spot.

KEKAHA KAI STATE PARK (KONA COAST STATE PARK) ★

This beach is about 2 miles north of the Kona Airport on Queen Kaahumanu Highway; turn left at a sign pointing improbably down a bumpy road. You won't need a four-wheel-drive vehicle to make it down here—just drive slowly and watch out for potholes. At the end you'll find 5 miles of shoreline with a half-dozen long, curving beaches and a big cove on Mahaiula Bay, as well as archaeological and historical sites. The series of well-protected coves is excellent for swimming, and there's great snorkeling and diving offshore; the big winter waves attract surfers. Facilities include restrooms, picnic tables, and barbecue pits; you'll have to bring your own drinking water. The beach is open daily from 8am to 8pm (the closing time is strictly enforced, and there's no overnight camping).

WHITE SANDS BEACH ★

Don't blink as you cruise Alii Drive, or you'll miss White Sands Beach. This small white-sand pocket beach about 4½ miles south of Kailua-Kona is sometimes called Disappearing Beach because it does just that, especially at high tide or during storms. It vanished completely when Hurricane Iniki hit in 1991, but it's now back in place (at least it was the last time I looked). On calm days, the water is perfect for swimming and snorkeling. Locals use the elementary waves to teach their children how to surf and boogie board. In winter, the waves swell to expert levels, attracting surfers and spectators. Facilities include restrooms, showers, lifeguards, and a small parking lot.

The Kohala Coast

ANAEHOOMALU BAY (A-BAY) ★★

The Big Island makes up for its dearth of beaches with a few spectacular ones, such as Anaehoomalu, or A Bay, as the locals call it. This popular gold-sand beach, fringed by a grove of palms and backed by royal fish ponds still full of mullet, is one of Hawaii's most beautiful. It fronts the Waikoloa Beach Marriott Resort and is enjoyed by guests and locals alike (it's busier in summer, but doesn't ever get truly crowded). The beach slopes gently from shallow to deep water; swimming, snorkeling, diving, kayaking, and windsurfing are all excellent here. At the far edge of the bay, snorkelers and divers can watch endangered green sea turtles line up and wait their turn to have small fish clean them. Equipment rental and snorkeling, scuba, and windsurfing instruction are

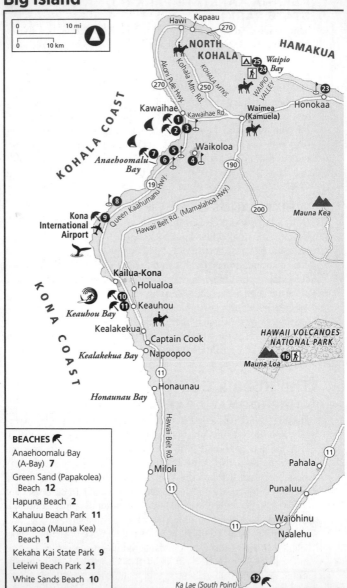

Beaches & Outdoor Activities on the Big Island

NORTH KOHALA

HAMAKUA

Hawi — Kapaau — 270

Akoni Pule Hwy.

Kohala Mtn. Rd.

Kohala Mtns.

270 — 250

KOHALA COAST

Kawaihae — Kawaihae Rd.

1
2 3

7 5
6
4

Waikoloa

Anaehoomalu Bay

19

8

Kona International Airport

9

Queen Kaahumanu Hwy.

Hawaii Belt Rd. (Mamalahoa Hwy.)

190

200

Mauna Kea

Waipio Bay
25
24

Waipio Valley

Waimea (Kamuela)

23

Honokaa

Kailua-Kona

Holualoa

10
11

Keauhou

Keauhou Bay

Kealakekua

Captain Cook

Napoopoo

Kealakekua Bay

11

Honaunau

Honaunau Bay

Hawaii Belt Rd.

Miloli

HAWAII VOLCANOES NATIONAL PARK

16

Mauna Loa

Pahala

11

Punaluu

Waiohinu

Naalehu

Ka Lae (South Point)

12

BEACHES

Anaehoomalu Bay (A-Bay) **7**

Green Sand (Papakolea) Beach **12**

Hapuna Beach **2**

Kahaluu Beach Park **11**

Kaunaoa (Mauna Kea) Beach **1**

Kekaha Kai State Park **9**

Leleiwi Beach Park **21**

White Sands Beach **10**

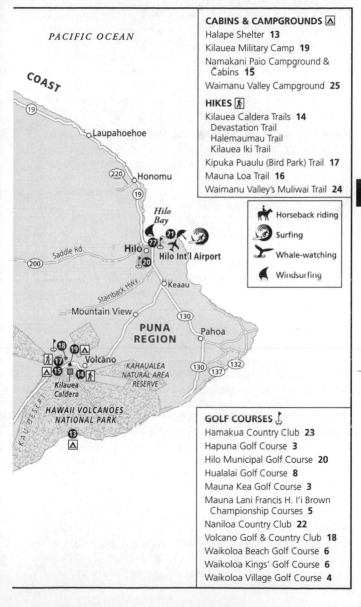

CABINS & CAMPGROUNDS ⚠
Halape Shelter **13**
Kilauea Military Camp **19**
Namakani Paio Campground & Cabins **15**
Waimanu Valley Campground **25**

HIKES 🏃
Kilauea Caldera Trails **14**
  Devastation Trail
  Halemaumau Trail
  Kilauea Iki Trail
Kipuka Puaulu (Bird Park) Trail **17**
Mauna Loa Trail **16**
Waimanu Valley's Muliwai Trail **24**

🐎 Horseback riding
🌊 Surfing
🐋 Whale-watching
🏄 Windsurfing

GOLF COURSES 🏌
Hamakua Country Club **23**
Hapuna Golf Course **3**
Hilo Municipal Golf Course **20**
Hualalai Golf Course **8**
Mauna Kea Golf Course **3**
Mauna Lani Francis H. I'i Brown Championship Courses **5**
Naniloa Country Club **22**
Volcano Golf & Country Club **18**
Waikoloa Beach Golf Course **6**
Waikoloa Kings' Golf Course **6**
Waikoloa Village Golf Course **4**

PACIFIC OCEAN

COAST

Laupahoehoe

Honomu

Hilo Bay

Hilo

Hilo Int'l Airport

Saddle Rd.

Keaau

Stainback Hwy.

Mountain View

PUNA REGION

Pahoa

Volcano

KAHAUALEA NATURAL AREA RESERVE

Kilauea Caldera

HAWAII VOLCANOES NATIONAL PARK

KAU DESERT

available at the north end of the beach. Facilities include restrooms, showers, picnic tables, and plenty of parking.

HAPUNA BEACH ★★★
Just off Queen Kaahumanu Highway, south of the Hapuna Beach Prince Hotel, lies this crescent of gold sand—big, wide, and a half-mile long. In summer, when the beach is widest, the ocean calmest, and the crowds biggest, this is the island's best beach for swimming, snorkeling, and bodysurfing. But beware of Hapuna in winter, when its thundering waves, strong rip currents, and lack of lifeguards can be dangerous. Facilities include A-frame cabins for camping, pavilions, restrooms, showers, and plenty of parking.

KAUNAOA BEACH (MAUNA KEA BEACH) ★★★
Everyone calls this gold-sand beach Mauna Kea Beach (it's at the foot of Mauna Kea Beach Hotel), but its real name is Hawaiian for "native dodder," a lacy, yellow-orange vine that once thrived on the shore. A coconut grove sweeps around this golden crescent, where the water is calm and protected by two black-lava points. The sandy bottom slopes gently into the bay, which often fills with tropical fish, sea turtles, and manta rays, especially at night, when the hotel lights flood the shore. Swimming is excellent year-round, except in rare winter storms. Snorkelers prefer the rocky points, where fish thrive in the surge. Facilities include restrooms, showers, and ample parking, but there are no lifeguards.

Hilo
LELEIWI BEACH PARK ★
Hilo's beaches may be few, but Leleiwi is one of Hawaii's most beautiful. This unusual cove of palm-fringed black-lava tide pools, fed by freshwater springs and rippled by gentle waves, is a photographer's delight—and the perfect place to take a plunge. In winter, big waves can splash these ponds, but the shallow pools are generally free of currents and ideal for families with children, especially in the protected inlets at the center of the park. Leleiwi often attracts endangered sea turtles, making this one of Hawaii's most popular snorkeling spots. The beach is 4 miles out of town on Kalanianaole Avenue. Facilities include restrooms, showers, lifeguards, picnic pavilions, and paved walkways. There's also a marine-life exhibit here.

South Point
GREEN SAND BEACH (PAPAKOLEA BEACH) ★
Hawaii's famous green-sand beach is located at the base of Puu o Mahana, an old cinder cone spilling into the sea. The place has its problems: It's difficult to reach; the open bay is often rough; there

are no facilities, fresh water, or shade from the relentless sun; and howling winds scour the point. Nevertheless, each year the unusual green sands attract thousands of oglers, who follow a well-worn four-wheel-drive-only road for 2½ miles to the top of a cliff, which you have to climb down to reach the beach. The sand is crushed olivine, a green semiprecious mineral found in eruptive rocks and meteorites. If the surf's up, check out the beach from the cliff's edge, if the water's calm, it's generally safe to swim

To get to Green Sand Beach from the boat ramp at South Point, follow the four-wheel-drive trail; even if you have a four-wheel-drive vehicle, you may want to walk because the trail is very, very bad in parts. Make sure you have appropriate closed-toed footwear: tennis shoes or hiking boots. The trail is relatively flat, but you're usually walking into the wind as you head toward the beach. The beginning of the trail is lava. After the first 10 to 15 minutes of walking, the lava disappears and the trail begins to cross pasture-land. After about 30 to 40 minutes more, you'll see an eroded cinder cone by the water; continue to the edge, and there lie the green sands below.

The best way to reach the beach is to go over the edge from the cinder cone. (It looks like walking around the south side of the cone would be easier, but it's not.) From the cinder cone, go over the overhang of the rock, and you'll see a trail.

Going down to the beach is very difficult and treacherous, as you'll be able to see from the top. You'll have to make it over and around big lava boulders, dropping down 4 to 5 feet from boulder to boulder in certain spots. And don't forget that you'll have to climb back up. Look before you start; if you have any hesitation, don't go down (you get a pretty good view from the top, anyway).

Warning: When you get to the beach, watch the waves for about 15 minutes and make sure they don't break over the entire beach. If you walk on the beach, always keep one eye on the ocean and stick close to the rock wall. There can be strong rip currents here, and it's imperative to avoid them. Allow a minimum of 2 to 3 hours for this entire excursion.

WATERSPORTS

If you want to rent beach toys, such as snorkel gear or boogie boards, the beach concessions at all the big resorts, as well as tour desks and dive shops, offer equipment rentals and sometimes lessons for beginners. The cheapest place to get great rental equipment is **Snorkel Bob's,** in the parking lot of Huggo's restaurant at 75–5831 Kahakai Rd., at Alii Drive, Kailua-Kona (© **808/329-0770;** www.snorkelbob.com), and in the New Industrial Area, 73–4976 Kamanu St. (© **808/329-0771**).

Boating

For fishing charters, see "Sport Fishing: The Hunt for Granders," later on p. 109.

Body Glove Cruises ★★ The *Body Glove*, a 55-foot trimaran that carries up to 100 passengers, runs an adventurous sail-snorkel-dive cruise at a reasonable price. You'll be greeted with fresh Kona coffee, fruit, and breakfast pastries; you'll then sail north of Kailua to Pawai Bay, a marine preserve where you can snorkel, scuba-dive, swim, or just hang out on the deck for a couple of hours. After a buffet deli lunch spread, you might want to take the plunge off the boat's water slide or diving board before heading back to Kailua Pier. The boat departs daily from the pier at 9am and returns at 1:30pm. The only thing you need to bring is a towel; snorkeling equipment (and scuba equipment, for a fee, if you choose to dive) is provided. *Money-saving tip:* The afternoon trip is cheaper.

Kailua Pier. © **800/551-8911** or 808/326-7122. www.bodyglovehawaii.com. Morning cruises $120 adults, $78 children 6–12, free for children 5 and under; afternoon cruises $78 adults, $58 children 6–12, free for children 5 and under; extra $61 for certified scuba divers with own equipment, $74 without own equipment; extra $84 for introductory scuba. Whale-watching cruises (Dec–Apr) $78 adults, $58 children 6–12, free for children 5 and under.

Captain Dan McSweeney's Year-Round Whale-Watching Adventures ★★★ Hawaii's most impressive visitors—45-foot humpback whales—return to the waters off Kona every winter. Capt. Dan McSweeney, a whale researcher for more than 25 years, works daily with the whales, so he has no problem finding them. Frequently, he drops an underwater microphone into the water so you can listen to their songs, or uses an underwater video camera to show you what's going on. In humpback season—roughly December 26 through April—Dan makes two 3-hour trips daily. From November to December 20, he schedules one morning trip on Tuesday, Thursday, and Saturday to look for pilot, sperm, false killer, melon-headed, pygmy killer, and beaked whales. Captain Dan guarantees a sighting, or he'll take you out again for free. No cruises in May and October.

Honokohau Harbor. © **888/942-5376** or 808/322-0028. www.ilovewhales.com. Whale-watching cruises $80 adults, $70 children under 90 pounds.

Captain Zodiac If you'd prefer to take a **snorkel cruise to Keal-akekua Bay** in a small boat, go in Captain Zodiac's 16-passenger,

24-foot inflatable rubber life raft. The boat takes you on a wild ride 14 miles down the Kona Coast to Kealakekua, where you'll spend about an hour snorkeling in the bay and then enjoy snacks and beverages at the picnic snorkel site. Trips are twice daily, from 8:15am to 12:15pm and from 12:45 to 5pm. *Warning:* Pregnant women and those with bad backs should avoid this often-bumpy ride.

Gentry's Marina, Honokohau Harbor. ℂ **808/329-3199.** www.captainzodiac. com. 4-hr. snorkel cruises $93 adults, $70 children 3–12; 3 hr. whale watching cruises $65 adults, $59 children 4–12. Book online for discounts.

Fair Wind Snorkeling & Diving Adventures ★★★ ☺ One of the best ways to snorkel Kealakekua Bay, the marine-life preserve that's one of the top snorkel spots in Hawaii, is on Fair Wind's half-day **sail-and-snorkel cruise to Kealakekua Bay.** The company recently added the *Hula Kai,* the latest (state-of-the-art) 55-foot foil-assist catamaran (the first on the Big Island), which offers an upscale experience and a faster, smoother ride on a boat full of luxury. I recommend the *Hula Kai* 5-hour snorkel-and-dive morning cruise, which includes a light breakfast, a gourmet barbecue lunch, two snorkeling sites, a guided tour, and optional scuba diving ($155 adults; minimum age 18). The *Fair Wind II,* a 60-foot catamaran that holds up to 100 passengers, offers a morning cruise that leaves from Keauhou Bay at 9am and returns at 1:30pm; it includes a light breakfast, lunch, snorkel gear, and lessons ($125 adults, $75 kids 4–12, $29 toddlers). The afternoon cruise runs from 2 to 6:30pm and includes a barbecue lunch, sailing, snorkeling, and equipment ($109 adults, $69 kids 4–12, free for kids 3 and under). Also on the *Fair Wind II* is a shorter (and cheaper) snack, sail-and-snorkel cruise for $75 adults and $45 children—there's no lunch, just fruit and a snack plus snorkeling equipment.

78-7130 Kaleiopapa St., Kailua-Kona. ℂ **800/677-9461** or 808/322-2788. www. fair-wind.com. Snorkel cruises $75-$155 adults, $45-$75 children 4–12, prices vary depending on cruise.

Kamanu Charters ★★ This sleek catamaran, 36 feet long and 22 feet wide, provides a laid-back sail-and-snorkel cruise from Honokohau Harbor to Pawai Bay. The 3½-hour trip includes a tropical lunch (deli sandwiches, chips, fresh fruit, and beverages), snorkeling gear, and personalized instruction for first-time snorkelers. The *Kamanu* sails (weather permitting) at 9am and 1:30pm; it can hold up to 24 people.

Honokohau Harbor. ℂ **800/348-3091** or 808/329-2021. www.kamanu.com. Sail-and-snorkel cruises $90 adults, $50 children 12 and under.

FROMMER'S favorite BIG ISLAND EXPERIENCES

Creeping Up to the Ooze (p. 152). Since Kilauea's ongoing eruption began in 1983, lava has been bubbling and oozing in a mild-mannered way that lets you walk right up to the creeping flow for an up-close encounter.

Going Underwater at Kealakekua Bay (p. 108). The island has lots of extraordinary snorkel and dive sites, but none is so easily accessible as mile-wide Kealakekua Bay, an uncrowded marine preserve on the South Kona Coast. Here you can swim with dolphins, sea turtles, octopuses, and every species of tropical fish that calls Hawaii's waters home.

Discovering Old Hawaii at Puuhonua O Honaunau National Historical Park (p. 131). Protected by a huge rock wall, this sacred Honaunau site was once a refuge for ancient Hawaiian warriors. Today you can walk the consecrated grounds and glimpse a former way of life in a partially restored 16th-century village, complete with thatched huts, canoes, forbidding idols, and a temple that holds the bones of 23 Hawaiian chiefs.

Stargazing from Mauna Kea (p. 136). A jacket, beach mat, and binoculars are all you need to see every star and planet in this ultraclean atmosphere, where the visibility is so good that 11 nations have set up telescopes (two of them the biggest in the world) to probe deep space.

Watching for Whales. Humpback whales pass through waters off the Kona Coast every December through April. To spot them from shore, head down to the Natural Energy Laboratory of Hawaii Authority (p. 127), just south of Kona Airport, and keep your eyes peeled as you walk the shoreline. To get here, follow Queen Kaahumanu Highway (Hwy. 19) toward the airport; 6 miles outside of town, look for the sign NATURAL ENERGY LAB and turn left. Just after the road takes a sharp turn to the right, there's a small paved parking area with restrooms; a beach trail is on the ocean side of the lot.

Body Boarding (Boogie Boarding) & Bodysurfing

On the Kona side of the island, the best beaches for body boarding and bodysurfing are **Hapuna Beach, White Sands Beach,** and **Kekaha Kai State Park** (Kona Coast State Park). On the east side, try **Leleiwi Beach.**

Savoring a Cup of Kona Coffee. It's just one of those things you have to do while you're on the Big Island. For a truly authentic cup of java, head upcountry to **Holuakoa Café,** on Mamalahoa Hwy. (Hwy. 180) in Holualoa (© **808/322-2233**).

Hanging Out in Waipio Valley (p. 143). Pack a picnic and head for this gorgeously lush valley that time forgot. Delve deep into the jungle on foot, comb the black-sand beach, or just laze the day away by a babbling stream, the tail end of a 1,000-foot waterfall.

Chasing Rainbows at Akaka Falls (p. 140). When the light is right, a perfect prism is formed and a rainbow leaps out of this spectacular 442-foot waterfall, about an 11-mile drive from Hilo. Take time to roam through the surrounding rainforest, where you're sure to have close encounters with exotic birds, aromatic plumeria trees, and shocking red-torch ginger.

Gawking at the Day's Catch in Honokohau Harbor. Every afternoon between 4 and 5pm, local fishermen pull into the fuel dock to weigh in their big-game fish. 1,000-pound blue marlins, 150-pound yellowfin tunas, plenty of scale-tipping mahimahi, ono (also known as wahoo), and others. Sit in the bleachers and check out these magnificent creatures.

Hunting for Petroglyphs. The majority of Hawaii's ancient rock carvings are found in the 233-acre Puako Petroglyph Archaeological District (p. 133), near Mauna Lani Resort. The best time to go looking is in the cool early morning or late afternoon. There are more than 3,000 petroglyphs in this area alone—see how many you can spot.

Shopping at the Hilo Farmers Market (p. 168). For a handful of dollars, you can buy a pound of rambutan (a sweet Indonesian fruit), a bouquet of tropical orchids, and a couple of tasty foot-long Hawaiian laulau (pork, chicken, or fish steamed in ti leaves). But be sure to arrive early (the market opens at sunrise)—many of the 60 or so vendors quickly sell out.

Ocean Kayaking

Imagine sitting at sea level, eye to eye with a turtle, a dolphin, even a whale—it's possible in an oceangoing kayak. Anyone can kayak in calm waters: Just get in, find your balance, and paddle. After a few minutes of instruction and a little practice in a calm area (like the lagoon in front of **King Kamehameha's Kona Beach Hotel**), you'll be ready to explore. Beginners can practice their skills in **Kailua Bay;** intermediates might try paddling from **Honokohau Harbor** to **Kekaha Kai State Park;** the **Hamakua Coast** is a challenge for experienced kayakers.

You can rent one- and two-person kayaks (and other ocean toys) from **Aloha Kayak ★★★** (© **877/322-1444** or 808/322-2868; www.alohakayak.com). Half-day rates are $25 for a single and $45 for a double; full-day rates are $35 for a single and $60 for a double. Aloha Kayak also has a unique tour from Keauhou Bay and the Captain Cook Monument, with Hawaiian guides showing you sea caves and snorkeling areas full of fish and turtles. The tours last either 4 hours ($89 adults, $45–$65 children 11 and under) or 6 hours ($159 adults, $80 children 11 and under) and include all equipment, beverages, snorkeling gear, and lunch or snacks.

Parasailing

Get a bird's-eye view of Hawaii's pristine waters with **UFO Parasail** (© **800/FLY-4-UFO** or 808/325-5836; www.ufoparasail. net), which offers parasail rides daily from 8am to 2pm from Kailua Pier. The cost is $65 for the standard flight of 7 minutes of air time at 600 feet, and $75 for a deluxe 10-minute ride at 800 feet. You can go up alone or with a friend; no experience is necessary. *Tip:* Take the early-bird special at 8am (when the light is fantastic and the price is right) for just $60 for 400 feet, or $70 for 800 feet.

Scuba Diving

The Big Island's leeward coast offers some of the best diving in the world; the water is calm, warm, and clear. Want to swim with fast-moving game fish? Try **Ulua Cave** at the north end of the Kohala Coast. There are nearly two dozen dive operators on the west side of the Big Island, plus a couple in Hilo. They offer everything from scuba-certification courses to guided boat dives.

"This is not your mother or father's dive shop," says the owner Simon Key of the newly opened **Kona Diving Company,** in the Old Industrial area, 74–5467 Luhia St., Kailua-Kona (© **808/331-1858;** www.bottomtimehawaii.com). "This is a dive shop for today's diver." Simon claims what sets Kona Diving Company apart is its willingness to take its 34-foot catamaran (complete with showers, TV, and restrooms) to unusual dive sites and "not those sites just 2 minutes from the mouth of the harbor." Kona Diving also offers introductory dives in enriched air (Nitrox) for an additional $10; two-tank dives for $120 to $130.

One of Kona's oldest dive shops, **Jack's Diving Locker,** 75–5813 Alii Dr. (© **800/345-4807** or 808/329-7585; www. jacksdivinglocker.com), recently purchased another longtime dive shop, Kona Coast Divers, and combined the two businesses into one. Plus, it expanded its former 600-square-foot retail store into an 8,000-square-foot dive center with swimming pool (featuring underwater viewing windows), classrooms, full-service rentals, and full-service sports-diving and technical-diving facility. It offers the classic two-tank dive for $125 and a two-tank manta-ray night dive for $145.

Hot-Lava Dives Hilo's **Nautilus Dive Center,** 382 Kamehameha Ave., between Open Market and the Shell gas station (② **808/935-6939;** www.nautilusdivehilo.com), offers a very unusual opportunity for advanced divers: diving where the lava flows into the ocean. "Sometimes you can feel the pressure from the sound waves as the lava explodes," owner Bill De Rooy says. "Sometimes you have perfect visibility to the color show of your life." As we went to press, Bill was doing these dives when the conditions were right (an unstable collapse of a recent lava field sent 20 acres of lava into the ocean; fortunately, no one was injured). Call to see if Bill is doing the dives; a two-tank dive goes for as much as $500 per person.

Night Dives with Manta Rays ★★ A little less risky—but still something you'll never forget—is swimming with manta rays on a night dive. These giant, harmless creatures, with wingspans that reach up to 14 feet, glide gracefully through the water to feed on plankton. **Jack's Diving Locker,** 75–5819 Alii Dr. (② **800/345-4807** or 808/329-7585; www.jacksdivinglocker.com), offers its "Manta Ray Madness" for $145 for a two-tank dive and $95 for snorkelers. Everyone from beginners through experts will love this dive. Jack's cannot guarantee that these wild creatures will show up every night, but does boast a more than 90% sightings record.

If Jack's is booked, try **Sandwich Isle Divers,** 75–5729 Alii Dr., in the back of the Kona Marketplace (② **888/743-3483** or 808/329-9188; www.sandwichisledivers.com). It offers two-tank nighttime manta dives for $165 (including equipment), or $140 if you have your own gear.

Weeklong Dives If you're looking for an all-diving vacation, you might think about spending a week on the 80-foot **Kona Aggressor II ★** (② **800/344-5662** or 808/329-8182; www.aggressor.com), a live-aboard dive boat that promises to provide unlimited underwater exploration, including day and night dives, along 85 miles of the Big Island's coastline. You might spot harmless 70-foot whale sharks, plus not-so-harmless tiger and hammerhead sharks, as well as dolphins, whales, monk seals, and sea turtles. Fourteen divers are accommodated in six staterooms. Guided dives are available, but as long as you're certified, just log in with the dive master and you're free to follow the limits of your dive computer. It's $1,995 for 7 days (without gear), double occupancy, which includes excellent accommodations and all meals. Rental gear, from cameras (starting at $100 a week) to dive gear ($120) to computers ($125), is available.

Snorkeling

If you come to Hawaii and don't snorkel, you'll miss half the fun. The year-round calm waters along the Kona and Kohala coasts are home to spectacular marine life. Some of the best snorkeling areas on the Kona-Kohala coasts include **Hapuna Beach Cove,** at the foot of the Hapuna Beach Prince Hotel, a secluded little cove where you can snorkel with schools of yellow tangs, needlefish, and green sea turtles. But if you've never snorkeled in your life, **Kahaluu Beach Park** is the best place to start. Just wade in and look down at the schools of fish in the bay's black-lava tide pools. Another "hidden" snorkeling spot is off the rocks north of the boat launch ramp at **Honaunau Bay.** Other great snorkel sites include **White Sands Beach, Kekaha Kai State Park,** and **Hookena, Honaunau, Puako,** and **Spencer** beach parks.

In addition to **Snorkel Bob's,** mentioned in the intro to this section, you can rent gear from **Kona Coast Divers ★**, Honokohau Marina, Kailua-Kona (✆ **808/329-8802;** www.konacoast divers.com). Note that some snorkel charter operations closed in the wake of the 2011 tsunami, but most likely they'll have reopened by the time you're booking your trip.

Snorkeling Cruises to Kealakekua Bay ★★★ Probably the best snorkeling for all levels can be found in **Kealakekua Bay.** The calm waters of this underwater preserve teem with a wealth of marine life. Coral heads, lava tubes, and underwater caves all provide an excellent habitat for Hawaii's vast array of tropical fish, making mile-wide Kealakekua the Big Island's best accessible spot for snorkeling and diving. Without looking very hard, you can see octopuses, free-swimming moray eels, parrotfish, and goat fish; once in a while, a pod of spinner dolphins streaks across the bay. Kealakekua is reachable only by boat; in addition to **Fair Wind** (p. 103) and **Captain Zodiac** (p. 102), check out **Sea Quest Snorkeling and Rafting Adventures** (✆ **808/329-RAFT;** www.seaquesthawaii.com), which offers unique coastal adventures through sea caves and lava tubes on the Kona Coast, as well as snorkeling plunges into the ocean at the historic Place of Refuge in Honaunau and at the Captain Cook Monument at Kealakekua. The six-passenger, rigid-hull, inflatable rafts can go where larger boats can't. The 4-hour morning tour is

$92 for adults and $75 for children, while the 3-hour afternoon tour goes for $72 for adults and $62 for children. During whale season, there's a 3-hour whale-watching cruise for $56 for adults and children. Children under 6 years old, pregnant women, and people with bad backs are not allowed.

Snuba

If you're not quite ready to make the commitment to scuba but you want more time underwater than snorkeling allows, **Big Island Water Sports** (© 808/326-7446; www.snubabig island.com) may be the answer. Just like in scuba, the diver wears a regulator and mask; however, the tank floats on the surface on a raft and is connected to the diver's regulator by a hose that allows the diver to go 20 to 25 feet down. You need only 15 minutes of instruction before you're ready to go. Snuba can actually be easier than snorkeling, as the water is calmer beneath the surface. It costs $89 for a 1½-hour dive from the beach, $145 for one dive from a boat, and $170 for two dives from a boat; children must be at least 8 years old.

Sport Fishing: The Hunt for Granders ★★

If you want to catch fish, it doesn't get any better than the Kona Coast, known internationally as the marlin capital of the world. Big-game fish, including gigantic blue marlin and other Pacific billfish, tuna, mahi-mahi, sailfish, swordfish, ono (also known as wahoo), and giant trevallies (ulua), roam the waters here. When anglers catch marlin that weigh 1,000 pounds or more, they call them "granders"; there's even a "wall of fame" on Kailua-Kona's Waterfront Row, honoring 40 anglers who've nailed more than 20 tons of fighting fish.

Nearly 100 charter boats with professional captains and crew offer fishing charters out of **Keauhou, Kawaihae, Honokohau,** and **Kailua Bay harbors.** If you're not an expert angler, the best way to arrange a charter is through a booking agency such as the **Charter Desk at Honokohau Marina** (© **888/566-2487** or 808/329-1800; www.charterdesk.com) or **Charter Services Hawaii** (© **800/567-2650** or 808/334-1881; www.konazone. com). Either one will sort through the more than 40 different types of vessels, fishing specialties, and personalities to match you with the right boat. Prices range from $750 to $3,500 or so for a full-day exclusive charter (you and up to five of your friends have the entire boat to yourselves), or for $95 you can share a boat with others and rotate your turn at pulling in the big one.

4

FUN ON & OFF THE BEACH | Watersports

Serious sport-fishers should call the boats directly. They include **Anxious** (© 808/326-1229; www.alohazone.com) and **Marlin Magic** (© 808/325-7138; www.marlinmagic.com). If you aren't into hooking a 1,000-pound marlin or 200-pound tuna and just want to go out to catch some smaller fish and have fun, I recommend **Reel Action Light Tackle Sportfishing ★★** (© 808/325-6811). Light-tackle anglers and saltwater fly-fishermen should contact **Sea Genie II ★★** (© 808/325-5355; www.seageniesportfishing.com), which has helped several anglers set world records. All of the above outfitters operate out of Honokohau Harbor.

Most big-game charter boats carry six passengers max, and the boats supply all equipment, bait, tackle, and lures. No license is required. Many captains now tag and release marlins; other fish caught belong to the boat (not to you, but to the charter)—that's Island style. If you want to eat your catch or have your trophy marlin mounted, arrange it with the captain before you go.

Note: A handful of the charter fishing operations were closed due to the effects of the 2011 tsunami that rocked Japan. Most of them will likely have returned to business as usual by the time of your visit. Check with individual operators to confirm that business is up and running.

Submarine Dives

This is the stuff movies are made of: venturing 100 feet below the sea in a high-tech 65-foot submarine. On a 1-hour trip, you'll be able to explore a 25-acre coral reef that's teeming with schools of colorful tropical fish. Look closely and you might catch glimpses of moray eels—or even a shark—in and around the reef. On selected trips, you'll watch as divers swim among these aquatic creatures, luring them to the view ports for face-to-face observation. Call **Atlantis Submarines ★**, 75–5669 Alii Dr. (across the street from Kailua Pier), Kailua-Kona (© 800/548-6262; www.atlantis adventures.com). Trips leave daily between 10am and 1pm. The cost is $99 for adults and $45 for children under 12 (book on their website for a discount). *Note:* The ride is safe for everyone, but skip it if you suffer from claustrophobia.

Surfing

Most surfing off the Big Island is for the experienced only. As a general rule, the beaches on the north and west shores of the island get northern swells in winter, while those on the south and east shores get southern swells in summer. Experienced surfers should check out the waves at **Pine Trees** (north of Kailua-Kona), **Lyman's** (off Alii Dr. in Kailua-Kona), and **Banyan's** (also off Alii

Dr.); reliable spots on the east side of the island include **Honolii Point** (outside Hilo), **Hilo Bay Front Park,** and **Keaukaha Beach Park.** But there are a few sites where beginners can catch a wave, too: You might want to try **Kahaluu Beach Park,** where the waves are manageable most of the year, other surfers are around to give you pointers, and there's a lifeguard on shore.

Ocean Eco Tours (© 808/324-SURF; www.oceaneco tours.com), owned and operated by veteran surfers, is one of the few companies on the Big Island that teaches surfing. Private lessons cost $150 per person (including all equipment) and usually last a minimum of 2 hours; 2- to 3-hour group lessons go for $95 (also including all equipment), with a maximum of four students. Both teachers love this ancient Hawaiian sport, and their enthusiasm is contagious. The minimum age is 8, and you must be a fairly good swimmer.

Your only Big Island choice for surfboard rentals is **Pacific Vibrations,** 75–5702 Likana Lane (just off Alii Dr., across from the pier), Kailua-Kona (© **808/329-4140;** www.laguerdobros. com/pacvib/pacificv.html), where short boards go for $15 and long boards for $20 per day.

HIKING & CAMPING

For information on camping and hiking, contact **Hawaii Volcanoes National Park,** P.O. Box 52, Hawaii National Park, HI 96718 (© 808/985-6000; www.nps.gov/havo); **Puuhonua O Honaunau National Historical Park,** Honaunau, HI 96726 (© 808/328-2288; www.nps.gov/puho); the **State Division of Forestry and Wildlife,** 19 E. Kawili St., Hilo, HI 96720 (© 808/974-4221; www.dofaw.net); the **State Division of Parks,** P.O. Box 936, Hilo, HI 96721 (© 808/974-6200; www. hawaiistateparks.org); the **County Department of Parks and Recreation,** 101 Pauahi St., Suite 6, Hilo, HI 96720 (© 808/961-8311; www.hawaii-county.com/parks/parks.htm); or the **Hawaii Sierra Club** (© 808/538-6616; www.hi.sierraclub.org/Hawaii/excomm.html).

Camping equipment is *not* available for rent on the Big Island. Plan to bring your own or buy it at the **Hilo Surplus Store,** 148 Mamo St., Hilo (© **808/935-6398**).

Guided Day Hikes A guided day hike is a great way to discover natural Hawaii without having to sleep under a tree. Call the following outfitters ahead of time (before you arrive) for a schedule of trips; they fill up quickly.

A longtime resident of Hawaii, Dr. Hugh Montgomery of **Hawaiian Walkways** ★, Honokaa (© **800/457-7759** or

808/775-0372; www.hawaiianwalkways.com), formerly named "Tour Operator of the Year" by the Hawaii Ecotourism Association of Hawaii, offers a variety of options, ranging from excursions that skirt the rim of immense valleys to hikes through the clouds on the volcano. Hikes range from $119 to $169 for adults, $99 to $119 for kids. Custom hikes are available for one to four hikers from $600. Prices include food, beverages, and equipment.

Naturalist and educator Rob Pacheco of **Hawaii Forest & Trail ★★**, 74–5035-B Queen Kaahumanu Hwy. (behind the Chevron station), Kailua-Kona (✆ **800/464-1993** or 808/331-8505; www.hawaii-forest.com), offers fully outfitted day trips to some of the island's most remote, pristine areas, some of which he has exclusive access to. Rob's fully trained staff narrates the entire trip, offering extensive natural, geological, and cultural commentary (and more than a little humor). Tours are limited to 10 people and are highly personalized to meet the group's interests and abilities. Options include waterfall adventures, rainforest discovery hikes, birding tours, volcanoes, and even an off-road adventure in a 6×6 Pinzgauer Scrambler that allows you to explore hard-to-reach places. Each tour involves 2 to 4 hours of easy-to-moderate walking, over terrain manageable by anyone in average physical condition. Half-day trips, including snacks, beverages, water, and gear, start at $125 for adults, and $95 for children ages 8 to 12. Full-day adventures are $149 to $189 adults, and $119 to $149 children, but keep in mind that full-day hikes are 8- to 11-hour days, which may be too strenuous for younger children.

Guided Night Hikes For an off-the-beaten-track experience, **Arnott's Lodge,** 98 Apapane Rd., Hilo (✆ **808/969-7097;** www.arnottslodge.com), offers a daylong tour of Hawaii Volcanoes National Park, followed by a night lava hike right up to the fiery flow. The 9½-hour tour leaves the lodge at noon and spends most of the afternoon in the park. The lava hike (a 4-hr., somewhat strenuous round-trip hike) takes place as the sun is setting, so you can see the glow of the flow both during and after sunset. The cost is $85.

Hawaii Volcanoes National Park ★★★

This national park is a wilderness wonderland. Miles of trails not only lace the lava, but also cross deserts, rainforests, beaches, and, in winter, snow at 13,650 feet. Trail maps (highly recommended) are sold at park headquarters. Check conditions before you head out. Come prepared for sun, rain, and hard wind any time of year. Always wear sunscreen and bring plenty of drinking water.

For complete coverage of the national park, see p. 147. **Warning:** If you have heart or respiratory problems or if you're pregnant, don't attempt any hike in the park; the fumes will bother you.

TRAILS IN THE PARK

Kilauea Iki Trail   You'll experience the work of the volcano goddess, Pele, firsthand on this hike. The 4-mile trail begins at the visitor center, descends through a forest of ferns into still-fuming Kilauea Iki Crater, and then crosses the crater floor past the vent where a 1959 lava blast shot a fountain of fire 1,900 feet into the air for 36 days. Allow 2 hours for this fair-to-moderate hike.

Halemaumau Trail   This moderate 3.5-mile hike starts at the visitor center, goes down 500 feet to the floor of Kilauea Crater, crosses the crater, and ends at Halemaumau Overlook.

Devastation Trail   Up on the rim of Kilauea Iki Crater, you can see what an erupting volcano did to a once-flourishing ohia forest. The scorched earth with its ghostly tree skeletons stands in sharp contrast to the rest of the lush forest. Everyone can take this .5-mile hike on a paved path across the eerie bed of black cinders. The trail head is on Crater Rim Road at Puu Puai Overlook.

Kipuka Puaulu (Bird Park) Trail   This easy 1.5-mile, hour-long hike lets you see native Hawaiian flora and fauna in a little oasis of living nature in a field of lava. For some reason, the once red-hot lava skirted this miniforest and let it survive. At the trail head on Mauna Loa Road, there's a display of plants and birds you'll see on the walk. Go early in the morning or in the evening (or, even better, just after a rain) to see native birds such as the apapane (a small, bright-red bird with black wings and tail) and the iiwi (larger and orange-vermilion colored, with a curved orange bill). Native trees along the trail include giant ohia, koa, soapberry, kolea, and mamani.

Mauna Loa Trail   Probably the most challenging hike in Hawaii, this trail goes 7.5 miles from the lookout to a cabin at 10,035 feet and then 12 more miles up to the primitive Mauna Loa summit cabin at 13,250 feet, where the climate is subarctic and overnight temperatures are below freezing year-round. This 4-day round-trip requires advance planning, great physical condition, and registration at the visitor center. Call © **808/985-6000** for maps and details. The trail head begins where Mauna Loa Road ends, 14 miles north of Hwy. 11.

CAMPGROUNDS & WILDERNESS CABINS IN THE PARK

The only park campground accessible by car is **Namakani Paio**, which has a pavilion with picnic tables and a fireplace (no wood is provided). Tent camping is free; no reservations are required. Stays are limited to 7 days per year. Backpack camping at hiker shelters and cabins is available on a first-come, shared basis, but you must register at the visitor center.

Kilauea Military Camp (www.kmc-volcano.com), a mile from the visitor center, is a rest-and-recreation camp for active and retired military personnel. Facilities include 75 one- to three-bedroom cabins with fireplaces (some with a Jacuzzi), cafeteria, bowling alley, bar, general store, weight room, and tennis and basketball courts. Rates are based on rank, ranging from $72 to $240 a night. Call © 808/967-8333 on the Big Island.

The following cabins and campgrounds are the best of what the park and surrounding area have to offer:

Halape Shelter This backcountry site, about 7 miles from the nearest road, is the place for those who want to get away from it all and enjoy their own private white-sand beach. The small, three-sided stone shelter, with a roof but no floor, can accommodate two people comfortably, but four's a crowd. You could pitch a tent inside, but if the weather is nice, you're better off setting up outside. There's a catchment water tank, but check with rangers on the water situation before hiking in (sometimes they don't have accurate information on the water level; bring extra water just in case). The only other facility is a pit toilet. Go on weekdays if you're really looking for an escape. It's free to stay here, but you're limited to 3 nights. Permits are available at the visitor center on a first-come, first-served basis, no earlier than noon on the day before your trip. For more information, call © 808/985-6000.

Namakani Paio Campgrounds & Cabins As we went to press, these affordable cabins and campgrounds, located just 5 miles west of the park entrance, were temporarily closed due to the remodeling of the Volcano House (which also manages the cabins and campgrounds). The Volcano House is scheduled to reopen in 2011; call the number below to make sure. If you are a camper you will love the open grassy field in a eucalyptus forest for tent camping. The trail to Kilauea Crater is just a half-mile away. No permit is needed, but stays are limited to 7 days. Facilities include pavilions with barbecues and a fireplace, picnic tables, outdoor dishwashing areas, restrooms, and drinking water. There are also 10 cabins that accommodate up to four people each. Every cabin has a covered picnic table at the entrance and a fireplace with a grill. Toilets, sinks, and hot showers are available in a separate building. You can get groceries and gas in the town of Volcano, 4 miles away. Make cabin reservations through **Volcano House,** P.O. Box 53, Hawaii National Park, HI 96718 (© **808/967-7321**); the cost is

$40 per night for two adults (and two children), $48 for three adults, and $56 for four adults.

Waimanu Valley's Muliwai Trail

This difficult 2- to 3-day backpacking adventure—only for the hardy—takes you to a hidden valley some call Eden, with virgin waterfalls and pools and spectacular views. The trail, which goes from sea level to 1,350 feet and down to the sea again, takes more than 9 hours to hike in and more than 10 hours to hike out. Be prepared for clouds of bloodthirsty mosquitoes, and look out for wild pigs. If it's raining, forget it: You'll have 13 streams to cross before you reach the rim of Waimanu Valley, and rain means flash floods.

You must get permits online (https://camping.ehawaii.gov/camping/welcome.html) to camp in Waimanu Valley. Permits to the nine designated campsites are assigned by number. They're $18 for up to two people, and you're limited to a 6-day stay. Facilities are limited to two composting pit toilets. The best water in the valley is from the stream on the western wall, a 15-minute walk up a trail from the beach. All water must be treated before drinking. The water from the Waimanu Stream drains from a swamp, so skip it. Be sure to pack out what you take in.

For information on Muliwai Trail, visit the Na Ala Hele website at www.hawaiitrails.org. To get to the trail head, take Hwy. 19 to the turnoff for Honokaa; drive 9½ miles to the Waipio Valley Lookout. Unless you have four-wheel-drive, this is where your hike begins. Walk down the road and wade the Wailoa Stream; then cross the beach and go to the northwest wall. The trail starts here and goes up the valley floor, past a swamp, and into a forest before beginning a series of switchbacks that parallel the coastline. These switchbacks go up and down about 14 gulches. At the ninth gulch, about two-thirds of the way along the trail, is a shelter. After the shelter, the trail descends into Waimanu Valley, which looks like a smaller version of Waipio Valley but without signs of human intrusion.

GOLF & OTHER OUTDOOR ACTIVITIES

The not-for-profit group **Friends for Fitness,** P.O. Box 1671, Kailua-Kona, HI 96745 (© **808/322-0033**), offers a free brochure on physical activities (from aerobics to yoga) in West Hawaii; they will gladly mail it to you upon request.

Golf

For last-minute and discount tee times, call **Stand-by Golf** (© **888/645-BOOK** or 808/322-BOOK; www.standbygolf.com)

from 7am to 2:30pm and 6 to 10pm. Stand-by Golf offers discounted (10%–40% off), guaranteed tee times for same-day or next-day golfing.

If your game's a little rusty, head for the **Swing Zone,** 74-5562 Makala Blvd. (at Kuikuni Hwy., by the Old Airport Park), Kailua-Kona (© **808/329-6909**). The driving range has 27 mats and 10 grass tee spaces, the practice putting green and chipping area is free with a bucket of balls (60 balls for $7) and the pro shop sells limited supplies (rental clubs are available, too, for just $2.75 each or $11 a set). For $15, including a putter and a ball, you can play a round on the 18-hole, putting course built in the shape of the Big Island.

In addition to the courses below, I love the fabulous **Hualalai Golf Course ★★★** at the Four Seasons Resort Hualalai (p. 36). Unfortunately, it's open only to resort guests—but for committed golfers, this Jack Nicklaus–designed championship course is reason enough to pay the sky-high rates.

THE KOHALA COAST

Hapuna Golf Course ★★★ Since its opening in 1992, this 18-hole championship course has been named the most environmentally sensitive course by *Golf* magazine, as well as "Course of the Future" by the U.S. Golf Association. Designed by Arnold Palmer and Ed Seay, this 6,027-yard, links-style course extends from the shoreline to 700 feet above sea level, with views of the pastoral Kohala Mountains and the Kohala coastline. The elevation changes on the course keep it challenging (and windy at the higher elevations). There are a few elevated tee boxes and only 40 bunkers. Facilities include putting greens, driving ranges, lockers, showers, a pro shop, and restaurants.

At the Hapuna Beach Prince Hotel, Mauna Kea Resort, off Hwy. 19 (near mile marker 69). © **808/880-3000.** www.princeresortshawaii.com. Greens fees $250 ($235 for resort guests), twilight (after 1:30pm) $155.

Mauna Kea Golf Course ★★★ This breathtakingly beautiful, par-72, 7,114-yard championship course, designed by Robert Trent Jones, Jr., is consistently rated one of the top golf courses in the United States. The signature 3rd hole is 175 yards long; the Pacific Ocean and shoreline cliffs stand between the tee and the green, giving every golfer, from beginner to pro, a real challenge. Another par-3 that confounds duffers is the 11th hole, which drops 100 feet from tee to green and plays down to the ocean, into the steady trade winds. When the trades are blowing, 181 yards might as well be 1,000 yards. Book ahead; the course is very popular, especially for early weekend tee times. *Note:* As we went to press, Mauna Kea's greens, tees, fairways, and rough had just been replaced with new hybrids of turf that can be groomed for the skill levels of both

IMPROVE YOUR golf game IN 2½ HOURS

Darrin Gee's Spirit of Golf Academy ★★★, P.O. Box 2308, Kohala (ⓒ **866/GOLF-433** or 808/887-6800; www.spiritofgolf hawaii.com), has developed a program for the inner, mental game of golf that will improve your score in just 2½ hours, whether you're a beginner or you've been swinging clubs for years. Unlike the majority of golf schools, which focus on the mechanics of the golf swing, for just $250 you will learn how to improve your mental game, using Gee's Seven Principles of Golf, which means learning how to increase your focus and concentration, how to relax under pressure, and how to play to your potential. The small clinics (four players to one instructor) are available at championship golf courses on the Big Island.

resort and professional golfers, and the bunkers were restored to their original configuration.

At the Mauna Kea Beach Hotel, Mauna Kea Resort, off Hwy. 19 (near mile marker 68). ⓒ **808/882-5400.** www.princeresortshawaii.com. Greens fees $250 ($225 for resort guests), twilight (after 1:30pm) $155.

Mauna Lani Francis H. I'i Brown Championship Courses ★★★ The **South Course,** a 7,029-yard par-72, has an unforgettable ocean hole: the downhill, 221-yard, par-3 7th, which is bordered by the sea, a salt-and-pepper sand dune, and lush kiawe trees. The **North Course** may not have the drama of the oceanfront holes, but because it was built on older lava flows, the more extensive indigenous vegetation gives the course a Scottish feel. The hole that's cursed the most is the 140-yard, par-3 17th: It's absolutely beautiful but plays right into the surrounding lava field. Facilities include two driving ranges, a golf shop (with teaching pros), a restaurant, and putting greens.

At the Mauna Lani Resort, Mauna Lani Dr., off Hwy. 19 (20 miles north of Kona Airport). ⓒ **808/885-6655.** www.maunalani.com. Greens fees $260 ($160 for resort guests). Check website for specials.

Waikoloa Beach Golf Course ★ This pristine 18-hole, par-70 course certainly reflects the motto of designer Robert Trent Jones, Jr.: "Hard par, easy bogey." Most golfers remember the par-5, 505-yard 12th hole, a sharp dogleg left with bunkers in the corner and an elevated tee surrounded by lava. Facilities include a golf shop, restaurant, and driving range.

At the Waikoloa Beach Resort, 1020 Keana Place (adjacent to the Waikoloa Beach Marriott Resort and the Hilton Waikoloa Village). © **877/WAIKOLOA** or 808/886-6060. www.waikoloabeachresort.com. Greens fees $165 ($135 for resort guests); twilight rates (after 2pm) $85.

Waikoloa Kings' Golf Course ★ This sister course to the Waikoloa Beach Golf Course is about 500 yards longer. Designed by Tom Weiskopf and Jay Morrish, the 18-hole links-style tract features a double green at the 3rd and 6th holes, and several carefully placed bunkers that often come into play due to the ever-present trade winds. Facilities include a pro shop and showers.

At the Waikoloa Beach Resort, 600 Waikoloa Beach Dr. (adjacent to the Waikoloa Beach Marriott Resort and the Hilton Waikoloa Village). © **877/WAIKOLOA** or 808/886-7888. www.waikoloabeachresort.com. Greens fees $165 ($135 for resort guests); twilight rates (after 2pm) $85.

Waikoloa Village Golf Course This semiprivate 18-hole course, with a par-72 for each of the three sets of tees, is hidden in the town of Waikoloa and usually overshadowed by the glamour resort courses along the Kohala Coast. Not only is it a beautiful course with great views, but it also offers some great golfing. The wind can play havoc with your game here (like most Hawaii golf courses). Robert Trent Jones, Jr., designed this challenging course, inserting his trademark sand traps, slick greens, and great fairways. I'm particularly fond of the 18th hole: This par-5, 490-yard thriller doglegs to the left, and the last 75 yards up to the green are water, water, water. Enjoy the fabulous views of Mauna Kea and Mauna Loa, and—on a very clear day—Maui's Haleakala in the distance.

Waikoloa Rd., off Hwy. 19 (18 miles north of Kona Airport), Waikoloa Village. © **808/883-9621.** www.waikoloa.org/golf. Greens fees $84. Turn left at the Waikoloa sign; it's about 6 miles up, on the left.

THE HAMAKUA COAST

Hamakua Country Club 🏷 As you approach the sugar town of Honokaa, you can't miss this funky 9-hole course, built in the 1920s on a very steep hill overlooking the ocean. It's a par-33, 2,520-yard course. Architect Frank Anderson managed to squeeze in 9 holes by crisscrossing holes across fairways—you may never see a layout like this again. But the best part about Hamakua is the price: just $15 for 18 holes (you play the 9-hole course twice). You don't need a tee time; just show up, and if no one's around, drop your $15 in the box and head out. Carts aren't allowed because of the steep hills.

On the ocean side of Hwy. 19 (41 miles from Hilo), Honokaa. © **808/775-7244.** Greens fees $15 for 18 holes (you play the 9-hole course twice).

Golf & Other Outdoor Activities

FUN ON & OFF THE BEACH

HILO

Hilo Municipal Golf Course   This is a great course for the casual golfer: It's flat, scenic, and often fun. **Warning:** Don't go after a heavy rain (especially in winter), when the fairways can get really soggy and play can slow way down. The rain does keep the course green and beautiful, though. Wonderful trees (monkey pods, coconuts, eucalyptus, banyans) dot the grounds, and the views—of Mauna Kea on one side and Hilo Bay on the other—are breathtaking. There are four sets of tees, with a par-71 from all; the back tees give you 6,325 yards of play. Getting a tee time can be a challenge; weekdays are your best bet.

340 Haihai St. (btw. Kinoole and Iwalani sts.). ✆ **808/959-7711.** Greens fees $29 Mon–Fri, $34 Sat–Sun and holidays; carts $16. From Hilo, take Hwy. 11 toward Volcano; turn right at Puainako St. (at Prince Kuhio Plaza), left on Kinoole, and then right on Haihai St.

Naniloa Country Club   At first glance, this semiprivate 9-hole course looks pretty flat and short, but once you get beyond the 1st hole—a wide, straightforward, 330-yard par-4—things get challenging. The tree-lined fairways require straight drives, and the huge lake on the 2nd and 5th holes is sure to haunt you. This course is very popular with locals and visitors alike. Rental clubs are available.

120 Banyan Dr. (at the intersection of Hwy. 11 and Hwy. 19). ✆ **808/935-3000.** Greens fees $15 walking for 18 holes, $30 with cart.

VOLCANO VILLAGE

Volcano Golf & Country Club   Located at an altitude of 4,200 feet, this public course got its start in 1922, when the Blackshear family put in a green using old tomato cans for the holes. It now has three sets of tees to choose from, all with a par of 72. The course is unusually landscaped, making use of the pine and ohia trees scattered throughout. It's considered challenging by locals. Some tips from the regulars: Because the course is at such a high altitude, the ball travels farther than you're probably used to, so club down. If you hit the ball off the fairway, take the stroke—you don't want to look for your ball in the forest and undergrowth. Also, play a pitch-and-run game—the greens are slick.

Hwy. 11, on the right side, just after the entrance to Hawaii Volcanoes National Park. ✆ **808/967-7331.** www.volcanogolfshop.com. Greens fees $55.

Biking

For mountain- and cross-training bike rentals in Kona, go to **Hawaiian Pedals** ★, Kona Inn Shopping Village, Alii Drive,

Kailua-Kona (© **808/329-2294**), or **Hawaiian Pedals Bike Works,** Hale Hana Centre, 74–5583 Luhia St., Kailua-Kona (© **808/326-2453;** www.hawaiianpedals.com); both have a huge selection of bikes: cruisers ($20 a day), mountain bikes ($40 a day), hybrids ($20 a day), and racing bikes and front-suspension mountain bikes ($60 a day). Bike racks go for $5 a day, and you pay only for the days you actually use it. The folks at the shops are friendly and knowledgeable about cycling routes all over the Big Island.

Guided Bike Tours Check out **Kona Coast Cycling** (© **877/592-BIKE** or 808/327-1133; www.cyclekona.com), which offers half-day (3–4 hr.) and full-day (4–6 hr.) bicycling tours, ranging from a casual ride to intense mountain biking at its best to 6-day bike tours of the Big Island. The locations are diverse, from the rolling hills of a Kona coffee farm to awesome views of the Waipio Valley Lookout. Most tours include round-trip transportation from hotels, van support, tour guide, helmet, gloves, water, snacks, and lunch on the full-day trips. Prices range from $125 to $145 for the day tours and $2,195 to $2,695 for the 6- to 8-day tours (includes airport pickup, accommodations, breakfast and lunch, bicycle, helmet, and tour guide).

Contact the **Big Island Mountain Bike Association,** P.O. Box 6819, 318 E. Kawili St., Hilo, HI 96720 (© **808/961-4452**), for a copy of John Alford's *Mountain Biking the Hawaiian Islands,* which includes maps and descriptions of bike rides for all of the islands.

Birding

Native Hawaiian birds are few—and dwindling. But Hawaii still offers extraordinary birding for anyone nimble enough to traverse the tough, mucky landscape. And the best birding is on the Big Island; birders the world over come here hoping to see three Hawaiian birds, in particular: the akiapolaau, a woodpecker wannabe with a war club–like head; the nukupuu, an elusive little yellow bird with a curved beak, one of the crown jewels of Hawaiian birding; and the alala, a critically endangered Hawaiian crow that's now almost impossible to see in the wild.

If you don't know an apapane from a nukupuu, go with someone who does. Contact **Hawaii Forest & Trail,** 74–5035-B Queen Kaahumanu Hwy. (behind the Chevron station), Kailua-Kona (© **800/464-1993** or 808/331-8505; www.hawaii-forest.com), to sign up for the **Rainforest & Dryforest Adventure ★★**, led by naturalist Rob Pacheco. On this tour, you'll venture into the pristine rainforest to see rare and endangered Hawaiian birds. The guide will also point out Hawaii's unique botany and evolution. The full-day (11-hour) tour costs $179 and includes a midmorning snack with coffee, lunch, beverages, daypack, binoculars, walking stick, and rain gear.

If you want to head out on your own, good spots to see native Hawaiian and other birds include the following:

Hawaii Volcanoes National Park   The best places for accomplished birders to go on their own are the ohia forests of this national park, usually at sunrise or sunset, when the little forest birds seem to be most active. The Hawaiian nene goose can be spotted at the park's Kipuka Nene Campground, a favorite nesting habitat. Geese and pheasants sometimes appear on the Volcano Golf Course in the afternoon.

Hakalau Forest National Wildlife Refuge   The first national wildlife refuge established solely for forest bird management is on the eastern slope of Mauna Kea above the Hamakua Coast. It's open for birding on Saturday, Sunday, and state holidays, using the public access road only. You must call ahead of time to get the gate combinations of the locked gates and to register. Every visitor to Upper Maulua is required to have a reservation. Reservations can be made by calling the Hakalau Forest NWR office (© 808/443-2300) between 8am and 4pm Monday through Friday at least 1 week prior to entry. Visitors will be asked to provide (1) their telephone number; (2) the number of people in their group; (3) the license plate numbers(s) of vehicle(s) to be used; and (4) a description of vehicle(s) to be used. A four-wheel-drive vehicle is required for the 50-mile trip, which takes almost 2 hours each way from Hilo or Kona. More information is available at www.fws.gov/hakalauforest.

Hilo Ponds   Ducks, coots, herons (night and great blue), cattle egrets, and even Canada and snow geese fly into these popular coastal wetlands in Hilo, near the airport. Take Kalanianaole Highway about 3 miles east, past the industrial port facilities to Loko Waka Pond and Waiakea Pond.

Horseback Riding

Kohala Naalapa ★, on Kohala Mountain Road (Hwy. 250), mile marker 11 (ask for directions to the stables at the security-guard station; © **808/889-0022;** www.naalapastables.com), offers unforgettable journeys into the rolling hills of Kahua and Kohala ranches, past ancient Hawaiian ruins, through lush pastures with grazing sheep and cows, and along mountaintops with panoramic coastal views. The horses and various riding areas are suited to everyone from first-timers to experienced equestrians. There are two trips a day: a 2½-hour tour at 8:30am for $89 and a 1½-hour tour at 1:30pm for $68. No kids under 8, pregnant women, or riders over 230 pounds permitted.

Experienced riders should sign up for a trip with **Kings' Trail Rides, Tack, and Gift Shop ★★**, Hwy. 11 at mile marker 111, Kealakekua (© **808/323-2388**; www.konacowboy.com). These 4-hour trips, with 2 hours of riding, are limited to four people. You'll head down the mountain along Monument Trail to a small bay just north of Kealakekua Bay, where you'll stop for lunch and an hour of snorkeling. The price ($135) includes lunch and gear.

To see Waipio Valley on horseback, call **Waipio Naalapa Trail Rides ★** (© **808/775-0419**; www.naalapastables.com). The 2½-hour tours of this gorgeous tropical valley depart Monday through Saturday at 9am and 12:30pm (don't forget your camera). The guides are well versed in Hawaiian history and provide running commentary as you move through this historic place. The cost is $89 for adults. No kids under 8, pregnant women, or riders over 230 pounds permitted.

Visitors can explore **Parker Ranch** (© **808/885-7655**; www.parkerranch.com), a vast 175,000-acre working cattle ranch. You'll learn firsthand about the ranch, its history, and its variety of plant life, and you may even catch glimpses of pheasant, francolins, or wild pigs. Rides (suitable for beginners) are available twice daily at 8:15am and 12:15pm, for $79 per person. Morning and noon rides are 2 hours. Kids must be at least 7 years old. Riders will feel like Hawaiian *paniolo* (cowboys) as they ride through stone corrals where up to 5,000 Hereford cattle were rounded up after being brought down from the slopes of Mauna Kea. A visit to the racetrack where Parker Ranch thoroughbreds were trained and still hold the record for speed is included in the excursion. The rides all begin at the Blacksmith Shop on Pukalani Road.

Tennis

You can play for free at any Hawaii County tennis court; for a detailed list of all courts on the island, contact **Hawaii County Department of Parks and Recreation,** 101 Pauahi St., Suite 6, Hilo, HI 96720 (© **808/961-8311;** www.hawaii-county.com/parks/parks.htm). The best courts in Hilo are at the Hoolulu Tennis Stadium, located next to the Civic Auditorium on Manono Street (© **808/961-8720, ext. 28**). Most resorts in the Kona and Kohala areas do not allow nonguests to use their tennis facilities.

SEEING THE SIGHTS

I f you want nothing more than a fabulous beach to lie on and a perfectly mixed mai tai, you're coming to the right place. But if you want more out of your vacation, read on. On the Big Island, you can visit fascinating historic sites, hunt for petroglyphs, climb to the top of Mauna Kea, learn about the local flora at a botanical garden or national park, and much more. This chapter will help you get the most from your Big Island experience.

THE KONA COAST

GUIDED WALKING TOURS The **Kona Historical Society** (© 808/323-3222; www.konahistorical.org) hosts two historical walking tours in the Kona region. All walks must be booked in advance; call for reservations and departure locations. If you can put together a group of 10 or more, try the 75-minute **Historic Kailua Village Walking Tour ★** (© 808/938-8825), the most comprehensive tour of the Kona Coast. It takes you all around Kailua-Kona, from King Kamehameha's last seat of government to the summer palace of the Hawaiian royal family and beyond, with lots of Hawaiian history along the way. Tickets are $15 for adults, $10 for children 5 to 12, and include a 24-page booklet with more than 40 archival photographs of Kailua village. The self-guided **Kona Coffee Living History Tour** takes you through the everyday life of a Japanese family on the Uchida Coffee Farm during the 1920s to 1940s. Interact with costumed interpreters as they go about life on a coffee farm. The tour is offered Monday through Thursday on the hour from 10am to 2pm; $20 adults and $7.50 kids 5 to 12. Meet at the Kona Historical Society office, 81–6551 Mamalahoa Hwy. (next to Kona Specialty Meats), across from mile marker 110, Kealakekua.

EXPERIENCE HOW THE LOCALS LIVE (and eat!)

"Go local for a day" is the mantra of **Home Tours Hawaii ★★★** (℃ **877/325-5772** or 808/325-5772; www.hometourshawaii. com), which features Chef Ann Sutherland, who was born and raised in Hawaii and earned her sterling reputation as a gourmet chef here. She invites visitors to experience what it's like to live (and, most important, eat) in Hawaii for a day. Chef Ann and her partner, Pat, pick you up in an air-conditioned van and then escort you to various private homes in the Kona region (from an upscale, multimillion-dollar oceanfront home to a handmade cottage in the middle of a coffee plantation to a luxury estate) with a progressive brunch, prepared using local products, at each home you visit. Chef Ann is a funny storyteller who enter- tains you with history and trivia as you drive from one home to the next. Don't be too shocked when you hear the astronomical prices of real estate in Hawaii. You won't want to miss this insid- er's look at how residents live in Hawaii. Chef Ann's mouth- watering masterpieces are worth the price alone. The 4-hour tour, with transportation, brunch, and a gift bag of local prod- ucts to take home with you, is $139.

SELF-GUIDED DRIVING TOURS Big Island Audio Tour (℃ **808/883-2670;** www.bigislandaudiotour.com), a self-guided audio tour on CD, features 36 tracks of information, including directions to the well-known sights plus tracks on beaches, short hikes, side trips, and information on Hawaiian language, history, and culture. The cost is $20 plus $2 for shipping.

If you're interested in seeing how your morning cup of joe goes from beans to brew, get a copy of the **Coffee Country Driving Tour.** This self-guided drive will take you farm by farm through Kona's famous coffee country; it also features a fascinating history of the area, the lowdown on coffee-making lingo, some insider tips on how to make a great cup, and even a recipe for Kona coffee macadamia-nut chocolate-chunk pie (goes great with a cup of java). The free brochure is available at the **Big Island Visitors Bureau,** 250 Keawe St., Hilo, HI 96720 (℃ **808/961-5797;** www.bigisland.org).

IN & AROUND KAILUA-KONA ★★★

Ellison S. Onizuka Space Center ☺ This small museum has a real moon rock and memorabilia in honor of Big Island–born astronaut Ellison Onizuka, who died in the 1986

Kailua-Kona Town

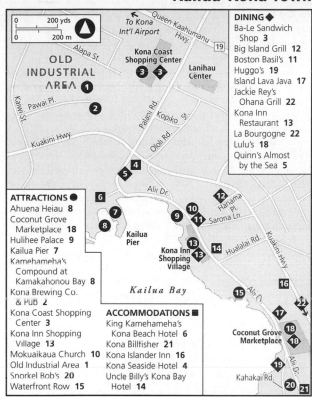

0 | 200 yds
0 | 200 m

To Kona Int'l Airport

DINING ◆
Ba-Le Sandwich Shop **3**
Big Island Grill **12**
Boston Basil's **11**
Huggo's **19**
Island Lava Java **17**
Jackie Rey's Ohana Grill **22**
Kona Inn Restaurant **13**
La Bourgogne **22**
Lulu's **18**
Quinn's Almost by the Sea **5**

ATTRACTIONS ●
Ahuena Heiau **8**
Coconut Grove Marketplace **18**
Hulihee Palace **9**
Kailua Pier **7**
Kamehameha's Compound at Kamakahonou Bay **8**
Kona Brewing Co. & PUB **2**
Kona Coast Shopping Center **3**
Kona Inn Shopping Village **13**
Mokuaikaua Church **10**
Old Industrial Area **1**
Snorkel Bob's **20**
Waterfront Row **15**

ACCOMMODATIONS ■
King Kamehameha's Kona Beach Hotel **6**
Kona Billfisher **12**
Kona Islander Inn **16**
Kona Seaside Hotel **4**
Uncle Billy's Kona Bay Hotel **14**

5

Challenger space-shuttle disaster. Displays include a gravity well, which illustrates orbital motion, and an interactive rocket-propulsion exhibit, where you can launch your own miniature space shuttle.

At Kona International Airport, Kailua-Kona. ℂ **808/329-3441.** www.hawaii museums.org/mc/ishawaii_astronaut.htm. Admission $3 adults, $1 children 18 and under. Daily 8:30am–4:30pm. Parking in airport lot $2 per hour.

Hulihee Palace ★★   This two-story New England–style mansion of lava rock and coral mortar, built in 1838 by the Big Island's governor, John Adams Kuakini, overlooks the harbor at Kailua-Kona. The largest, most elegant residence on the island when it was erected, Hulihee became a home to Hawaii's royalty, making it the other royal palace in the United States (the most famous being

Oahu's Iolani Palace). Now run by Daughters of Hawaii, it features many 19th-century mementos and gorgeous koa furniture. You'll get lots of background and royal lore on the guided tour (no photography allowed). There was some damage to this historic structure in the 2006 earthquake, but all is scheduled to be repaired by the time you read this.

The palace hosts 12 free **Hawaiian music and hula concerts** a year, each dedicated to a Hawaiian monarch, at 4pm, generally on the third Sunday of the month (except June and Dec, when the performances are held in conjunction with King Kamehameha Day and Christmas). Check the website for dates.

Across the street is **Mokuaikaua Church** (✆ **808/329-1589**), the oldest Christian church in Hawaii. It's constructed of lava stones, but its architecture is New England style all the way. The 112-foot steeple is still the tallest manmade structure in Kailua-Kona.

Note: The Hulihee Palace was temporarily closed due to basement flooding after the 2011 tsunami. However, it should be reopened by the time you read this.

75-5718 Alii Dr., Kailua-Kona. ✆ **808/329-1877.** www.daughtersofhawaii.com. Admission $6 adults, $4 seniors, $1 children. Wed–Sat 10am–3pm. Tours held throughout the day (arrive at least 1 hr. before closing).

Kailua Pier This is action central for water adventures. Fishing charters, snorkel cruises, and party boats all come and go here. Stop by around 4pm, when the captains weigh in with the catch of the day, usually huge marlin—the record-setters often come in here. It's also a great place to watch the sunset.

On the waterfront outside Honokohau Harbor, Kailua-Kona. ✆ **808/329-7494.**

Kamehameha's Compound at Kamakahonu Bay ★★ On the ocean side of the Kona Beach Hotel is a restored area of deep spiritual meaning to Hawaiians. This was the spot that King Kamehameha the Great chose to retreat to in 1812 after conquering the Hawaiian Islands. He stayed until his death in 1819. The king built a temple, **Ahuena Heiau,** and used it as a gathering place for his *kahuna* (priests) to counsel him on governing his people in times of peace. It was on this sacred ground in 1820 that Kamehameha's son Liholiho as king, sat down to eat with his mother, Keopuolani, and Kamehameha's principal queen, Kaahumanu, thus breaking the ancient *kapu* (taboo) against eating with women; this act established a new order in the Hawaiian kingdom. The temple grounds are now just a third of their original size, but they're still impressive. You're free to wander the grounds, envisioning the days when King Kamehameha appealed to the gods to help him rule with the spirit of humanity's highest nature.

On the grounds of King Kamehameha's Kona Beach Hotel, 75–5660 Palani Rd., Kailua-Kona. ℂ **808/329-2911.** www.konabeachhotel.com/history.cfm.

Kona Brewing Co. & Pub   This microbrewery is the first of its kind on the Big Island. Spoon and Pops, a father-and-son duo from Oregon, brought their brewing talents here and now produce about 25 barrels (about 124,000 gal.) per year. Drop by anytime during their business hours and take a quick, informal tour of the brewery, after which you get to taste the product. A brewpub on the property serves gourmet pizza, salads, and fresh-brewed Hawaiian ales.

75–5629 Kuakini Hwy. (entry on Pawai Place), Kailua-Kona. ℂ **808/334-BREW.** www.konabrewingco.com. Free tours and tastings. Tours daily 10:30am and 3pm. Turn north on Kuakini Hwy. (from Palani Rd.) and drive approximately ½ mile to the 1st stop sign, Kaiwi St., and turn right. Take the 1st right on Pawai Place and follow it until it ends at the brewery parking lot. Watch for directional signs along the way.

Natural Energy Laboratory of Hawaii Authority (NELHA)   Technology buffs should consider a visit to NELHA, where the hot tropical sun, in combination with a complex pumping system that brings 42°F (6°C) ocean water from 2,000 feet deep up to land, is used to develop innovations in agriculture, aquaculture, and ocean conservation. The interesting 75-minute tour takes in all areas of the high-tech ocean science and technology park, including the seawater delivery system, the energy conversion process, and some of the park's more interesting tenants, from Maine lobsters to giant clams.

73–4460 Queen Kaahumanu Hwy. (at mile marker 94), Kailua-Kona. ℂ **808/329-8073.** www.nelha.org. Public presentation tours $8 adults, free for children 8 and under. Mon–Thurs and the 3rd Sat of every month 10–11:30am; reservations required.

UPCOUNTRY KONA: HOLUALOA ★★

On the slope of Hualalai volcano above Kailua-Kona sits the small village of Holualoa, which attracts travelers weary of super-resorts. Here you'll find a little art and culture—and shade.

   This funky upcountry town, centered on two-lane Mamalahoa Highway, is nestled amid a lush, tropical landscape where avocados grow as big as footballs. Little more than a wide spot in the road, Holualoa is a cluster of brightly painted, tin-roofed plantation shacks enjoying a revival as B&Bs, art galleries, and quaint shops (see "Shops & Galleries," later in this chapter, for details). In 2 blocks, it manages to pack in two first-rate galleries, a frame shop, a potter, a glassworks, a goldsmith, an old-fashioned general store, a vintage 1930s gas station, a tiny post office, a Catholic church, and the **Kona Hotel,** a hot-pink clapboard structure that looks like a Western movie set—you're welcome to peek in, and you should.

The cool up-slope village is the best place in Hawaii for a coffee break. That's because Holualoa is in the heart of the coffee belt, a 20-mile-long strip at an elevation of between 1,000 and 1,400 feet, where all the Kona coffee in the world is grown in the rich volcanic soil of the cool uplands (see "Kona Coffee Craze!" on p. 78). Everyone's backyard seems to teem with glossy green leaves and ruby-red cherries (which contain the seeds, or beans, used to make coffee), and the air smells like an espresso bar. **Holuakoa Café,** on Mamalahoa Highway (Hwy. 180) in Holualoa (𝒞 **808/322-2233**), is a great place to get a freshly brewed cup and a bite to eat.

To reach Holualoa, follow narrow, winding Hualalai Road up the hill from Hwy. 19; it's about a 15-minute drive.

SOUTH KONA ★★★

Kona Historical Society Museum ★★   This well-organized museum is housed in the historic Greenwell Store, built in 1875 by Henry Nicholas Greenwell out of native stone. Antiques, artifacts, and photos tell the story of this fabled coast. The museum is filled with items that were common to everyday life here when coffee-growing and cattle-raising were the main industries. Stocked with accurate reproductions of goods that filled the shelves and hung from the ceiling joists, the store offers a glimpse of the past, complete with storekeepers dressed in period costumes, offering visitors St. Jacobs Oil to cure their arthritis or rheumatism. Before you leave, the shopkeeper may share some gossip about local people and events.

The Historical Society has another project in the works: the Kona Heritage Ranch, an outdoor museum about the daily life of a rancher in 1890, which will be located next door to the Greenwell Store. As part of the project, the society has created a replica of an 1890 Portuguese stone oven, the first of several structures and programs planned for the Kona Heritage Ranch. Portuguese from the Azores or Madeira started coming to Kona in the 1870s to help develop and manage dairies, a key phase of the ranching industry in Hawaii. The outdoor hive-type oven, made with cemented stone, was a constant presence wherever the Portuguese dairymen (and sugar-industry workers) settled. They brought with them both their knowledge of dairying on tropical islands and their love of freshly baked stone-oven bread. An informal group gathers every Thursday to learn about wood-fired baking techniques.

Serious history buffs should sign up for one of the museum's walking tours (see "Guided Walking Tours" on p. 123).

Hwy. 11, btw. mile markers 111 and 112, Kealakekua. © **808/323-3222** or 808/323-2006. www.konahistorical.org. Free admission (donations accepted); admission to the Greenwell Store is $7 adults and $3 children ages 5–12 years. Mon–Thurs 10am–2pm. Parking on grassy area next to Kona Specialty Meats parking lot.

Kula Kai Caverns & Lava Tubes ★★ 🎒

Before you trudge up to Pele's volcanic eruption, take a look at her underground handiwork. Ric Elhard and Rose Herrera have explored and mapped out the labyrinth of lava tubes and caves, carved out over the past 1,000 years or so, that crisscross their property on the southwest rift zone on the slopes of Mauna Loa near South Point. Options range from an easy half-hour tour on a well-lit underground route to a more adventuresome 2-hour caving trip (recommended minimum age is 8). Helmets, lights, gloves, and knee pads are all included. Sturdy shoes are recommended for caving.

Off Hwy. 11, btw. mile markers 78 and 79, Ocean View. © **808/929-9725**. www.kulakaicaverns.com. Half-hour tour $15 adults, $10 children 6–12; 2- to 3-hr. tour $95 per person. Reservations required.

The Painted Church ★ 🎒

Oh, those Belgian priests—what a talented lot. In the late 1800s, Father John Berchman Velghe borrowed a page from Michelangelo and painted biblical scenes inside St. Benedict's Catholic Church so the illiterate Hawaiians could visualize the white man's version of creation.

Walking Through Thurston Lava Tube at Hawaii Volcanoes National Park (p. 148)   It's scary, it's spooky, and most kids love it. You hike downhill through a rainforest full of little chittering native birds to enter this huge, silent black hole full of drips, cobwebs, and tree roots that stretch underground for almost a half-mile.

Snorkeling Kahaluu Beach Park (p. 108)   The shallow, calm waters off Kahaluu Beach are the perfect place to take kids snorkeling. The waters are protected by a barrier reef, and the abundance of fish will keep the kids' attention. You can pick up a fish identification card at any dive shop and make a game out of seeing how many fish the kids can find.

Riding a Submarine into the Underwater World (p. 110)   The huge viewing windows on Atlantis's 48-passenger sub will have the kids enthralled as the high-tech craft leaves the surface and plunges 120 feet down through the mysterious Neptunian waters. The trip isn't too long—just an hour—and there are plenty of reef fish and prehistoric-looking corals to hold the young ones' attention.

Launching Your Own Space Shuttle (p. 124)   Okay, it's a model of a space shuttle, but it's still a real blast. The Ellison S. Onizuka Space Center has dozens of interactive displays to thrill budding young astronauts, such as a hands-on experience with gyroscopic stabilization. Great video clips of astronauts working and living in space may inspire your kids as well.

Hunting for Petroglyphs (p. 132)   There's plenty of space to run around and discover ancient stone carvings at either the Puako Petroglyph Archaeological District (at Mauna Lani Resort) or the Kings' Trail (by the Waikoloa Beach Marriott Resort). And finding the petroglyphs is only part of the game—once you find them, you have to guess what the designs mean.

Watching the Volcano (p. 147)   Any kid who doesn't get a kick out of watching a live volcano set the night on fire has been watching too much television. Take snacks, bottled water, flashlights, and sturdy shoes and follow the ranger's instructions on where to view the lava safely.

84-5140 Painted Church Rd., Capt. Cook. ✆ **808/328-2227.** www.thepainted church.org. Turn off Hwy. 11 (toward the ocean) at about the 104 mile marker on to Rte. 160. Go on about a mile to the first turnoff to the right. Watch for the King

Kamehameha sign opposite. Continue along a narrow, winding road about ¼ mile to sign and turn right.

Puuhonua O Honaunau National Historical Park ★★★

With its fierce, haunting idols, this sacred site on the black-lava Kona Coast certainly looks forbidding. To ancient Hawaiians, however, Puuhonua O Honaunau served as a 16th-century place of refuge, providing sanctuary for defeated warriors and *kapu* (taboo) violators. A great rock wall—1,000 feet long, 10 feet high, and 17 feet thick—defines the refuge where Hawaiians found safety. On the wall's north end is Hale O Keawe Heiau, which holds the bones of 23 Hawaiian chiefs. Other archaeological finds include burial sites, old trails, and a portion of an ancient village. On a self-guided tour of the 180-acre site—which has been restored to its precontact state—you can see and learn about reconstructed thatched huts, canoes, and idols, and feel the *mana* (power) of old Hawaii.

A cultural festival, usually held in June, allows you to join in games, learn crafts, sample Hawaiian food, see traditional hula, and experience life in precontact Hawaii. Every Labor Day weekend, one of Hawaii's major outrigger canoe races starts here and ends in Kailua-Kona. Call for details on both events.

Note: Puuhonua O Honaunau National Historical Park sustained a fair amount of damage in the tsunami of 2011. The park remains closed indefinitely while the government assesses the damage and makes plans for repairs. Please contact them in advance of your visit to learn of the latest developments.

Hwy. 160 (off Hwy. 11 at mile marker 104), Honaunau. ℂ **808/328-2288.** www. nps.gov/puho. Admission $5 per vehicle, good for 7 days. Visitor center daily 8am–5:30pm; park daily 7am–8pm. From Hwy. 11, it's 3½ miles to the park entrance.

The Kohala Coast ★★★

Puukohola Heiau National Historic Site ★★★

This seacoast temple, called "the hill of the whale," is the single most imposing and dramatic structure of the early Hawaiians. It was built by Kamehameha I from 1790 to 1791. The *heiau* stands 224 feet long by 100 feet wide, with three narrow terraces on the seaside and an amphitheater to view canoes. Kamehameha built this temple after a prophet told him he would conquer and unite the islands if he did so; 4 years later, he fulfilled his kingly goal. The site also includes an interactive visitor center, the house of John Young (a trusted advisor of Kamehameha), and, offshore, the submerged ruins of Hale O Ka Puni, a shrine dedicated to the shark gods.

Hwy. 270, near Kawaihae Harbor. ℂ **808/882-7218.** www.nps.gov/puhe. Free admission. Daily 7:30am–4:30pm. The visitor center is on Hwy. 270; the *heiau* is a short walk away. The trail is closed when it's too windy, so call ahead if you're in doubt.

ANCIENT HAWAIIAN FISH PONDS

Like their Polynesian forebears, Hawaiians were among the first aquaculturists on the planet. Scientists still marvel at the ways they used the brackish ponds along the shoreline to stock and harvest fish. There are actually two different types of ancient fish ponds (or *loko i'a*). Closed ponds, located inshore, were closed off from the ocean. Open ponds used rock walls as a barrier to the ocean and sluice gates that connected the ponds to the ocean. The gates were woven vines, with just enough room for juvenile fish to swim in at high tide while keeping the bigger, fatter fish from swimming out. Generally, the Hawaiians kept and raised mullet, milkfish, and shrimp in these open ponds; juvenile manini, papio, eels, and barracuda occasionally found their way in, too.

The **Kalahuipuaa Fish Ponds,** at Mauna Lani Resort (© **808/885-6622**), are great examples of both types of ponds in a lush tropical setting. South of the Mauna Lani Resort are **Kuualii** and **Kahapapa Fish Ponds,** at the Waikoloa Beach Marriott Resort (© **808/885-6789**). Both resorts have taken great pains to restore the ponds to their original states and to preserve them for future generations; call ahead to arrange a free guided tour.

KOHALA COAST PETROGLYPHS

The Hawaiian petroglyphs are a great enigma of the Pacific—no one knows who made them or why. They appear at 135 different sites on six inhabited islands, but most of them are found on the Big Island.

At first glance, the huge slate of pahoehoe looks like any other smooth black slate of lava on the seacoast of the Big Island—until gradually, in slanting rays of the sun, a wonderful cast of characters

Into Another Dimension

What could be better than 3-D? How about 4-D? The 24-seat **Great 4-D Movie Ride** at the Shops at Mauna Lani features films that not only look lifelike, they make you feel as though you're a part of the action—think surround sound, full-range motion seats, and blown air and water spray for an experience that will trip all your senses. At press time, screenings included *Yogi's Wild Ride* and *National Geographic Sea Monsters;* call © **786/320-8884** or visit www.shopsatmaunalani.com for updated titles and show times. Tickets are $5 before 5pm and $7 after.

IS EVERYONE hawaiian IN HAWAII?

The plantations brought so many different people to Hawaii that the state is now a rainbow of ethnic groups: Living here are Caucasians, African Americans, American Indians, Eskimos, Japanese, Chinese, Filipinos, Koreans, Tahitians, Vietnamese, Hawaiians, Samoans, Tongans, and other Asian and Pacific Islanders. Add to that a few Canadians, Dutch, English, French, Germans, Irish, Italians, Portuguese, Scottish, Puerto Ricans, and Spaniards.

In combination, it's a remarkable potpourri. Many people retain an element of the traditions of their homeland. Some Japanese Americans in Hawaii, generations removed from the homeland, are more traditional than the Japanese of Tokyo. And the same is true of many Chinese, Koreans, Filipinos, and others, making Hawaii a kind of living museum of various Asian and Pacific cultures.

leaps to life before your eyes. You might see dancers and paddlers, fishermen and chiefs, hundreds of marchers all in a row. Pictures of the tools of daily life are everywhere: fish hooks, spears, poi pounders, canoes. The most common representations are family groups. There are also post–European contact petroglyphs of ships, anchors, horses, and guns.

The largest concentration of these stone symbols in the Pacific lies within the 233-acre **Puako Petroglyph Archaeological District ★**, near Mauna Lani Resort. A total of 3,000 designs have been identified. The 1.5-mile **Malama Trail** starts north of Mauna Lani Resort; take Hwy. 19 to the resort turnoff and drive toward the coast on North Kaniku Drive, which ends at a parking lot; the trail head is marked by a sign and interpretive kiosk. Go in the early morning or late afternoon, when it's cool.

The **Kings' Shops** (© 808/886-8811), at the Waikoloa Beach Resort, offers a free 1-hour tour of the surrounding petroglyphs every Thursday through Sunday at 10:30am. Just show up at the stage in the center of the shopping center by 10:30am.

Visitors with disabilities, as well as others, can explore petroglyphs at **Kaupulehu Petroglyphs ★** in the Kona Village Resort, Queen Kaahumanu Highway (© 808/325-5555). Free guided tours are offered twice a week, but reservations a week in advance are required (or you won't get past the gatehouse). Here you can see some of the finest images in the Hawaiian Islands. There are many petroglyphs of sails, canoes, fish, and chiefs in headdresses, plus a burial scene. Kite motifs—rare in rock art—similar to those found in New Zealand are also here. This is Hawaii's only ADA-accessible petroglyph trail. *Note:* The area in front of the petroglyphs is ADA accessible; however, the 10- to 15-minute walk from the parking area is across coral rock and can be a challenge.

Warning: The petroglyphs are thousands of years old and easily destroyed. Do not walk on them or attempt to take a rubbing (there's a special area in the Puako Preserve for doing so). The best way to capture a petroglyph is with a photo in the late afternoon, when the shadows are long.

North Kohala ★★★

Lapakahi State Historical Park ★ ☺ This 14th-century fishing village, on a hot, dry, dusty stretch of coast, offers a glimpse into the lifestyle of the ancients. Lapakahi is the best-preserved fishing village in Hawaii. Take the self-guided 1-mile loop trail past stone platforms, fish shrines, rock shelters, salt pans, and restored *hale* (houses) to a coral-sand beach and the deep-blue sea (good snorkeling). Wear good hiking or tennis shoes; it's a hearty 45-minute walk. Go early in the morning or late in the afternoon to beat the heat.

Hwy. 270, Mahukona. ✆ **808/327-4958.** www.hawaiistateparks.org/parks/hawaii/Index.cfm?park_id=50. Free admission. Daily 8am–4pm. Guided tours by appointment.

Mookini Luakini Heiau ★★ 📷 The 1,500-year-old Mookini Heiau, once used by kings to pray and offer human sacrifices, is Hawaii's oldest, largest, and most sacred religious site (and now a national historic landmark). The massive three-story stone temple, dedicated to Ku, the Hawaiian god of war, was erected in A.D. 480; each stone is said to have been passed hand to hand from Pololu Valley, 14 miles away, by 18,000 men who worked from sunset to sunrise. Kamehameha, born nearby under Halley's Comet, sought spiritual guidance here before embarking on his campaign to unite Hawaii. You can see the temple only by appointment. To set up an appointment for a tour, call the Mookini Preservation Foundation, on Oahu (✆ **808/373-8000**).

On the north shore, near Upolu Point Airport.

Original King Kamehameha Statue ★★ Here stands King Kamehameha the Great, right arm outstretched, left arm holding a spear, as if guarding the seniors who have turned a century-old New England–style courthouse into an airy center for their golden years. The center is worth a stop just to meet the town elders, who are quick to point out the local sights, hand you a free *Guide to*

North Kohala & Waimea

Historic North Kohala, and give you a brief tour of the courthouse, whose walls are covered with the faces of innocent looking local boys killed in World War II, Korea, and Vietnam.

But the statue's the main attraction here. There's one just like it in Honolulu, across the street from Iolani Palace, but this is the original: an 8-foot, 6-inch bronze by Thomas R. Gould, a Boston sculptor. It was cast in Europe in 1880 but was lost at sea on its way to Hawaii. A sea captain eventually recovered the statue, which was placed here, near Kamehameha's Kohala birthplace, in 1912.

Kamehameha was born in 1750, became ruler of Hawaii in 1810, and died in Kailua-Kona in 1819. His burial site remains a mystery.

Hwy. 270, Kapaau.

Pololu Valley Lookout ★★★ At this end-of-the-road scenic lookout, you can gaze at the vertical jade-green cliffs of the Hamakua Coast and two islets offshore. The view may look familiar once you get here—it often appears on travel posters. Linger if you can; adventurous travelers can take a switchback trail (a good

45-min. hike) to a secluded black-sand beach at the mouth of a wild valley once planted in taro; bring water and bug spray.

At the end of Hwy. 270, Makapala.

Pua Mau Place ☺   Perched on the sun-kissed western slopes of the Kohala Mountains and dotted with deep, craggy ravines is one of Hawaii's most unusual botanical gardens, Pua Mau Place, a 45-acre oasis with breathtaking views of both the ocean and the majestic mountains. It's dedicated to plants that are "ever blooming," an expansive collection of continuously flowering tropical flowers, trees, and shrubs. The gardens also have an aviary of exotic birds and a unique hibiscus maze planted with some 200 varieties of hibiscus. This is a great place for families; children are invited to feed the birds in the aviary. Visitors can take the self-guided tour (along with a booklet filled with the names and descriptions of all the plants) along mulched pathways meandering through the gardens, where every plant is clearly marked.

10 Ala Kahua Dr., Kawaihae. ✆ **808/882-0888.** www.puamau.com. Admission $10 adults, $8 seniors and students, free for children 12 and under. Daily 9am–4pm. Located off Hwy. 270 on Ala Kahua Dr. (in Kohala Estates), just north of Kawaihae. Turn at mile marker 6, ½ mile up the hill to the gate at a lava rock wall.

Waimea (Kamuela) ★★★

Kamuela Museum   It takes only about an hour to explore tiny Kamuela Museum. Its eclectic collection includes an early Hawaiian dogtooth death cup, a piece of rope used on the *Apollo* mission, and ancient artifacts from the royal family.

At the junction of Hwy. 19 and Hwy. 250, Waimea. ✆ **808/885-4724.** www. hawaiimuseums.org/mc/ishawaii_kamuela.htm. Admission $5 adults, $2 children 11 and under. Daily 8am–5pm.

Mauna Kea ★★★

The summit of Mauna Kea, the world's tallest mountain if measured from its base on the ocean floor, is the best place on earth for astronomical observations because its mid-Pacific site is near the equator and because it enjoys clear, pollution-free skies and pitch-black nights with no urban light to interfere. That's why Mauna Kea is home to the world's largest telescope—but the stargazing from here is fantastic even with the naked eye.

SETTING OUT   You'll need a four-wheel-drive vehicle to climb to the peak, Observatory Hill. A standard car will get you as far as the visitor center, but check your rental agreement before you go; some agencies prohibit you from taking your car on the Saddle Road, which is narrow and rutted, and has a soft shoulder.

pidgin: 'EH FO'REAL, BRAH

If you venture beyond the tourist areas, you might hear another local tongue: pidgin English, a conglomeration of slang and words from the Hawaiian language. "Broke da mouth" (tastes really good) is the favorite pidgin phrase and one you might hear; "'Eh fo'real, brah" means "It's true, brother." You could be invited to hear an elder "talk story" (relating myths and memories). But because pidgin is really the province of the locals, your visit to Hawaii is likely to pass without your hearing much pidgin at all.

SAFETY TIPS Always check the weather and Mauna Kea road conditions before you head out (© **808/961-5582**). Dress warmly; the temperatures drop into the 30s (around 0°C) after dark. Drink as much liquid as possible, avoiding alcohol and coffee, in the 36 hours surrounding your trip to avoid dehydration. Don't go within 24 hours of scuba diving—you could get the bends. The day before you go, avoid gas-producing foods, such as beans, cabbage, onions, soft drinks, or starches. If you smoke, take a break for 48 hours before to allow the carbon monoxide in your bloodstream to dissipate—you need all the oxygen you can get. Wear dark sunglasses to avoid snow blindness, and use lots of sunscreen and lip balm. Pregnant women and anyone under 13 or with a heart condition or lung ailment are advised to stay below. Once you're at the top, don't overexert yourself; it's bad for your heart. Take it easy up here.

ACCESS POINTS & VISITOR CENTERS It's about an hour from Hilo or Waimea to the visitor center and another 30 to 45 minutes from here to the summit. Take the Saddle Road (Hwy. 200) from Hwy. 190, it's about 19 miles to Mauna Kea State Recreation Area, a good place to stop and stretch your legs. Go another 9 miles to the unmarked Summit Road turnoff, at mile marker 28 (about 9,300 ft.), across from the Hunter's Check-in Station. People usually start getting lightheaded after the 9,600-foot marker (about 6¼ miles up the Summit Rd.), the site of the last comfort zone and the **Onizuka Visitor Information Station** (© **808/961-2180;** www.ifa.hawaii.edu/info/vis). Named in memory of Hawaii's fallen astronaut, a native of the Big Island and a victim of the 1986 *Challenger* explosion, the center is open daily from 9am to 10pm.

TOURS & PROGRAMS If you'd rather not go it alone to the top, you can caravan up as part of a **free summit tour,** offered

Saturday and Sunday at 1pm from the visitor center (returns at 5pm). You must be 16 or older and in good health (no cardiopulmonary problems), not be pregnant, and have a four-wheel-drive vehicle. The tours explain the development of the facilities on Mauna Kea and include a walking tour of an observatory at 13,796 feet. Call ☎ **808/961-2180** if you'd like to participate.

Every night from 6 to 10pm, you can do some serious **stargazing** from the Onizuka Visitor Information Station. There's a free lecture at 6pm, followed by a video, a question-and-answer session, and your chance to peer through 11-, 14-, and 16-inch telescopes. Bring a snack and, if you've got them, your own telescope or binoculars — along with a flashlight with a red filter. Dress for 30° to 40°F (–1° to 4°C) temperatures, but call ☎ **808/961-5582** for the weather report first. Families are welcome.

At the **Keck Telescope Control Center,** 65–1120 Mamalahoa Hwy. (Hwy. 19), across from the North Hawaii Community Hospital, Waimea (☎ **808/885-7887;** www.keckobservatory.org), you can see a model of the world's largest telescope, which sits atop Mauna Kea. The center is open Monday through Friday from 8am to 4:30pm. A 12-minute video explains the Keck's search for objects in deep space.

The **W. M. Keck Observatory** at the summit does not offer tours, but it does provide a visitor gallery with a 12-minute video, informational panels on the observatory layout and science results, two public restrooms, and a viewing area with partial views of the Keck telescope and dome. Gallery hours are Monday through Friday from 10am to 4pm.

MAKING THE CLIMB If you're heading up on your own, stop at the visitor center for about a half-hour to get acquainted with the altitude. Walk around, eat a banana, and drink some water before you press onward and upward in low gear, engine whining. It takes about 30 to 45 minutes to get to the top from here. The trip is a mere 6 miles, but you climb from 9,000 to nearly 14,000 feet.

AT THE SUMMIT Up here, 11 nations, including Japan, France, and Canada, have set up peerless infrared telescopes to look into deep space. Among them sits the **Keck Telescope,** the world's largest. Developed by the University of California and the California Institute of Technology, it's eight stories high, weighs 150 tons, and has a 33-foot-diameter mirror made of 36 perfectly attuned hexagon mirrors, like a fly's eye, rather than one conventional lens.

Also at the summit, up a narrow footpath, is a cairn of rocks; from it, you can see across the Pacific Ocean in a 360-degree view that's beyond words and pictures. When it's socked in, you get a surreal look at the summits of Mauna Loa and Maui's Haleakala poking through the puffy white cumulus clouds beneath your feet.

Inside a cinder cone just below the summit is **Lake Waiau,** the only glacial lake in the mid-Pacific and, at 13,020 feet above sea level, one of the highest lakes in the world. The lake never dries up, even though it gets only 15 inches of rain a year and sits in porous lava where there are no springs. Nobody quite knows what to make of this, but scientists suspect the lake is replenished by snowmelt and permafrost from submerged lava tubes. You can't see the lake from Summit Road; you must take a brief high-altitude hike. But it's easy: On the final approach to the summit area, upon regaining the blacktop road, go about 600 feet to the major switchback and make a hard right turn. Park on the shoulder of the road (which is at 13,200 ft.). No sign points the way, but there's an obvious .5-mile trail that goes down to the lake about 200 feet across the lava. Follow the base of the big cinder cone on your left; you should have the summit of Mauna Loa in view directly ahead as you walk.

The Hamakua Coast ★★★

The sugar industry's rich 117-year history, along the scenic 45-mile coastline from Hilo to Hamakua, comes alive in the interpretive *Hilo-Hamakua Heritage Coast* drive guide found on the **Hawaii Island Economic Development Board**'s website, 117 Kiawe St., Hilo, HI 96720 (✆ **808/935-2180;** www.hiedb.org; info@hiedb.org). The downloadable guide not only points out the historic sites and museums, scenic photo opportunities, restaurants and stores, and even restrooms along the Hawaii Belt Road (Hwy. 19), but also has corresponding brown-and-white points-of-interest

EXPERIENCING WHERE THE
gods live

"The ancient Hawaiians thought of the top of Mauna Kea as heaven, or at least where the gods and goddesses lived," according to Monte "Pat" Wright, owner and chief guide of **Mauna Kea Summit Adventures.** Wright, the first guide to take people up to the top of Mauna Kea, the world's tallest mountain when measured from the base and an astonishing 13,796 feet when measured from sea level, says he fell in love with this often-snowcapped peak the first time he saw it.

Mauna Kea Summit Adventures offers a luxurious trip to the top of the world. The 7- to 8-hour adventure begins midafternoon, when guests are picked up along the Kona-Kohala coasts in a brand-new $65,000 custom four-wheel-drive turbo-diesel van. As the passengers make the drive up the mountain, the extensively trained guide discusses the geography, geology, natural history, and Hawaiian culture along the way.

The first stop is at the Onizuka Visitor Information Station, at 9,000 feet, where guests can stretch, get acclimatized to the altitude, and eat dinner. As they gear up with Mauna Kea Summit Adventures' heavy arctic-style hooded parkas and gloves (the average temperature on the mountain is 30°F/–1°C), the guide describes why the world's largest telescopes are located on Mauna Kea and also tells stories about the lifestyle of astronomers who live for a clear night sky.

After a dinner of gourmet sandwiches, vegetarian onion soup, and hot chocolate, coffee, or tea, everyone climbs back into the van for the half-hour ride to the summit. As the sun sinks into the

signs on the highway. Visitor centers anchored at either end in Hilo and in Hamakua offer additional information on the area.

NATURAL WONDERS ALONG THE COAST

Akaka Falls ★★★   See one of Hawaii's most scenic waterfalls via an easy 1-mile paved loop through a rainforest, past bamboo and ginger, and down to an observation point. You'll have a perfect view of 442-foot Akaka and nearby Kahuna Falls, which is a mere 100-footer. Keep your eyes peeled for rainbows. The noise you hear is the sound of coqui frogs, an alien frog from Puerto Rico that has become a pest on the Big Island.

On Hwy. 19, **Honomu** (8 miles north of Hilo). Turn left at Honomu and head 3½ miles inland on Akaka Falls Rd. (Hwy. 220).

Pacific nearly 14,000 feet below, the guide points out the various world-renowned telescopes as they rotate into position for the night viewing.

After the last trace of sunset colors has disappeared from the sky, the tour again descends down to midmountain, where the climate is more agreeable, for stargazing. Each tour has Celestron Celestar 8 deluxe telescopes, which are capable of 30× to 175× magnification and gather up to 500 times more light than the unaided eye.

Wright advises people to book the adventure early in their vacation. "Although we do cancel about 25 trips a year due to weather, we want to be able to accommodate everyone," he says. If guests book at the beginning of their holiday and the trip is canceled due to weather, then Mauna Kea Summit Adventures will attempt to reschedule another day.

Note that the summit's low oxygen level (40% less oxygen than at sea level) and the diminished air pressure (also 40% less air pressure than at sea level) can be a serious problem for people with heart or lung problems or for scuba divers who have been diving in the previous 24 hours. Pregnant women, children under 13, and obese people should not travel to the summit due to the decreased oxygen. Because the roads to the summit are bumpy, anyone with a bad back might want to opt out, too.

The cost for this celestial adventure is $200 including tax (15% off if you book online 2 weeks in advance). For more information, call ✆ **888/322-2366** or 808/322-2366, or go to www.maunakea.com.

Hawaii Tropical Botanical Garden ★★ More than 1,800 species of tropical plants thrive in this little-known Eden by the sea. The 40-acre garden, nestled between the crashing surf and a thundering waterfall, has the world's largest selection of tropical plants growing in a natural environment, including torch gingers (which tower on 12-ft. stalks), a banyan canyon, an orchid garden, a banana grove, a bromeliad hill, and a golden bamboo grove, which rattles like a jungle drum in the trade winds. Some endangered Hawaiian specimens, such as the rare *Gardenia remyi*, are flourishing in this habitat. The gardens are seldom crowded; you can wander around by yourself all day. ✓

Co-*key,* Co-*key:* What Is That Noise?

That loud noise you hear after dark, especially on the eastern side of the Big Island, is the cry of the male coqui frog looking for a mate. A native of Puerto Rico, where the frogs are kept in check by snakes, the coqui frog came to Hawaii in some plant material, found no natural enemies, and spread across the Big Island (and Maui). A chorus of several hundred coqui frogs is deafening (up to 163 decibels, or the noise level of a jet engine from 100 ft.). In some places, such as Akaka Falls, there are so many frogs that they are now chirping during daylight hours.

Off Hwy. 19 on the 4-mile Scenic Route (8 miles north of Hilo), Onomea Bay. © 808/964-5233. www.htbg.com. Admission $15 adults, $5 children 6–16, free for children 5 and under. Daily 9am–5pm.

Laupahoehoe Beach Park ★ This idyllic place holds a grim reminder of nature's fury. In 1946, a tidal wave swept across the village that once stood on this lava-leaf (that's what *laupahoehoe* means) peninsula and claimed the lives of 20 students and four teachers. A memorial in this pretty little park recalls the tragedy. The land here ends in black sea stacks that resemble tombstones. It's not a place for swimming, but the views are spectacular.

Off Hwy. 19, Laupahoehoe Point exit.

World Botanical Gardens ★★ Just north of Hilo is Hawaii's largest botanical garden, with some 5,000 species. When the fruits are in season, the staff hands out free chilled juices. One of the most spectacular sights is the .25-mile rainforest walk (wheelchair accessible), along a stream on a flower-lined path to the viewing area of the three-tiered, 300-foot Umauma Falls. Parents will appreciate the large children's maze, where the "prize" is a playing field near the exit. The mock-orange hedge, which defines the various paths in the maze, is only 5 feet tall, so most parents can peer over the edge to keep an eye on their *keiki.* Other terrific walks include the "rainbow walk," through an ethnobotanical garden, and one through a wellness garden with medicinal Hawaiian plants. There's also an arboretum. Still under construction as we went to press is a phylogenetic garden with plants and trees arranged in roughly the same sequence in which they first appeared on earth.

Off Hwy. 19 near mile marker 16, Umauma. © 808/963-5427. www.world botanicalgardens.com. Admission $13 adults, $6 teens 13–19, $3 children 5–12, free for children 4 and under. Guided tours $40 per person, lunch included (24-hr. advance reservation). Daily 9am–5:30pm.

HONOKAA ★★★

Honokaa is worth a visit to see the remnants of plantation life, when sugar was king. This is a real place that hasn't yet been boutiqued into a shopping mall; it looks as if someone has kept it in a bell jar since 1920. There's a real barbershop, a real Filipino store, some good shopping (see "Shops & Galleries," p. 156), and a hotel with creaky floorboards that dishes up hearty food. The town also serves as the gateway to spectacular Waipio Valley (see below).

Honokaa has no attractions, per se, but you might want to check out the **Katsu Goto Memorial,** next to the library at the Hilo end of town. Katsu Goto, one of the first indentured Japanese immigrants, arrived in Honokaa in the late 1800s to work on the sugar plantations. He learned English, quit the plantation, and aided his fellow immigrants in labor disputes with American planters. On October 23, 1889, he was hanged from a lamppost in Honokaa, a victim of local-style justice.

THE END OF THE ROAD:
WAIPIO VALLEY ★★★

Long ago, this lush, tropical place was the valley of kings, who called it the valley of "curving water" (which is what *waipio* means). From the black-sand bay at its mouth, Waipio sweeps 6 miles between sheer, cathedral-like walls that reach almost a mile high. Once 40,000 Hawaiians lived here, amid taro, red bananas, and wild guavas in an area etched by streams and waterfalls. Only about 50 Hawaiians live in the valley today, tending taro, fishing, and soaking up the ambience of this old Hawaiian place.

The sacred valley is steeped in myth and legend. Many of the ancient royals are buried here; some believe they rise up to become Marchers of the Night, whose chants reverberate through the valley. The caskets of Hawaiian chiefs Liloa and Lono Ika Makahiki, stolen from the Bishop Museum, are believed to have been brought here by Hawaiians.

To get to Waipio Valley, take Hwy. 19 from Hilo to Honokaa, and then Hwy. 240 to the **Waipio Valley Lookout ★★★**, a grassy park on the edge of Waipio Valley's sheer cliffs with splendid views of the wild oasis below. This is a great place for a picnic; you can sit at old redwood picnic tables and watch the white combers race along the black-sand beach at the mouth of the valley. From the lookout, you can hike down into the valley.

Warning: Do not attempt to drive your rental car down into the valley (even if you see someone else doing it). The problem is not so much going down as coming back up. Every day, rental cars have to be "rescued" and towed back up to the top, at great expense to the driver. Instead, hop on the **Waipio Valley Shuttle**

Volunteering on Vacation

If you are looking for a different type of experience during your next vacation to Hawaii, you might want to consider becoming a volunteer and leaving the islands a little nicer than when you arrived. People interested in volunteering at beach and ocean cleanups can contact the **University of Hawaii Sea Grant College Program** (☎ **808/397-2651,** ext. 256) or **Hawaii Wildlife Fund** (☎ **808/756-1808**). For ecovolunteering on land, contact **Malama Hawaii** (www.malamahawaii.org/get_involved/volunteer.php), a statewide organization dedicated to *malama* (taking care) of the culture and environment of Hawaii. At this site you will find a range of opportunities on various islands, such as weeding gardens and potting plants in botanical gardens, restoring taro patches, cleaning up mountain streams, bird-watching, and even hanging out at Waikiki Beach helping with a reef project.

(☎ **808/775-7121**) for a 90- to 120-minute guided tour, offered Monday through Saturday from 9am to 3pm. Get your tickets at **Waipio Valley Artworks,** on Hwy. 240, 2 miles from the lookout (☎ **808/775-0958;** www.waipiovalleyartworks.com). Tickets are $55 for adults, $28 for kids 12 and under.

You can also explore the valley with **Waipio Valley Wagon Tours** (☎ **808/775-9518;** www.waipiovalleywagontours.com), which offers narrated 90-minute historical rides by mule-drawn surrey. Tours are offered daily at 10:30am, 12:30pm, and 2:30pm. It costs $55 for adults, $50 for seniors, and $25 for children 4 to 12; call for reservations.

If you want to spend more than a day in the valley, plan ahead. A few simple B&Bs are situated on the ridge overlooking the valley and require advance reservations (see p. 36 for listings).

Hilo ★★★

Contact or stop by the **Downtown Hilo Improvement Association,** 329 Kamehameha Ave., Hilo, HI 96720 (☎ **808/935-8850;** www.downtownhilo.com), for a copy of its very informative self-guided walking tour of Hilo, which focuses on 18 historic sites dating from the 1870s to the present.

ON THE WATERFRONT

Old banyan trees shade **Banyan Drive ★★**, the lane that curves along the waterfront to the Hilo Bay hotels. Most of the trees were planted in the mid-1930s by memorable visitors such as Cecil B. DeMille (who was here in 1933 filming *Four Frightened People*),

Babe Ruth (his tree is in front of the Hilo Hawaiian Hotel), King George V, Amelia Earhart, and other celebrities whose fleeting fame didn't last as long as the trees themselves.

It's worth a stop along Banyan Drive—especially if the coast is clear and the summit of Mauna Kea is free of clouds—to make the short walk across the concrete-arch bridge in front of the Naniloa Hotel to **Coconut Island ★**, if only to gain a panoramic sense of the place.

Also along Banyan Drive is **Liliuokalani Gardens ★★**, the largest formal Japanese garden this side of Tokyo. This 30-acre park, named for Hawaii's last monarch, Queen Liliuokalani, is as pretty as a postcard, with bonsai, carp ponds, pagodas, and a moongate bridge. Admission is free; open 24 hours.

OTHER HILO SIGHTS

Lyman Museum & Mission House ★ ☺   The oldest wood-frame house on the island was built in 1839 by David and Sarah Lyman, a missionary couple who arrived from New England in 1832. This hybrid combined New England–style and Hawaiian-style architecture and is built of hand-hewn koa planks and native timbers. Here the Lymans received such guests as Mark Twain and Hawaii's monarchs. The well-preserved house is the best example of missionary life and times in Hawaii. You'll find lots of artifacts from the 19th century, including furniture and clothing from the Lymans and one of the first mirrors in Hilo.

The **Earth Heritage Gallery,** in the complex next door, continues the story of the islands with geology and volcanology exhibits, a mineral-rock collection that's rated one of the best in the country, and a section on local flora and fauna. The **Island Heritage Gallery** features displays on Hawaiian culture, including a replica of a grass *hale* (house), as well as on other cultures transplanted to Hawaii's shores. A special gallery features changing exhibits on the history, art, and culture of Hawaii.

276 Haili St. (at Kapiolani St.). ℂ **808/935-5021.** www.lymanmuseum.org. Admission $10 adults, $8 seniors 61 and over, $3 children 6–17; $21 per family. Mon–Sat 10am–4:30pm. Tours at 11am and 2pm (call to reserve a space).

Maunaloa Macadamia Nut Factory   Explore this unique factory to learn how Hawaii's favorite nut is grown and processed. And, of course, you'll want to try a few samples.

Macadamia Nut Rd., off Hwy. 11 (8 miles from Hilo). ℂ **888/MAUNALOA** or 808/966-8618. www.maunaloa.com. Free admission; self-guided factory tours. Daily 8:30am–5pm. From Hwy. 11, turn on Macadamia Nut Rd.; go 3 miles down the road to the factory.

Naha Stone   This 2½-ton stone was used as a test of royal strength: Ancient legend said that whoever could move the stone

imiloa: EXPLORING THE UNKNOWN

Absolutely do *not* miss the **Imiloa: Astronomy Center of Hawaii** ★★★. The 300 exhibits in the 12,000-square-foot gallery make the connection between the Hawaiian culture and its explorers, who "discovered" the Hawaiian Islands, and the astronomers who explore the heavens from the observatories atop Mauna Kea. *Imiloa,* which means "explorer" or "seeker of profound truth," is the perfect name for this architecturally stunning center, located on 9 landscaped acres overlooking Hilo Bay in the University of Hawaii at Hilo Science and Technology Park campus, 600 Imiloa Place (© **808/969-9700;** www.imiloahawaii.org). Plan to spend at least a couple of hours here; a half-day would be better, to allow time to browse the excellent interactive exhibits as well as take in one of the planetarium shows, which boast a state-of-the-art digital projection system. Open Tuesday through Sunday from 9am to 4pm; admission is $18 for adults and $9.50 for children 4 to 12.

would conquer and unite the islands. As a 14-year-old boy, King Kamehameha the Great moved the stone—and later fulfilled his destiny. The Pinao stone, next to it, once guarded an ancient temple.

In front of the Hilo Public Library, 300 Waianuenue Ave.

Nani Mau Gardens ★   Just outside Hilo is Nani Mau (Forever Beautiful), where Makato Nitahara, who turned a 20-acre papaya patch into a tropical garden, claims to have every flowering plant in Hawaii. His collection includes more than 2,000 varieties, from fragile hibiscus, whose blooms last only a day, to durable red anthuriums imported from South America. There are also Japanese gardens, an orchid walkway, a botanical museum, a house full of butterflies, and a restaurant that's open for lunch.

421 Makalika St. © **808/959-3500.** www.nanimau.com. Admission $10 adults, $5 children 4-10. Tram tours $7 extra for adults, $5 extra for children (for the tram, you must have a min. of 4 people, and you must reserve at least 2 days prior to arrival). Daily 8am–5pm. Go 3 miles south of Hilo Airport on Hwy. 11, turn on Makalika St., and continue ¾ mile.

Pacific Tsunami Museum ★   The most interesting artifacts here are not the exhibits, but the volunteers who survived Hawaii's most deadly "walls of water" in 1946 and 1960, both of which reshaped the town of Hilo. Visitors can listen to their stories of terror and view a range of exhibits, from interactive computers to a display on what happens when a local earthquake triggers a seismic wave, as it did in 1975 during the Big Island's last tsunami.

130 Kamehameha Ave. ℂ **808/935-0926.** www.tsunami.org. Admission $8 adults, $7 seniors, $4 children 6–17. Mon–Sat 9am–4pm.

Panaewa Rainforest Zoo ★ ☺ This 12-acre zoo, nestled in the heart of the Panaewa Forest Reserve south of Hilo, is the only outdoor rainforest zoo in the United States. Some 50 species of animals from rainforests around the globe call Panaewa home—including several endangered Hawaiian birds. All of them are exhibited in a natural setting. This is one of the few zoos where you can observe Sumatran tigers, Brazilian tapirs, and the rare pygmy hippopotamus, an endangered "minihippo" found in western Africa.

Stainback Hwy. (off Hwy. 11). ℂ **808/959-7224.** www.hilozoo.com. Free admission. Daily 9am–4pm. Petting zoo Sat 1:30–2:30pm; tiger feeding 3:30pm daily.

Papahānaumokuākea: Discovery Center for Hawaii's Remote Coral Reefs ☺ ✄ This 4,000-square-foot center is perfect for children, who can explore the Northwest Hawaiian Islands coral reef ecosystem, which was added to the United Nation's World Heritage sites in 2010. Through interactive displays, engaging three-dimensional models, and an immersion theater, the kids can learn natural science, culture, and history while having a great time. A 2,500-gallon saltwater aquarium provides a habitat for a collection of fish from the Northwest Hawaiian Islands reefs. Lots of fun at a terrific price: free!

308 Kamehameha Ave., Ste. 109. ℂ **808/933-8195** or 808/933-8180. www.hawaiireef.noaa.gov. Free admission. Tues–Sat 9am–4pm.

Rainbow Falls ★ 📷 Go in the morning, around 9 or 10am, just as the sun comes over the mango trees, to see Rainbow Falls at its best. The 80-foot Falls spill into a big round natural pool surrounded by wild ginger. According to legend, Hina, the mother of Maui, lives in the cave behind the Falls. Unfortunately, swimming in the pool is no longer allowed.

West on Waianuenue Ave., past Kaumana Dr.

Hawaii Volcanoes National Park ★★★

Yellowstone, Yosemite, and other national parks are spectacular, no doubt about it. But in my opinion, they're all ho-hum compared to this one: Here nothing less than the miracle of creation is the daily attraction.

In the 19th century, before tourism became Hawaii's middle name, the islands' singular attraction for visitors wasn't the beach,

A Desert Crossing

If you follow Hwy. 11 counterclockwise from Kona to the volcano, you'll get a preview of what lies ahead in the national park: hot, scorched, quake-shaken, bubbling-up new/dead land. This is the great Kau Desert, layer upon layer of lava flows, fine ash, and fall-out. As you traverse the desert, you cross the Great Crack and the Southwest Rift Zone, a major fault zone that looks like a giant groove in the earth, before you reach Kilauea Volcano.

but the volcano. From the world over, curious spectators gathered on the rim of Kilauea's Halemaumau crater to see one of the greatest wonders of the globe. Nearly a century after it was named a national park (in 1916), Hawaii Volcanoes remains the state's premier natural attraction.

Hawaii Volcanoes has the only rainforest in the U.S. National Park system—and it's the only park that's home to an active volcano. Most people drive through the park (it has 50 miles of good roads, some of them often covered by lava flows) and call it a day. But it takes at least 3 days to explore the whole park, including such oddities as **Halemaumau Crater ★★★**, a still-fuming pit of steam and sulfur; the intestinal-looking **Thurston Lava Tube ★★★**; **Devastation Trail ★★★**, a short hike through a desolated area destroyed by lava; and, finally, the end of **Chain of Craters Road ★★★**, where lava regularly spills across the man-made two-lane blacktop to create its own red-hot freeway to the sea. In addition to some of the world's weirdest landscapes, the park has hiking trails, rainforests, campgrounds, a historic old hotel on the crater's rim, and that spectacular, still-erupting volcano.

NOTES ON THE ERUPTING VOLCANO Volcanologists refer to Hawaii's volcanic eruptions as "quiet" eruptions because gases escape slowly instead of building up and exploding violently all at once. Hawaii's eruptions produce slow-moving, oozing lava that provides excellent, safe viewing most of the time.

Even so, the volcano has still caused its share of destruction. Since the current eruption of Kilauea began on January 3, 1983, lava has covered some 16,000 acres of lowland and rainforest, threatening rare hawks, honeycreeper birds, spiders, and bats, while destroying power and telephone lines and eliminating water service possibly forever. Some areas have been mantled repeatedly and are now buried underneath 80 feet of lava. At last count, the lava flow had destroyed nearly 200 homes and businesses, wiped out Kaimu Black Sand Beach (once Hawaii's most photographed

Hawaii Volcanoes National Park

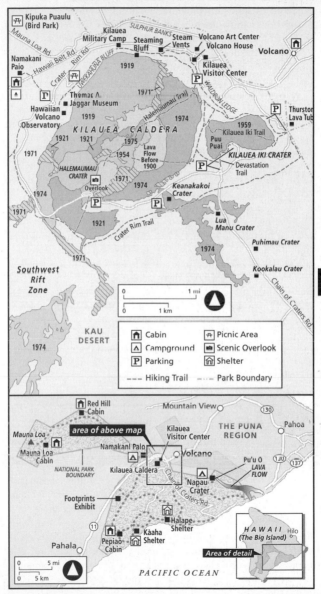

0   1 mi
0   1 km

Cabin 🏠 **Picnic Area** 🎋
Campground ⛺ **Scenic Overlook** 📷
Parking 🅿 **Shelter** 🏠
--- Hiking Trail -·-·- Park Boundary

beach) and Queen's Bath, obliterated entire towns and subdivisions (Kalapana, Royal Gardens, Kalapana Gardens, and Kapaahu Homesteads), and buried natural and historic landmarks (a 12th-c. *heiau,* the century-old Kalapana Mauna Kea Church, Wahaulu Visitor Center, and thousands of archaeological artifacts and sites). The cost of the destruction—so far—is estimated at $100 million. But how do you price the destruction of a 700-year-old temple or a 100-year-old church?

However, Kilauea hasn't just destroyed parts of the island; it has also added to it—more than 560 acres of new land. The volume of erupted lava over the last 2 decades measures nearly 2 billion cubic yards—enough new rock to pave a two-lane highway 1¼ million miles long, circling the earth some 50 times. Or, as a spokesperson for the park puts it: "Every 5 days, there is enough lava coming out of Kilauea volcano's eruption to place a thin veneer over Washington, DC—all 63 square miles."

The most prominent vent of the eruption has been Puu Oo, a 760-foot-high cinder-and-spatter cone. The most recent flow—the one you'll be able to see, if you're lucky—follows a 7-mile-long tube from the Puu Oo vent area to the sea. This lava flow has extended the Big Island's shoreline seaward and added hundreds of acres of new land along the steep southern slopes. Periodically, the new land proves unstable, falls under its own weight, and slides into the ocean. (These areas of ground gained and lost are not included in the tally of new acreage—only the land that sticks counts.)

Scientists are also keeping an eye on Mauna Loa, which has been swelling since its last eruption in 1984. If there's a new eruption, there could be a fast-moving flow down the southwest side of the island, possibly into South Kona or Kau.

WHAT YOU'RE LIKELY TO SEE   With luck, the volcano will still be streaming rivers of red lava when you visit the park, but a continuous eruption of this length (more than 2 decades) is setting new ground, so to speak. Kilauea continues to perplex volcanologists because most major eruptions in the past have ended abruptly after only several months.

But neither Mother Nature nor Madame Pele (the volcano goddess) runs on a schedule. The volcano could be shooting fountains of lava hundreds of feet into the air on the day you arrive, or it could be completely quiet—there are no guarantees. On many days, the lava flows right by accessible roads, and you can get as close as the heat will allow; sometimes, however, the flow is in underground tubes where you can't see it, or miles away from the nearest access point, visible only in the distance. Always ask the park rangers for advice before you set out on any lava-viewing expeditions.

A Volcano-Visiting Tip

Thanks to its higher elevation and windward (rainier) location, this neck of the woods is always colder than it is at the beach. If you're coming from the Kona side of the island in summer, expect it to be at least 10° to 20° cooler at the volcano; bring a sweater or light jacket. In the winter months, expect temperatures to be in the 40s or 50s (single digits to midteens Celsius), and dress accordingly. Always have rain gear on hand, especially in winter.

VOLCANO VOCABULARY The volcano has its own unique, poetic vocabulary that describes in Hawaiian what cannot be said so well in English. The lava that looks like swirls of chocolate cake frosting is called **pahoehoe** (pa-*hoy*-hoy); it results from a fast-moving flow that curls artistically as it moves. The big, blocky, jumbled lava that looks like a chopped-up parking lot is called **aa** (ah-ah); it's caused by lava that moves slowly, pulling apart as it overruns itself.

Newer words include **vog,** which is volcanic smog made of volcanic gases and smoke from forests set on fire by aa and pahoehoe. **Laze** results when sulfuric acid hits the water and vaporizes, and mixes with chlorine to become, as any chemistry student knows, hydrochloric acid. Both vog and laze sting your eyes and can cause respiratory illness; don't expose yourself to either for too long. Anyone with heart or breathing trouble, as well as women who are pregnant, should avoid both vog and laze.

JUST THE FACTS

WHEN TO GO The best time to go is when Kilauea is really pumping. If you're lucky, you'll be in the park when the volcano is active and there's a fountain of lava; mostly, the lava runs like a red river downslope into the sea. If you're on another part of the island and hear a TV news bulletin that the volcano is acting up, head to Hilo to see the spectacle. You won't be sorry—and your favorite beach will still be there when you get back.

ACCESS POINTS Hawaii Volcanoes National Park is 29 miles from Hilo, on Hawaii Belt Road (Hwy. 11). If you're staying in Kailua-Kona, it's 100 miles, or about a 2½-hour drive, to the park. At press time, admission was still $10 per vehicle, but the park was proposing to double that to $20 per car; once you pay the fee, you can come and go as often as you want for 7 days. Hikers and bicyclists pay $5; bikes are allowed only on roads and paved trails.

VISITOR CENTERS & INFORMATION Contact **Hawaii Volcanoes National Park,** P.O. Box 52, Hawaii Volcanoes

Not So Close! They Hardly Know You

In the excitement of seeing a whale or a school of dolphins, don't forget that they're protected under the Marine Mammals Protection Act. You must stay at least 300 feet (the length of a football field) away from all whales, dolphins, and other marine mammals. This applies to swimmers, kayakers, and windsurfers. And, yes, visitors have been prosecuted for swimming with dolphins! If you have any questions, call the **National Marine Fisheries Service** (© 808/541-2727) or the **Hawaiian Islands Humpback Whale National Marine Sanctuary** (© 800/831-4888).

National Park, HI 96718 (© **808/985-6000;** www.nps.gov/havo). The **Kilauea Visitor Center** is at the entrance to the park, just off Hwy. 11; it's open daily from 7:45am to 5pm.

ERUPTION UPDATES Everything you wanted to know about Hawaii's volcanoes, from what's going on with the current eruptions to where the next eruption is likely to be, is now available on the Hawaiian Volcano Observatory's new website, **http:// volcanoes.usgs.gov/hvo/activity/kilaueastatus.php**. The site is divided into areas on Kilauea (the currently erupting volcano), Mauna Loa (which last erupted in 1984), and Hawaii's other volcanoes. Each section provides photos, maps, eruption summaries, and historical information.

You can also get the latest on volcanic activity in the park by calling the park's **24-hour hot line** (© **808/985-6000**). Updates on volcanic activity are posted daily on the bulletin board at the visitor center.

HIKING & CAMPING IN THE PARK Hawaii Volcanoes National Park offers a wealth of hiking and camping possibilities. See "Hiking & Camping," p. 111, for details.

ACCOMMODATIONS IN & AROUND THE PARK If camping isn't your thing, don't worry. There's a hotel, **Volcano House** (p. 66), within the park boundary, on the rim of Halemaumau Crater. Volcano Village, just outside the park, has plenty of comfortable and convenient hotels and restaurants; see p. 63 for hotel listings and p. 93 for restaurant listings.

SEEING THE HIGHLIGHTS

Your first stop should be **Kilauea Visitor Center ★★**, a rustic structure in a shady grove of trees just inside the entrance to the park. Here you can get up-to-the-minute reports on the volcano's activity, learn how volcanoes work, see a film showing blasts from the past, get information on hiking and camping, and pick up the obligatory postcards.

Filled with a new understanding of volcanology and the volcano goddess, Pele, you should then walk across the street to **Volcano House;** go through the lobby and out the other side, where you can get a look at **Kilauea Caldera ★★★**, a 2½-mile wide, 500-foot-deep hole. The caldera used to be a bubbling pit of fountaining lava; today you can still see wisps of steam that might, while you're standing there, turn into something more.

Now get out on the road and drive by the **Sulphur Banks ★**, which smell like rotten eggs, and the **Steam Vents ★★★**, where trails of smoke, once molten lava, rise from within the inner reaches of the earth. This is one of the places where you feel that the volcano is really alive.

Stop at the **Thomas A. Jaggar Museum ★★★** (daily 8:30am–5pm; free admission) for a good look at Halemaumau Crater, which is a half-mile across and 1,000 feet deep. On a clear day, you might also see Mauna Loa, 20 miles to the west. The museum shows video from days when the volcano was really spewing, explains the Pele legend in murals, and monitors earthquakes (a precursor of eruptions) on a seismograph.

When you've seen the museum, drive around the caldera to the south side, park your car, and take the short walk to the edge of **Halemaumau Crater ★★★**, past stinky sulfur banks and steam vents, to stand at the overlook and stare in awe at this once-fuming old fire pit, which still generates ferocious heat out of vestigial vents.

If you feel the need to cool off, go to the **Thurston Lava Tube ★★★**, the coolest place in the park. You'll hike down into a natural bowl in the earth, a forest preserve the lava didn't touch—full of native birds and giant tree ferns. Then you'll see a black hole in the earth; step in. It's all drippy and cool here, with bare roots hanging down. You can either resurface into the bright daylight or, if you have a flashlight, poke on deeper into the tube, which goes for another .5 mile or so.

If you're still game for a good hike, try **Kilauea Iki Trail ★**, a 4-mile, 2-hour hike across the floor of the crater, which became a bubbling pool of lava in 1959 and sent fountains of lava 1,900 feet in the air, completely devastating a nearby ohia forest and leaving another popular hike ominously known as **Devastation Trail ★★★**. This .5-mile walk is a startling look at the powers of a volcanic eruption on the environment. (See "Hiking & Camping," on p. 111, for details on these and other park hikes.)

Check out ancient Hawaiian art at the **Puu Loa Petroglyphs ★**, around mile marker 15 down Chain of Craters Road.

Look for the stack of rocks on the road. A brief .5-mile walk will bring you to a circular boardwalk where you can see thousands of mysterious Hawaiian petroglyphs carved in stone. (**Warning:** It's very easy to destroy these ancient works of art. Do not leave the boardwalk, and do not walk on or around the petroglyphs. Rubbings of petroglyphs will destroy them; the best way to capture them is by taking a photo.) This area, Puu Loa, was a sacred place for generations. Fathers came here to bury their newborns' umbilical cords in the numerous small holes in the lava, thus ensuring a long life for the child.

THE VOLCANO AFTER DARK   If the volcano is erupting, be sure to see it after dark. Brilliant red lava snakes down the side of the mountain and pours into the sea, creating a vivid display you'll never forget. About 1½ hours before sunset, head out of the park and back down Volcano Highway (Hwy. 11). Turn onto Hwy. 130 at Keaau; go past Pahoa to the end of the road. (The drive takes the better part of an hour.) From here (depending on the flow), it's about a mile walk over sharp crusted lava; park rangers will tell you how to get to the best viewing locations, or you can call ahead (© **808/985-6000**) to check where the current eruption is and how to get there. Be forewarned that the flow changes constantly and, on some days, may be too far from the road to hike, in which case you'll have to be content with seeing it from a distance. Be sure to heed the rangers: In the past, a handful of hikers who ignored these directions died en route; new lava can be unstable and break off without warning. Take water, a flashlight, and your camera, and wear sturdy shoes.

A BIRD'S-EYE VIEW   The best way to see Kilauea's bubbling caldera is from up high, in a helicopter. This bird's-eye view puts the enormity of it all into perspective. I recommend **Blue Hawaiian Helicopters** ★★★ (© **800/745-BLUE** or 808/886-1768; www.bluehawaiian.com), a professionally run, locally based company with an excellent safety record; comfortable, top-of-the-line copters; and pilots who are extremely knowledgeable about everything from volcanology to Hawaii lore. The company flies out of both Hilo and Waikoloa (Hilo is cheaper because it's closer). From Hilo, the 45-minute **Circle of Fire Tour** ★★ takes you over the boiling volcano and then on to a bird's-eye view of the destruction the lava has caused as well as of remote beaches ($210 per person, or $183 online). From Waikoloa, the 2-hour **Big Island Spectacular** ★★★ stars the volcano, tropical valleys, Hamakua Coast waterfalls, and the Kohala Mountains (from $424, or $370 online, but worth every penny).

South Point: Land's End ★★★

At the end of 11 miles of bad road that peters out at Kaulana Bay, in the lee of a jagged, black-lava point, you'll find Land's End—the tail end of the United States. From the tip (beware of the big waves that lash the shore if you walk out there), the nearest continental landfall is Antarctica, 7,500 miles away.

It's a 2½-mile four-wheel-drive trip and a hike down a cliff from South Point to the anomaly known as **Green Sand Beach** ★, described on p. 100 in the "Beaches" section in chapter 4.

Back on the Mamalahoa Highway (Hwy. 11), about 20 miles east, is the small town of Pahoa; turn off the highway and travel about 5 miles through this once-thriving sugar plantation and beyond to the **Wood Valley Temple & Retreat Center** ★ (© **808/928-8539;** www.nechung.org), also known as Nechung Dorje Drayang Ling (Island of Melodious Sound). It's an oasis of tranquility tucked into the rainforest. Built by Japanese sugar-cane workers, the temple, retreat center, and surrounding gardens were rededicated by the Dalai Lama in 1980 to serve as a spiritual center for Tibetan Buddhism. You can walk the beautiful grounds, attend services, and breathe in the quiet mindfulness of this serene area.

6

SHOPS & GALLERIES

While chefs and farmers tout this island as fertile ground for crops and food, artists point to its primal, volcanic energy as a boost to their creative endeavors. Art communities and galleries are sprinkled across the Big Island, in villages such as Holualoa and Volcano, where fine works in pottery, wood-turning, handmade glass, and other two- and three-dimensional media are sold in serene settings.

Although the visual arts are flourishing on this island, the line between shop and gallery can often be too fine to determine. Too many self-proclaimed "galleries" sell schlock or a mixture of arts, crafts, and tacky souvenirs. T-shirts and Kona coffee mugs are a souvenir staple in many so-called galleries.

The galleries and shops below offer a broad mix in many media. Items for the home, jewelry and accessories, vintage Hawaiiana, and accoutrements at various prices and for various tastes can make great gifts to go, as can locally made food products such as preserves, cookies, flowers, Kona coffee, and macadamia nuts. You'll find that bowls made of rare native woods such as koa are especially abundant on the Big Island. This is an area in which politics and art intersect: Although reforestation efforts are underway to plant new koa trees, the decline of old-growth forests is causing many artists to turn to equally beautiful, and more environmentally sensitive, alternative woods.

THE KONA COAST
In & Around Kailua-Kona

Kailua-Kona's shopping prospects pour out into the streets in a festival atmosphere of T-shirts, trinkets, and dime-a-dozen souvenirs, with Alii Drive at the center of

Art Appreciation

The finest art on the Kona Coast hangs in, of all places, a bank. Award-winning **First Hawaiian Bank**, 74–5593 Palani Rd. ((✆ **808/329-2461**), has art lovers making special trips to view Hiroki Morinoue's mural, John Buck's prints, Chiu Leong's ceramic sculpture, Franco Salmoiraghi's photographs, Setsuko Morinoue's abstract fiber wall piece, and other works that were incorporated as part of the bank's design. Artists Yvonne Cheng and Sharon Carter Smith, whose works are included, assembled this exhibition, a sterling example of corporate sponsorship of the arts.

this activity. But the **Coconut Grove Market Place,** on Alii Drive, across the street from the seawall, has changed that image and added some great new shops around a sand volleyball court.

Shopping stalwarts in Kona are the **Kona Square,** across from **King Kamehameha's Kona Beach Hotel;** the hotel's shopping mall, with close to two dozen shops; and the **Kona Inn Shopping Village,** on Alii Drive. All include the usual assortment of T-shirt shops. One highlight is **Alii Gardens Marketplace** at the southern end of Kailua-Kona, a pleasant, tented outdoor marketplace with fresh fruit, flowers, imports, local crafts, and a wonderful selection of orchid plants. There's cheesy stuff here, too, but somehow it's less noticeable outdoors.

Another outdoor/indoor market, the **Kona International Market,** 74–5533 Luhia St. (near Kaiwi St.), in the Old Industrial Area, is a series of small open-air shops in a large pavilion with food vendors, similar to Waikiki's International Market. Unfortunately, with just a few exceptions, I find this "market" disappointing. I searched all the vendors looking for something made in Hawaii, and with very few exceptions (some jewelry), most of the trinkets sold here were not from the Big Island, and not even from Hawaii, and prices were not that attractive.

Honolua Surf Co. This shop targets the surf-and-sun enthusiast with good things for good times: towels, flip-flops, body boards, sunglasses, swimsuits, and everything else you need for ocean and shore action. Also popular is the full line of products with the Honolua Surf Co. label, including T-shirts, hats, bags, dresses, sweatshirts, aloha shirts, and swimwear. Kona Inn Shopping Village, 75-5744 Alii Dr. ✆ **808/329-1001.** www.honoluasurf.com.

Kailua Village Artists Gallery A co-op of four dozen Island artists, plus a few guest artists, displays its works in various media:

watercolors, paintings, prints, hand-blown and blasted glass, and photography. Books, pottery, and an attractive assortment of greeting cards are among the lower-priced items. Alii Sunset Plaza. 75-5799 Alii Dr. ℂ **808/329-6653.**

EDIBLES & EVERYDAY THINGS

The Big Island's **green markets** are notable for the quality of produce and the abundance of Island specialties at better-than-usual prices. Look for the cheerful green kiosks of the **Alii Gardens Marketplace,** 75–6129 Alii Dr. (at the south end), where local farmers and artists set up their wares, Wednesday to Saturday from 9am to 5pm. This is not your garden-variety marketplace; some vendors are permanent, some drive over from Hilo, and the owners have planted shade trees and foliage to make the 5-acre plot a Kona landmark. There are 40 to 50 vendors on any given day, selling jewelry, woodcrafts, produce, macadamia nuts, orchids, and—my favorite—the fresh juices of Kay Reeves, owner of Wau, who gets up before dawn to make her sensational lilikoi and lime juices. Kona Blue Sky Coffee is also here, as is Lynn Cappell, a fine painter of Island landscapes, and Laura de Rosa's sensational A'ala Dreams lotions and oils.

Java junkies jump-start their day at **Island Lava Java** (ℂ **808/327-2161**), the hot new magnet for coffee lovers at the Coconut Grove Market Place, on Alii Drive. At the other end of Kailua-Kona, in the New Industrial Area, between Costco and Home Depot, the handmade candies of the **Kailua Candy Company,** 73–5612 Kauhola St. (ℂ **808/329-2522,** or 800/622-2462 for orders), also beckon, especially the macadamia-nut clusters with ground ginger or the legendary macadamia-nut *honu* (turtle). Other products include truffles, pure Kona coffee, shortbread cookies, toffee, T-shirts, mugs, mustards, and other gift items.

Kona Wine Market, in the Kona Commons Shopping Center, 74–5450 Makala Blvd. (ℂ **808/329-9400**), has a noteworthy selection, including some esoteric vintages, at prices you'll love. This is a wine lover's store, with selections from California, Europe, and points beyond, as well as gift baskets, cheeses, cigars, oils and vinegars, specialty pastas and condiments, Riedel glassware, and friendly, knowledgeable service.

For everyday grocery needs, **KTA Super Stores** (in the Kona Coast Shopping Center, 74–5588 Palani Rd., and in the Keauhou Shopping Center, 78–6831 Alii Dr.) are always my first choice. Through its Mountain Apple brand, KTA sells hundreds of top-notch local products—from Kona smoked marlin and Hilo-grown rainbow trout to cookies, breads, jams and jellies, taro chips, and *kulolo,* the decadently dense taro-coconut steamed pudding—by dozens of local vendors. The fresh-fish department is always an adventure; if anything esoteric is running, such as the flashy red aweoweo, it's sure to be on KTA's counters, along with a large spread of prepared foods for sunset picnics and barbecues.

My other favorite is **Kona Natural Foods,** at the Crossroads Shopping Center, 75–1027 Henry St. (© **808/329-2296**). It's been upgraded from a health-food store to a full-on healthful supermarket. And it's the only full-service natural-food store for miles, selling bulk grains and cereals, vitamins, snacks, fresh-fruit smoothies, and sandwiches and salads from its takeout deli. Organic greens, grown in the South Kona area, are a small but strong feature of the produce section.

Upcountry Kona: Holualoa

Charming Holualoa, 1,400 feet and 10 minutes above Kailua-Kona at the top of Hualalai Road, is a place for strong espresso, leisurely gallery hopping, and nostalgic explorations across several cultural and time zones. One narrow road takes you across generations and cultures. **Paul's Place** is Holualoa's only all-purpose general store, a time warp tucked between frame shops, galleries, and studios.

Prominent Holualoa artists include the jewelry maker/sculptor Sam Rosen, who years ago set the pace for found-object art and today makes beautiful pieces at the rear of Chestnut Gallery; the furniture maker and wood sculptor Gerald Ben; the printmaker Nora Yamanoha; the glass artist Wilfred Yamazawa; the sculptor Cal Hashimoto; and Hiroki and Setsuko Morinoue of Studio 7 gallery. All galleries listed are on the main street, Mamalahoa Highway, and all are within walking distance of one another.

Dovetail Gallery & Design Located behind the old historic post office, Dovetail features contemporary and abstract art, as well as the works of high-end, fine craftsmen and furniture makers. But the gallery's custom woodworking shop separates it from all the other galleries lining the Mamalahoa Highway. It features top craftsmen and the design work of Gerald Ben, who not only is a skilled ceramicist, but also has been a custom woodworker for 22 years. His expertise is designing furniture and wood accessories for his clients, who include collectors, home owners, interior designers, and architects. 76–5942 Mamalahoa Hwy. © **808/322-4046.**

Holualoa Gallery Owners Matthew and Mary Lovein show their own work as well as the work of selected Hawaii artists in this roadside gallery in Holualoa. Sculptures, paintings, koa furniture, fused-glass bowls, raku ceramics, and creations in paper, bronze, metal, and glass are among the gallery's offerings. 76–5921 Mamalahoa Hwy. © **808/322-8484.** www.lovein.com.

Kimura Lauhala Shop   Everyone loves Kimura and the master-pieces of weaving that spill out of the tiny shop. It's lined with lauhala, from rolled-up mats and wide-brimmed hats to tote bags, coasters, and coin purses. The fragrant, resilient fiber, woven from the spiny leaves of the *hala* (pandanus) tree, is smooth to the touch and becomes softer with use. Lauhala also varies in color, accord-ing to region and growing conditions. Although Kimura employs a covey of local weavers who use the renowned *hala* leaves of Kona, some South Pacific imports bolster the supply. 77-996 Mamalahoa Hwy., at Hualalai Rd. ✆ **808/324-0053.**

Studio 7 🎁   Some of Hawaii's most respected artists, among them gallery owners Setsuko and Hiroki Morinoue, exhibit their works in this serenely beautiful studio. Smooth pebbles, stark woods, and a garden setting provide the backdrop for Hiroki's paintings and prints, and Setsuko's pottery, paper collages, and wall pieces. The Main Gallery houses multimedia art, the Print Gallery sculptural pieces and two-dimensional works, and the Ceramic Gallery the works of Clayton Amemiya, Chiu Leong, and Gerald Ben. This is the hub of the Holualoa art community; activities include workshops, classes, and special events by visiting artists. The studio is usually open Tuesday to Saturday, but call first. 76-5920 Mamalahoa Hwy. ✆ **808/324-1335.**

South Kona

In Kealakekua, the **Kamigaki Market,** on Hwy. 11 (Mamalahoa Hwy.), is a reliable source of food items, especially for regional specialties such as macadamia nuts and Kona coffee.

In Honaunau, farther south, keep an eye out for the **Bong Brothers Store,** on Hwy. 11 between mile markers 103 and 104 (www.bongbrothers.com), and its eye-catching selections of fresh local fruit—from cherimoya (in season) to star fruit and white Sugarloaf pineapples. The Bongs are known for their deli items, produce, and Kona coffee fresh from their own roasting room, but I think their black, very hip Bong Brothers and Bong Sistah T-shirts are the find of the region. The deli offers homemade soups and smoothies made with fresh local fruit.

In the town of Captain Cook, look for the big BANANA BREAD sign (you can't miss it) across the street from the fire station on Hwy. 11, and you'll come across the **Captain Cook Baking Company,** which bakes excellent banana bread with macadamia nuts, under the Auntie Helen's label. The bread is made with Big Island bananas and macadamia-nut honey, and baked right here in the kitchen. This bakery/sandwich shop also sells Lilikoi Gold passion butter, cheesecake brownies, and submarine sandwiches on its own house-made breads.

South Kona, one of the best growing regions on the Big Island, has a weekly **farmers market** every Saturday from 8am to noon at the **Keauhou Shopping Center** parking lot, near Ace Hardware. It's a true farmers market, selling only produce grown on the Big Island. Another great vegetable and fruit stand down south is the **South Kona Fruit Stand**, 84–4770 Mamalahoa Hwy. between mile markers 103 and 104, Captain Cook (✆ 808/328-8547), which sells some of the most unusual tropical produce from the Big Island.

Antiques & Orchids   Beverly Napolitan and her husband took over Captain Cook's oldest building (built in 1906) and filled it with an eclectic array of antiques, collectibles, and fresh orchids. There are a few vintage Hawaiian items, lots of teacups, raspberry-colored walls, linens, old kimonos, celadon, etched glass and crystal lamps, a Queen Liliuokalani lanai sofa from the 1800s, and a red wooden veranda where you can sit in the soft breeze and sip 100% Kona coffee. You can't miss this green building with white trim, on the mauka side of the highway in Captain Cook. Hwy. 11, Captain Cook. ✆ **808/323-9851.**

Kimura Store 🎁   This old-fashioned general store is one of those places you'll be glad you found—a store with spirit and character, plus everything you need and don't need. You'll see Hawaii's finest selection of yardage, enough cookware for a multicourse dinner, aspirin, Shiseido cosmetics, and an eye-popping assortment of buttons, zippers, and quilting materials. Irene Kimura, the family matriarch, who presided over the store for more than 60 years until she passed away recently, said she quit counting the fabric bolts at 8,000 but estimated there were more than 10,000. Kimura's is the spot for pareu and Hawaiian fabrics, brocades, silks, and offbeat gift items, such as Japanese china and *tabi*, the comfortable cloth footwear. Hwy. 11, Kainaliu. ✆ **808/322-3771.**

THE KOHALA COAST

Harbor Gallery ★★   Formerly Kohala Kollection, this two-story gallery has made a seamless transition, remaining a big draw next to Cafe Pesto in this industrial harbor area of Kawaihae. Frances Dennis's painted Island scenes on canvas are among the works by more than 150 artists, primarily from the Big Island. The range is vast—from jewelry to basketry, ceramics to heirloom-quality koa furniture. Kawaihae Shopping Center, Hwy. 270, just north of Hwy. 19, Kawaihae. © **808/882-1510**. www.harborgallery.biz.

Resort Shopping

Most Kohala Coast shops are concentrated in and around the resorts, listed below.

Hilton Waikoloa Village   Among the hotel's shops, **Sandal Tree** carries footwear with style and kick: Italian sandals at non-Italian prices, designer pumps, and other footwear to carry you from dockside to dance floor.

Kings' Shops   These stores are located at the entrance to the Waikoloa Beach Resort. A recent find here is **Walking in Paradise** (© 808/886-2600). The footwear—much of it made in France (Mephisto, Arche)—can be expensive, but it's worthwhile for anyone seeking comfort while exploring the harsh lava terrain of this island or the pedestrian culture of Kailua-Kona's Alii Drive. Toward the mauka (mountainside) end is **Noa Noa,** filled with exotic artifacts from Java and Borneo, plus tropical clothing for the easygoing life on the Pacific Rim. At **Under the Koa Tree,** some of the island's finest artists display their prints, woodcrafts, and paintings. For snacks, ice, sunscreen, wine, postcards, newspapers, and everyday essentials, there's the **Whalers General Store,** and for dining on the run, a small food court with pizza, plate lunches, and the **Jungle Edge Coffee** for a steaming cup of brew.

Queens' MarketPlace   The Queens' MarketPlace, located across the street from the Kings' Shops, offers a range of shops from Giggles, Lids, and Local Motion to eateries such as Sansei Seafood Restaurant & Sushi Bar, Charley's Thai Cuisine, Queen's Deli, Island Gourmet Markets, and Starbucks.

Hualalai Resort   The **Kaupulehu Store,** in the Four Seasons Resort Hualalai, is a perfect blend of high quality and cultural integrity. Located within the award-winning Kaupulehu Cultural Center, the store carries items made in Hawaii: handmade paper, hand-painted silks, seed leis, greeting cards, koa bowls, wreaths, John Kelly prints, and a selection of Hawaii-themed books. The **Hualalai Sports Club & Spa,** in the same resort, has a winning retail section of beauty and treatment products, including Hana Naia aromatherapy oils. The selection includes mango and jasmine perfumes, Bulgarian rose water, and herbal lotions and potions.

Mauna Lani Resort   The recently opened **Shops at Mauna Lani** is a high-end cluster of well-known name stores and a sprinkling of local, homegrown places such as terrific Monstera and Kimobean Hawaiian Coffee. Shops include Lahaina Galleries, Caché, Kohala Goldsmiths, and Foodland Farms. Chain eateries include Ruth's Chris Steak House and Tommy Bahama's Tropical Cafe.

NORTH KOHALA

Ackerman Gallery   Crafts and fine arts are housed in two separate galleries a few blocks apart. Artist Gary Ackerman and his wife, Yesan, display gifts, crafts, and the works of award-winning Big Island artists, including Ackerman's own Impressionistic paintings. There are Kelly Dunn's hand-turned Norfolk pine bowls, Jer Houston's heirloom-quality koa-and-ebony desks, and Wilfred Yamazawa's hand-blown-glass perfume bottles and sculptures. Primitive artifacts, Asian antiques, jewelry, and Cal Hashimoto's bamboo sculptures are also among the discoveries here. The crafts-and-gifts gallery, across from the King Kamehameha Statue, has recently doubled in size; it features gift ideas in all media and price ranges. Hwy. 270 (across from the Kamehameha Statue; also 3 blocks away, on the opposite side of the street), Kapaau. (C) **808/889-5971.** www.ackermangalleries.com.

As Hawi Turns   You never know what you'll find in this whimsical, delightful shop of women's clothing and accessories. The windows might be filled with painted paper lanterns in the shapes of stars, or retro-painted switch plates, or kicky straw hats paired with bias-cut silk dresses and quirky jewelry. This is the perfect place to pamper yourself with such fripperies as tatami zoris and flamboyant accessories for a colorful, tropical life. Hwy. 270 (Akoni Pule Hwy.), Hawi. (C) **808/889-5023.**

Elements   John Flynn designs jewelry, and his wife, Prakash, assembles fountains and other treasures, and together they've filled their quiet gallery with an assortment of arts and crafts from the Big Island. The lauhala accessories, jewelry, and fountains—simple bowls filled with smooth gemstones such as amethyst and rose quartz—make great gifts and accessories. Hwy. 270 (Akoni Pule Hwy.), Hawi. (C) **808/889-0760.**

WAIMEA

Waimea is lei country as well as the island's breadbasket, so look for protea, vegetables, vine-ripened tomatoes, and tuberose stalks here at reasonable prices.

Small and sublime, the **Waimea Farmers Market,** Hwy. 19, at mile marker 55 on the Hamakua side of Waimea town (on the lawn in front of the Department of Hawaiian Home Lands, West Hawaii office), draws a loyal crowd from 7am to noon on Saturday. At the other end of Waimea, the **Parker School Farmers Market,** held Saturday from 8am to 1pm, is smaller and more subdued, but with choice items as well. The Kalopa macadamia nuts are the sweetest and tastiest I've ever had.

Other shops in Waimea range from the small roadside storefronts lining Hwy. 19 and Hwy. 190, which intersect in the middle of town, to complexes such as the **Waimea Center,** where you'll find the trusty old **KTA Super Store,** 65–1158 Mamalahoa Hwy., the one-stop shop for all your basic necessities, plus a glorious profusion of interesting local foods. Across the street, with its upscale galleries and shops, **Parker Square,** 65–1279 Kawaihae Rd., will likely be your most rewarding stop.

Bentley's Home & Garden Collection To its lavish list of glassware, linens, chenille throws, home fragrances, stuffed animals, and Wild West gift wraps, Bentley's has added casual country clothing in linens and cottons. Dresses, sweaters, raffia hats, top-drawer Western shirts, handbags, and woven shoes adorn this fragrant, gardenlike shop. Parker Sq., Hwy. 19. (€) **808/885-5565.** www.bentleyshomecollection.com.

Gallery of Great Things Here's an eye-popping assemblage of local art and Pacific Rim artifacts. Browse under the watchful gaze of an antique Tongan war club (not for sale) and authentic rhinoceros- and deer-horn blowguns from Borneo, among the plethora of treasures from Polynesia, Micronesia, and Indonesia. You'll find jewelry, glassware, photographs, greeting cards, fiber baskets, and hand-turned bowls of beautifully grained woods. Photos by Victoria McCormick, the sketches of Kathy Long, feather masks by Beth McCormick, and the paintings of Yvonne Cheng are among the treasures by local artists. There are a few pieces of etched glass and vintage clothing, too, along with a small, gorgeous collection of antique kimonos. Parker Sq., Hwy. 19. (€) **808/885-7706.** www.galleryofgreatthingshawaii.com.

Sweet Wind Because the owner loves beauty and harmonious things, you'll find chimes, carved dolphins, crystals, geodes, incense (an excellent selection), beads, jewelry, gems, essential oils, and thoughtfully selected books worth more than a casual glance. The books cover self-help, health, metaphysics, Hawaiian spirituality, yoga, meditation, and other topics for wholesome living. Parker Sq., Hwy. 19. (€) **808/885-0562.**

Waimea General Store This charming, unpretentious country store offers a superb assortment of Hawaii-themed books, soaps and toiletries, cookbooks and kitchen accessories, candles, linens, greeting cards, dolls, Japanese *hapi* coats, Island teas, rare kiawe honey, preserves, cookies, and countless gift items, from the practical to the whimsical. Parker Sq., Hwy. 19. (€) **808/885-4479.**

THE HAMAKUA COAST
Honokaa

Honokaa Market Place I've noticed a proliferation of Balinese imports (not a good sign) mingling with the old and new Hawaiiana. The eclectic selection of Hawaiian, Asian, and Indonesian handicrafts includes wood crafts, Hawaiian prints, and Hawaiian quilts, from wall hangings and pillows to full-size quilts, plus a few pieces of jewelry. 45-3321 Mamane St. © **808/775-8255.**

Honokaa Trading Company "Rustic, tacky, rare—there's something for everyone," says owner Grace Walker, who has been in business for 24 years. Every inch of this labyrinthine 2,200-square-foot bazaar is occupied by antiques and collectibles, new and used goods, and countless treasures. You'll find plantation memorabilia, Hawaiiana, bark-cloth fabrics from the 1940s, rhinestone jewelry and rattan furniture from the 1930s, vintage ukuleles, Depression glass, dinnerware from Honolulu's landmark Willows restaurant, koa lamps, Francis Oda airbrush paintings, vintage kimonos, and linens. It's an unbelievable conglomeration, with surprises in every corner. Vigilant collectors make regular forays here to scoop up the 1950s ivory jewelry and John Kelly prints. Mamane St. © **808/775-0808.**

Taro Patch Gifts Taro Patch carries an eclectic assortment of Hawaiian music tapes and CDs, switch plates printed with Hawaiian labels, Kau coffee, local jams and jellies, soaps, pareu, books, ceramics, sushi candles, essential oils, and sportswear, such as Hawaiian-print cowboy shirts. 45-3599 Mamane St. © **808/775-7228.** www.taropatchgifts.com.

The End of the Road: Waipio Valley

Waipio Valley Artworks 🎁 Housed in an old wooden building at the end of the road before the Waipio Valley, this gallery/boutique offers treasures for the home. The focus here is strictly local, with a strong emphasis on woodwork—one of the largest selections, if not the largest, in the state. A recent expansion has brought more chests and tables and gift items by Big Island artists. All the luminaries of wood-turning have works here: Jack Straka, Robert Butts, Scott Hare, Kevin Parks. Their bowls, rocking chairs, and jewelry boxes exhibit flawless craftsmanship and richly burnished grains. More affordable are the pens and hair accessories. Deli sandwiches and Tropical Dreams ice cream are served in the expanded cafe. 48-5416 Kukuihaele Rd., Kukuihaele. © **808/775-0958.** www.waipiovalleyartworks.com.

HILO

Shopping in Hilo is centered on the **Kaikoo Mall,** 777 Kilauea Ave., near the state and county buildings; the **Prince Kuhio Plaza,** 111 E. Puainako St., just off Hwy. 11 on the road north to Volcano, where you'll find a supermarket, drugstore, Macy's, and other standards; the **Bayfront** area downtown, where the hippest new businesses have taken up residence in the historic buildings lining Kamehameha Avenue; and the new **Waiakea Plaza,** where the big-box retailers (Ross, OfficeMax, Borders, Walmart) have moved in. For practical needs, there's a **KTA Super Store** at 323 Keawe St. and another at 50 E. Puainako St.

Basically Books   This bookstore, affectionately called "the map shop," is a sanctuary for lovers of books, maps, and the environment. It has expanded its selection of Hawaii-themed gift items while maintaining the engaging selection of printed materials covering geology, history, topography, botany, mythology, and more. Get your bearings by browsing among the nautical charts, U.S. Geological Survey maps, street maps, raised relief maps, atlases, compasses, and books on travel, natural history, music, spirituality, and much more. This bountiful source of information, specializing in Hawaii and the Pacific, will enhance any visit to the islands. 160 Kamehameha Ave. ✆ **808/961-0144.** www.basicallybooks.com.

Dragon Mama 🎁   For a dreamy stop in Hilo, head for this haven of all-natural comforters, cushions, futons, meditation pillows, hemp yarns and shirts, antique kimonos and obi, tatami mats sold by the panel, and all manner of comforts in the elegantly spare Japanese esthetic. The bolts of lavish silks and pure, crisp cottons, sold by the yard, can be used for clothing or interior decorating. Dragon Mama also offers custom sewing, and you know she's good: She sewed the futon and bedding for the Dalai Lama when he visited the island a few years ago. 266 Kamehameha Ave. ✆ **808/934-9081.** www.dragonmama.com.

Hana Hou 🎁   Michele Zane-Faridi has done a superlative job of assembling, designing, and collecting objects of beauty that evoke old and new Hawaii. If you are looking for Hawaiian lauhala weaving, this is the place for mats, hats, purses, place mats, slippers, and even tissue-box covers. But that's not all: Vintage shirts, china, books, dresses, jewelry, handbags, accessories, Mundorff prints, 1940s sheet music, and fabrics are displayed in surprising corners. The feathered leis and collectibles—such as vintage silver-and-ivory jewelry by Ming—disappear quickly. 164 Kamehameha Ave. ✆ **808/935-4555.**

Part gallery, part retail store, and part consortium of the arts, the **East Hawaii Cultural Center,** 141 Kalakaua St., across from Kalakaua Park (© **808/961-5711; www.ehcc.org**), is run by volunteers in the visual and performing arts. Keep it in mind for gifts of Hawaii, or if you have any questions regarding the **Hawaii Concert Society, Hilo Community Players, Big Island Dance Council,** or **Big Island Art Guild.** The art gallery and gift shop exhibit locally made cards, jewelry, books, sculptures, and wood objects, including museum-quality works.

Hawaiian Force Artist Craig Neff and his wife, Luana, hang their shingle at the original location of Sig Zane Designs (good karma), where they sell wonderful bold T-shirt dresses, mamaki tea they gather themselves, lauhala fans and trivets, surf wear, aloha shirts, and jewelry made of opihi and Niihau shells. Everything here is Hawaiian, most of it made or designed by the Neffs. Their handsome two-tone T-shirt dresses are a Hawaiian Force signature, ideal for Island living, and very popular. 140 Kilauea Ave. © **808/934-7171.** www.hawaiianforce.com.

Sig Zane Designs 🎁 My favorite stop in Hilo, Sig Zane Designs evokes such loyalty that people make special trips from the outer islands for this inspired line of authentic Hawaiian wear. The spirit of this place complements the high esthetic standards; everyone involved is completely immersed in Hawaiian culture and dance. The partnership of Zane and his wife, the revered hula master Nalani Kanaka'ole, is stunningly creative. The shop is awash in gleaming woods, lauhala mats, and clothing and accessories—handmade house slippers, aloha shirts, pareu, muumuu, T-shirts, and high-quality crafts. They all center on the Sig Zane fabric designs. These bedcovers, cushions, fabrics, clothing, and custom-ordered upholstery will bring the rainforest into your room. To add to the delight, Sig and his staff take time to talk story and explain the significance of the images, or simply chat about Hilo, hula, and Hawaiian culture. 122 Kamehameha Ave. © **808/935-7077.** www.sigzane.com.

Edibles

Abundant Life Natural Foods Stock up here on healthful snacks, organic produce, vitamins and supplements, bulk grains, baked goods, and the latest in health foods. There's a sound selection of natural remedies and herbal body, face, and hair products.

The takeout deli makes fresh-fruit smoothies and sprout- and nutrient-rich sandwiches and salads. Seniors get a 10% discount. 292 Kamehameha Ave. ℭ **808/935-7411.** www.abundantlifenaturalfoods.com.

Big Island Candies Abandon all restraint: The chocolate-dipped shortbread and macadamia nuts, not to mention the free samples, will make it very hard to be sensible. Owner Alan Ikawa has turned cookie making into a spectator sport. Large viewing windows allow you to watch the hand-dipping from huge vats of chocolate while the aroma of butter fills the room. Ikawa uses eggs straight from a nearby farm, pure butter, Hawaiian cane sugar, no preservatives, and premium chocolate. Gift boxes are carted inter-island—or shipped all over the country—in staggering volumes. The Hawaiian Da-Kine line is irrepressibly local: *mochi* crunch, fortune cookies, animal crackers, and other morsels—all dipped in chocolate. By far the best are the shortbread cookies, dipped in chocolate, peanut butter, and white chocolate. If you get thirsty, there's a juice-and-smoothie bar. Outside are picnic tables on the manicured grounds. 585 Hinano St. ℭ **800/935-5510** or 808/935-8890. www.bigislandcandies.com.

Hilo Farmers Market 🎁 This has grown into the state's best farmers market, embodying what I love most in Hawaii: local color, good soil and weather, the mixing of cultures, and new adventures in taste. More than 120 vendors from around the island bring their flowers, produce, and baked goods to this teeming corner of Hilo every Wednesday and Saturday from sunrise to 4pm. Because many of the vendors sell out quickly, go as early as you can. Expect to find a stunning assortment: homegrown oyster mushrooms from Kona; the creamy, sweet, queenly Indonesian fruit called mango-steen; warm breads, from focaccia to walnut; an array of flowers; fresh aquacultured seaweed; corn from Pahoa; Waimea strawber-ries; taro products; foot-long, miso-flavored, and traditional Hawai-ian laulau; made-from-scratch tamales; and fabulous ethnic vegetables. The selection changes by the week, but it's always reasonable, fresh, and appealing, with a good cross-section of the island's specialties. Although it's open daily, Wednesday and Satur-day are the days when all the vendors are there. Kamehameha Ave. at Mamo St. ℭ **808/933-1000.**

HAWAII VOLCANOES NATIONAL PARK

Kilauea Kreations This is the quilting center of Volcano, a co-op made up of local Volcano artists and crafters who create quilts, jewelry, feather leis, ceramics, baskets, and fiber arts. Gift items made by Volcano artists are also sold here, but it's the quilts and quilting materials that distinguish the shop. Starter kits are available for beginners. I also like the Hawaiian seed leis and items made of lauhala, as well as the locally made soaps and bath products and the greeting cards, picture frames, and candles. 19-3972 Old Volcano Rd. ℭ **808/967-8090.** www.kilaueakreations.com.

Volcano Art Center The Volcano Island's frontier spirit and raw, primal energy have spawned a close-knit community of artists, and the Volcano Art Center (VAC) is the hub of the island's arts activity. Housed in the original 1877 Volcano House, VAC is a not-for-profit art-education center that offers exhibits and shows that change monthly, as well as workshops and retail space. Marian Berger watercolors of endangered birds, Dietrich Varez oils and block prints, Avi Kiriaty oils, Kelly Dunn and Jack Straka woods, Brad Lewis photography, Harry Wishard paintings, Ira Ono goddess masks, and Mike Riley furnishings are among the works you'll see. Of the 300 artists represented, 90% come from the Big Island. The fine crafts include baskets, jewelry, mixed-media pieces, stone and wood carvings, and the wood diaries of Jesus Sanchez, a third-generation Vatican bookbinder who has turned his skills to the island's woods. Hawaii Volcanoes National Park. ℭ **808/967-7565.** www.volcanoartcenter.org.

Volcano Store Walk up the wooden steps into a wonderland of flowers and local specialties. Tangy lilikoi butter (transportable, and worth a special trip) and flamboyant sprays of cymbidiums, tuberoses, dendrobiums, anthuriums, hanging plants, mixed bouquets, and calla lilies make a breathtaking assemblage in the enclosed front porch. Volcano residents are lucky to have these blooms at such prices. The flowers can also be shipped (orders are taken by phone); Marie and Ronald Onouye and their staff pack them meticulously (and if mainland weather is too humid or frosty for reliable shipping, they'll let you know). Produce, stone cookies (as in hard-as-stone) from Mountain View, Hilo taro chips, bottled water (a necessity in Volcano), local *poha* (gooseberry) jam, and bowls of chili rice (a local favorite) round out the selection. Even if you're just visiting the park for the day, it's worth turning off to stop for gas here; kindly clerks will give directions. Huanani Rd. and Old Volcano Rd. ℭ **808/967-7210.**

Volcano Winery Lift a glass of Volcano Blush or Macadamia Nut Honey and toast Pele at this boutique winery, where the local wines are made from tropical honey (no grapes) and tropical fruit blends (half-grape and half-fruit). It's open daily from 10am to 5:30pm; tastings are free. Plans are in the works to expand the winery to accommodate tours. You can order wines online. Pii Mauna

Dr., off Hwy. 11 at mile marker 30, all the way to the end. (℮ **808/967-7772.** www. volcanowinery.com.

Studio Visits

The airy Volcano studio/showroom of **Phan Barker** (℮ 808/985-8636), an international artist, is a mountain idyll and splendid backdrop for her art, which includes batik paintings on silk, acrylic painting on wood, oil on paper, dye on paper, and mixed-media sculptures. Her work has been exhibited in galleries and museums ranging from the Smithsonian to Saigon. In addition to studio visits (by appointment only), she offers beginner classes in silk painting and drawing.

Adding to the vitality of the Volcano arts environment are the studio visits offered once a year, usually around Thanksgiving, by the **Volcano Village Art Studios** (℮ 808/985-8979; http://volcanogardenarts.com/events-studiotour09.html). Several respected artists in various media open their studios to the public by appointment. Artists in the hui include **Ira Ono** (℮ 808/967-7261), who makes masks, water containers, fountains, paste-paper journals, garden vessels, and goddesses out of clay and found objects; and sculptor **Randy Takaki** (℮ 808/985-8756), who works in wood, metal, and ceramics.

THE BIG ISLAND AFTER DARK

There are a few pockets of entertainment on the Big Island, largely in the Kailua-Kona and Kohala Coast resorts. Your best bet is to check the local newspapers—Honolulu Advertiser and West Hawaii Today—for special shows, such as fundraisers, that are held at local venues. Other than that, regular entertainment in the local clubs usually consists of mellow Hawaiian music at sunset, small hula groups, or jazz trios.

Some of the island's best events are held at the **Kahilu Theatre,** in Waimea (✆ **808/885-6017;** www.kahilu theatre.org), so be on the lookout for any mention of it during your stay. Hula, the top Hawaiian music groups from all over Hawaii, drama, and all aspects of the performing arts use Kahilu as a venue.

BIG ISLAND LUAU

Kona Village Luau ★★★ 📷 The longest continuously running luau on the island is still the best—a combination of an authentic Polynesian venue with a menu that works, impressive entertainment, and the spirit of old Hawaii. The feast begins with a ceremony in a sandy kiawe grove, where the pig is unearthed after a full day of cooking in a rock-heated underground oven. In the open-air dining room, next to prehistoric lagoons and tropical gardens, you'll sample a Polynesian buffet: *poisson cru,* poi, laulau (butterfish, seasoned pork, and taro leaves cooked in ti leaves), lomi salmon, squid luau (cooked taro leaves with steamed octopus

AN EVENING UNDER THE stars

This is one of those unique Hawaii experiences that you will remember long after your tan has faded. Perched from the vantage point of 3,200 feet on the slopes of the Kohala Mountains, **"An Evening at Kahua Ranch"** is a night under the stars with wonderful food, great entertainment, fun activities, and storytelling around a traditional campfire.

The evening begins when you are picked up at your hotel. As you relax in the air-conditioned van, enjoying the scenic coastline, your guide spins stories about this historic area. Arriving at the 8,500-acre working cattle ranch, you are personally greeted by the ranch owner, John Richards. When the sun starts to sink into the Pacific, beer, wine, and soft drinks are served as John talks about how cattle ranching came to Hawaii and how they manage the ranch in the 21st century. A traditional ranch-style barbecue of sirloin steak, chicken, locally grown potatoes, Waimea corn-on-the-cob, baked beans, Big Island green salad, Kona coffee, and dessert is served shortly after sunset.

After dinner, the fun and games begin: Local entertainers pull out guitars, line dancing gets going on the dance floor, and several *paniolo* (cowboy) activities take place. You can choose from learning how to rope, playing a game of horse shoes, or trying your hand at branding (a cedar shingle, yours to take home as a souvenir). When the stars come out, look through an 8-inch telescope to gaze into the moon or search for distant planets. A campfire gets started, and the ranch's cowboys come over and start telling stories as you toast marshmallows for old-fashioned s'mores over a crackling campfire.

The entire experience, including transportation, dinner, and entertainment, is only $119 per person, children half-price. For more information, call ✆ **808/987-2108** or go to www.explore theranch.com.

and coconut milk), ahi poke, opihi (fresh limpets), coconut pudding, taro chips, sweet potatoes, chicken long rice, steamed bread fruit, and the shredded kalua pig. The Polynesian revue, a fast-moving, mesmerizing tour of South Pacific cultures, manages—miraculously—to avoid being clichéd or corny. **Note:** The Kona Village Resort sustained damage during the 2011 tsunami and at press time remained closed. Please call ahead of your visit to find out about repairs and reopening. At the Kona Village Resort.

© **808/325-5555.** www.konavillage.com. Reservations required. Part of the Full American Plan for Kona Village guests; for nonguests, $98 adults, $67 children 6–12, $40 children 2–5. AE, DC, MC, V. Wed and Fri 5pm.

Gathering of the Kings   The Fairmont Orchid's Polynesian show—a series of traditional dances and music, blended with modern choreography, Island rhythms, and high-tech lighting and set design—tells the story of the Polynesians' journey across the Pacific to Hawaii. It features the culture and arts of the islands of Samoa, Tahiti, New Zealand, and Hawaii. Complementing the show, the luau also highlights the cuisine of these Pacific islands. At the Fairmont Orchid, Mauna Lani Resort, 1 N. Kaniku Dr. © **808/329-8111.** www.islandbreezeluau.com. Reservations required. Show and luau $99 adults, $65 children 6–12, free for children 5 and under. AE, MC, V. Sat 4:30pm.

Firenesia   If you are unable to get into the luau at Kona Village, the Sheraton Keauhou Bay Resort's luau is my second pick. The food is fine, but you really come here for the show, created by Island Breeze Productions. Filled with lavish theatrics woven into Hawaiian chants, legends, hula, and acrobatic performing arts, this is definitely not your tired Polynesian revue. At the Sheraton Keauhou Bay Resort, 78-128 Ehukai St. © **808/326-4969.** www.sheratonkeauhou.com. Reservations required. Show and luau $80 adults, $50 children 5–12. AE, MC, V. Mon 5pm.

KAILUA-KONA

A host of bars and restaurants feature dancing and live music when the sun goes down, all of them on Alii Drive in Kailua-Kona. Starting from the south end of Alii Drive, **Huggo's on the Rocks** (© **808/329-1493**) has dancing and live music on weekends, and next door at **Huggo's** restaurant, there's jazz and blues and a piano bar.

Across the street in the Coconut Grove Market Place, **Lulu's** (© **808/321-2633**) draws a 20-something crowd with music and dancing Friday and Saturday until 1am.

THE KOHALA COAST

Evening entertainment here usually takes the form of a luau or indistinctive lounge music at scenic resort bars with scintillating sunset views. But newcomer Waikoloa Beach Marriott's **Clipper Lounge** is a bright new venue for local musicians, with live music most nights (call for schedule, © **808/886-6789**) from 8:30 to 11:30pm.

old-style HAWAIIAN ENTERTAINMENT

The plaintive drone of the conch shell pierces the air, calling all to assemble. A sizzling orange sun sinks slowly toward the cobalt waters of the Pacific. In the distance, the majestic mountain Mauna Kea reflects the waning sun's light with a fiery red that fades to a hazy purple and finally to an inky black as a voluptuous full moon dramatically rises over its shoulder.

It's **Twilight at Kalahuipua'a,** a monthly Hawaiian cultural celebration that includes storytelling, singing, and dancing on the oceanside grassy lawn at Mauna Lani Resort ((C) **808/885-6622;** www.maunalani.com/luxury-hawaii-resort-factsheet.htm). These full-moon events, created by Daniel Akaka, Jr., who is Mauna Lani Resort's director of cultural affairs, hearken back to another time in Hawaii, when family and neighbors gathered to sing, dance, and "talk story."

Each month, the guests, ranging from the ultra-well-known in the world of Hawaiian entertainment to the virtually unknown local *kupuna* (elder), gather to perpetuate the traditional folk art of storytelling, with plenty of music and dance thrown in.

Twilight at Kalahuipua'a, always set on a Saturday closest to the full moon, really gets underway at least an hour before the 5:30pm start, when people from across the island and guests staying at the hotel begin arriving. They carry picnic baskets, mats, coolers, babies, and cameras. A sort of oceanside, premusic tailgate party takes place with *kamaaina* (local resident) families sharing their plate lunches, sushi, and beverages with visitors, who have catered lunches, packaged sandwiches, and taro chips, in a truly old-fashioned demonstration of aloha.

The Wednesday and Friday luau at the **Kona Village Resort** (see above) is the best choice on the island. Otherwise, the resort roundup includes the Hilton Waikoloa Village's **Legends of the Pacific** ((C) **808/886-1234**) Tuesday, Friday, and Sunday dinner show ($99 adults, $89 teens, $51 children 5–12). The Hilton's newly opened **Malolo Lounge** also has nightly live entertainment with Hawaiian music (8–11pm).

If you get a chance to see the **Lim Family,** don't miss them. Immensely talented in hula and song, members of the family perform in the intimate setting of the Mauna Lani Bay Hotel's **Atrium Bar** most Friday and Saturday nights at 6pm ((C) **808/885-6622**).

Just beyond the resorts lies a great music spot—the **Blue Dragon,** 61–3616 Kawaihae Rd., Kawaihae (✆ **808/882-7771**), where you can enjoy an eclectic mix of music (jazz, rock, swing, Hawaiian, even big-band music) Wednesday through Sunday.

HILO

Hilo's most notable events are special or annual occasions such as the **Merrie Monarch Hula Festival,** the state's largest, which continues for a week after Easter Sunday. The festivities include hula competitions with participants from all over the world, demonstrations, and crafts fairs. A staggering spirit of pageantry takes over the entire town. Tickets are always hard to come by; call (✆ **808/935-9168;** www.merriemonarch.com) well ahead of time, and see the "Big Island Calendar of Events" (p. 10) for further information.

A special new venue is the old **Palace Theater,** 38 Haili St. (✆ **808/934-7010;** www.hilopalace.com), restored and back in action thanks to the diligent Friends of the Palace Theater. The neoclassical wonder first opened in 1925, was last restored in 1940, and has reopened for first-run movies while restoration continues. Film festivals, art movies, hula, community events, concerts (including the Slack Key Guitar Festival), and all manner of special entertainment take place here.

 Hey, No Smoking in Hawaii

Well, not *totally* no smoking, but Hawaii has one of the toughest laws against smoking in the U.S. It's against the law to smoke in public buildings, including airports, shopping malls, grocery stores, retail shops, buses, movie theaters, banks, convention facilities, and all government buildings and facilities. There is no smoking in restaurants, bars, and nightclubs. Most bed-and-breakfasts prohibit smoking indoors, and more and more hotels and resorts are becoming smoke-free even in public areas. Also, there is no smoking within 20 feet of a doorway, window, or ventilation intake (so no hanging around outside a bar to smoke—you must go 20 ft. away). Even some beaches have no-smoking policies (and at those that do allow smoking, you'd better pick up your butts and not use the sand as your own private ashtray—or else face stiff fines). Breathing fresh, clear air is "in," while smoking in Hawaii is "out."

VOLCANO VILLAGE

Tucked into the rainforest of Volcano Village is the **Volcano Art Center's Niaulani Campus** (© **808/967-8222;** www.volcano artcenter.org). The word *niaulani,* which means "brushed by the heavens" or "billowing heavens," actually describes the way the clouds and fog move through the rainforest. The new 4,400-square-foot administration building houses an intimate great room with a fireplace, sofas, and large windows looking out to the fern forest outside. Check local listings for the free events, ranging from cultural talks to music and dance performances.

Index

See also Accommodations and Restaurant indexes, below.

General Index

Accommodations

Restaurants